Productive Advertising

PRODUCTIVE
ADVERTISING

BY

HERBERT W. HESS, A.B., Ph.D.

ASSISTANT PROFESSOR OF COMMERCE—ADVERTISING AND SALESMANSHIP DEPARTMENT—
WHARTON SCHOOL OF FINANCE AND COMMERCE, UNIVERSITY OF PENNSYLVANIA

84 ILLUSTRATIONS

PHILADELPHIA & LONDON
J. B. LIPPINCOTT COMPANY

PRINTED BY J. B. LIPPINCOTT COMPANY
AT THE WASHINGTON SQUARE PRESS
PHILADELPHIA, U. S. A.

THE AUTHOR RESPECTFULLY DEDI-
CATES THIS BOOK TO THOSE WHO
DREAM, HOPE, THINK AND WORK FOR
A CONSTANTLY IMPROVING WORLD
THRU PRODUCTIVE ADVERTISING

PREFACE

THE most difficult problem that a student of advertising has to face in attempting to gain a knowledge of the principles involved, is that kind of information which is logical in development and which leads him into a comprehensive evolutionary appreciation of the relations which exist. This book has been written with the idea of giving to the beginner in advertising a logically discussed text, which includes: first the psychology of advertising; second, the typography of advertising; third, the English of advertising; fourth, the economic implications of advertising; and fifth, throughout the entire work there is insisted upon, a certain philosophical interpretation of all the principles involved, which the progressive advertiser must ever observe in connection with any creative work he might attempt to perform.

Furthermore, there is an insistent demand that the student recognize the relationship between theory and practice as related to advertising. In other words, the principles as discussed with their suggested problems should reveal at least two things to the student who has faithfully carried out the foregoing outline: first, whether or not he himself possesses that quality of mind which will enable him creatively to compete in the actual formulation of advertising campaigns; or second, whether, not being creative, he is able to serve rather as an executive or as one fully appreciating the principles involved. In this latter attitude of mind he recognizes himself as one competent to work harmoniously and analytically with those who are initiatively interested in the successful selling phase of a particular business. In contrast to the two types of students thus ushered into a larger appreciation of the significance of advertising in our selling system, we have those students whose lack of appreciation in advertising values readily suggests interest in other phases of business more fixed in nature. Just as the business world under an efficiency system is compelled constantly to revalue and classify the abilities of its employees, so the spirit of this book should reveal to each student his particular adaptability or non-adaptability to the field of advertising.

The new instructor who uses this text should bear in mind that the ultimate meaning of this advertising course is the creation by the student of an advertising campaign related to some specific article or proposition. Now to introduce one into the field of advertising, it is quite impossible to consider the advertising campaign immediately; rather should he be instructed regarding the principles involved, which enable him to become critical in his appreciation of the advertising material being presented at a given time by the business world. Thus the new instructor should himself recognize the fact that the principles of psychology and typography are merely to formulate a standard for general criticism, the principles of which are to take a definite creative form immediately upon the introduction of the chapter on the "Advertising Campaign." A logical development of the course would insist that the advertising campaign be considered at the beginning of the second term. Thus the student's mind is turned from a critical to that of a creative attitude.

As I have intimated before, and it should be duly emphasized, productive advertising implies creating an impulse on the part of the student instantly to initiate himself into the practical interpretation of any advertising problem. The principles of this book, as facts, are merely to be looked upon as valuable accordingly as they can be used in the mastery of selling difficulties suggested in the problems.

In writing this book I am particularly indebted to several of my old students who have themselves become interested in the advertising field and who have thus been able to give such suggestions as would keep the work in touch with the young advertiser about to initiate himself into this realm. I am grateful to Mr. James Montgomery of the Foley Advertising Agency, whose suggestions regarding agency work have been invaluable; Mr. Frank Parker, law student and former assistant, for his legal analysis of the trade-mark. Mr. D. M. Johnson and Mr. Harvey Cassedy, my assistants, have been persistent in revising the text. Mr. Benjamin F. Emery, printer, has constantly guarded the printer's point of view, while Mr. Abbott McClure of the Industrial Art School and Mr. Jack Lit have given valuable suggestions in color. Mr. G. A. Pfeiffer has assisted in an intensive analysis of street car advertising. I am particularly grateful to Mr. F. C. Teller of the Onondago Lithographic Company, Syracuse, N. Y., for the practical chapter on "Illustration."   H. W. H.

PHILADELPHIA, July, 1915.

CONTENTS

ILLUSTRATIONS

PRODUCTIVE ADVERTISING

INTRODUCTION

THE HISTORY OF ADVERTISING

Advertising is as old as the human race, and throughout history we find its actions and reactions being relative to and coming directly from humanity. The unconscious beginning of advertising first manifested itself in the attempt of the individual to avail himself of the natural human forces and processes about him, in an endeavor to further his own economic ends. From this primal stage, advertising has evolved and developed in accordance and with the particular needs and desires of the various epochs which mark the progress of the world. With advertising intimately correlated to human development, it has in turn been affected and modified by the results of its own efforts. The power of advertising in its history, thus, at one time suggests retrogression and at another, advancement. For instance, the quack medicine advertisement has been as harmful, as advertised painless dentistry has been helpful, to humanity. Throughout the centuries the relation between advertising and evolution has been constant; only the form of advertising itself, as a highly specialized element in the creative processes of life, has changed. To-day, far from being a passive or an unconscious factor in human existence, and far from complacently following the vacillating course of the public's footsteps, advertising has become a positive and productive force,—a guiding factor in the shaping of the constantly changing public standards of life. It works with art and science in the evolution of human need and desire.

The date of the first advertisement, recognized as such, is unknown. However, during the period of civilization, when

1

for geographical and economic reasons the maintenance of an individual existence was simple and non-competitive, there was little or no interest in advertising. The thinness of the population and the abundance of food, together with the wide areas of unoccupied territory, enabled each family unit to live oblivious of the rest. Social forces as yet exerted no pressure on the individual. Accordingly, however, as economic conditions were slowly transformed, the direct consequence was the grouping of people into communities. At the same time, the social and economic pressure of community life began more or less to develop dependence in the gratification of human desires. This pressure soon resulted in a competitive business system based on the constantly increasing demands of humanity. The marketing of the family's output of commodities grew more difficult. Then it was discovered that by a broadcast proclamation of the excellence of wares, combined with the personality of a persuasive seller, the power of competition began to develop trade, wherefore traders hawked their wares unto the purchasing public.

Advertising grew with civilization. As communities developed into towns and towns into cities, the attendant congealing of the economic and social forces produced a stability and permanence in the merchant-trader's business location. Shops were opened: itinerancy lessened. So in a way the importance of the hawker, as such, dwindled until in time he was almost completely supplanted by that type of crier whose counterpart to-day is exemplified by the " barker." It was but a step from the latter to the public crier or *præcone,* an officer of the municipal or State government, as the case might be, charged with the proclamation of affairs of State as well as giving publicity to the shopkeeper, who was sagacious and prosperous enough to procure it. Finally, with the slow and steady advance of civilization and its consequent influence on the expansion of art and letters, the written advertisement appeared.

Three thousand years ago an Egyptian landowner wrote on a scrap of papyrus an advertisement for the return of a runaway slave. Exhumed from the ruins of Thebes, this papyrus is still preserved in the British Museum. It is not to be deduced, however, that written advertisements were of common occurrence at this time, for though the art of writing was being acquired by the populace, nevertheless the majority were still illiterate. Under such circumstances, therefore, written advertisements were of little avail; but as the center of civilization shifted from Palestine westward, absorbing the knowledge and the culture of each nation thru which it passed, written advertising became the more productive medium. Thus in the early Hebrew civilization practically all the advertising was done by word of mouth thru the public crier, although the utterances of the Kings and Prophets were inscribed on parchment and made prominent in the public places of the city.

The modes of advertising in Greece were apparently equally divided between the spoken and the written word. Here, the public crier survived in more accomplished splendor, always being accompanied by a musician, and using only the choicest rhetorical speech. Until this time the advertisements which were written partook of a public or quasi-public nature. Now in contrast with the Hebraic advertising, the distinguishing additional feature of the Greek publicity method was the well-defined existence of private advertisements in writing. On the exterior of private residences was a piece of whitened wall, the *luchoma*, and it received inscriptions relative to the affairs of the family residing therein.

Roman advertising in its general institutions resembled that of the two preceding nations. The public crier obtained, and the various means of disseminating news and information differed only in the elaborated details which an ever-increasing experience was bound to beget. The ruins of Pompeii and Herculaneum disclosed many houses and buildings to which were affixed on the pillars thereof, *tabellæ*, whereon public announcements were written, such as the formal dedication of a public bath. Police regulations, too, claimed their share in the details of advertising media, as for example the attempted prohibition of nuisances by the painting of two sacred serpents on a sign suspended from the wall. Streets in Rome were also known by

painted signs. Written private advertising in Rome assumed,
when viewed in the light of the same kind of advertising ante-
dating it, a diversity of forms. Bills named *libelli* were used
to acquaint the public with sales of estates, absconded debtors,
and things lost and found. Booksellers solicited the attention
of the prospective reader by having the titles of the new books
neatly inscribed on a placard placed prominently in the shop
window. Shows, exhibitions, and sales were given extensive
eminence at the public baths thru the medium of *libelli* and by
means of promiscuous writings on the walls; while premises
for sale or rent were usually advertised by inscriptions on the
piece of whitened wall commonly designated as the *album*. Nor
was the sign board lacking in conspicuousness; indeed, out of
the Roman *pot-pourri* of this species of advertising media came
the precursor of the famous medieval *rebus*.

Some signs were painted, but generally they were made of
stone or terra cotta relief and set in the pilasters at the front of
shops. The Roman custom of sculpturing on the tomb the tools
and implements typical of the deceased artificer's trade—the
classical example being the pickax and the lamp engraven on the
tomb of Diogenes—suggests the probability of these same insignia being used over the workshops and residences during the
mechanic's lifetime. Certain it is that the use of the insignia
on the tombstone had lost the inhibiting effect of a sacred posthu-
mous rite, for on the headstones of a later period the practice of
" punning " on the name was not infrequent. . The grave of
Onager was embellished with a wild ass, and that of Umbricus
was decorated with a shady tree.

The decay of the Roman civilization deflowered art and
science. As the vast hordes of Teutonic tribes inundated Western
Europe a gap was opened in the forward movement of the human
race. Letters, learning, sculpture, painting and science—all
were snuffed out by the flood of semi-barbarism. Advertising
met the same fate, and throughout the dark ages of illiteracy it
remained dormant.

Advertising, however, again went round its previous cycle
of evolution. The public crier of the Middle Ages betokened

its resuscitation; only this time there was an unusual strength and solidarity of interest manifested by this institution. As early as 1258 the public criers of France were organized and incorporated into a body which procured special prerogatives from the Crown; and similarly in England they constituted a national organization of no small repute. Of course, the cardinal duties of this functionary were intermingled primarily with matters of State, but this in nowise minimized his importance as a business transmitter from the merchant to the public at large. Tersely, the public crier became an advertising force. The Assizes of Jerusalem, which contained a code of the civil laws of the whole of civilized Europe during the twelfth and the thirteenth centuries, practically made it obligatory on people having things to sell to make an announcement thru the crier. Moreover, the crier was granted the exclusive right of proclaiming all sales by auction, and judicial sales of real and personal property. The obligation thus imposed upon the individual merchant desirous of gaining an audience for his goods was in no way a hardship. As yet the percentage of literacy was small, and therefore the oral announcement was really the only effective method of securing the precious publicity. At first the crier's vocal efforts concerned all kinds of goods, wares and merchandise, but his activities gradually extended until his announcements amounted to a verbal miscellany—things lost and found, sales, weddings, christenings and funerals were included therein. It was only a matter of time until the touter for the individual trader came,—pacing to and fro before the shop and shouting with the mature vigor of a vernacular expert, "What d'ye lack, sir? What d'ye lack?" The touter's energy eclipsed his picturesqueness. He vitalized the community.

Economic necessity created the *rebus*. Toward the close of the fourteenth century numbers for the houses did not exist and, hence, for the traveller, the sole means of identifying the household was the family coat-of-arms. Meanwhile the custom had arisen for the families, when moving from one residence to another, as the seasons of the year changed, to let the vacant country house as a hostelry, which likewise maintained its individuality principally thru the coat-of-arms. At length the coat-of-arms was imitated by the less pretentious inn-keepers who, though lacking the pedigree essential to a coat-of-arms, yet possessed the universal tendency to simulate that which gave distinction to the upper strata of society; and especially so in this case, since clever simulation meant more gold in their coffers. Red lions and green dragons all played their part in the scramble for public favor. Furthermore, so long as competition continued inoffensive a few symbols typical of the trade, so manipulated as to form an insignia, sufficed to establish the identity of the trader's shop. Here was the counterpart of the Roman signs. Thus a knife for a cutler, a hand for a glover, and a scissors for a tailor are instances in point. A more rigorous competition, segregation of traders to one locality, and the fact that the ability to read was still a rare acquirement,—these were the paramount factors in the arisal of the *rebus*. Animals, vegetables, portraits of great men, names of towns, and articles of dress,—all were used to serve the purpose. Incidentally, some neat quips were achieved: a hare and a bottle stood for Harebottle; while two cocks represented Cox.

The advent of the printing press about 1450 gave a further impetus to advertising as a science, which was just wakening unto its own power. The opportunity for augmenting the percentage of literacy was immediately enlarged; a broader, more comprehensive horizon opened on the advertiser's field. The printing press first turned out posters and handbills, and later, pamphlets and small books of news, which latter gave premonition of the coming of newspapers. However, it must not be assumed that the advent of printing garnered into the printing shops the complete production of the posters and pamphlets, for though the art of printing had become established and was daily decreasing the labor of the scribes, writing remained the supreme advertising media for two centuries longer.

Heralds of bill-board advertising of modern days, the posters, both written and printed, were used for all conceivable purposes. Usually these posters were called *siquis,* since the great proportion of them began with the words " if anybody," in Latin, *si quis.* William Caxton was the pioneer printer of England, having set up his press in Westminster Abbey in 1471; and nine years afterward he published one of the first *siquis* printed in the British Isles, the " Pyes of Salisbury Use," containing a collection of the rules as practised in the diocese of Salisbury. The original copy of this bill is still extant, being in the possession of the Bodelian library at Oxford. Books as well as the theatre sought to obtain the attention of the public thru the instrumentality of the *siquis;* tutors and companions, managers of boxing shows, and a host of other *entrepreneurs* of self, used the same means in their quest for notoriety. The *siquis* were nailed and posted wherever there was a recurring concourse of people, as for example on churches,—old St. Paul's Cathedral most famed of any,—in taverns, or at the town hall.

Meanwhile the crier and the touter were not extinct. They performed their customary activities with the same ardor and zeal. But a noticeable contraction was occurring in the field of their industry. Printing was gaining an ascendency.

Nearly two centuries of printing lay in back of the first so-called newspaper. As intimated previously, after the use of posters and handbills had become fixed, there came into existence small pamphlets and news-books, which in turn foreshadowed the newspaper. The limited means of communication, a comparative lack of a general system of public education, the scant facilities for printing rapidly and in volume, the inability to secure any widespread circulation on account of poor transportation, the heavy expenses involved in the procurement of paper, type and labor:—all of these affected newspaper development and confined its influence to a narrow sphere. Characteristic publications assumed the form of belated purveyors of news-gleanings,—some English papers even copying verbatim the contents of co-existent weeklies published on the Continent,—or of tracts giving vent to the individual convictions of its publisher in his essay to gain an audience sympathetic with his interpretation of the times.

Authentic records indicate that the first bona fide attempt at newspaper work in England was begun in May, 1622, under the direction of Nicholas Bourne and Thomas Archer. The paper was called the "Weekly News" and openly professed on its first page to be a transcription from the news books of Germany, France, Hungary and Bohemia. In August of the same year Nathaniel Butler, who was the first to try to establish a weekly newspaper on a permanent basis, founded an unnamed publication. Butler's idea was to collect and summarize weekly the news items from the Venetian gazettes, as a means of satisfying the unusual demand for news created by the Civil War. His scheme was at once subjected to all sorts of raillery and adverse criticism; and though his venture failed within a short time, nevertheless it had the effect of stimulating interest in a new form of enterprise. Many news-sheets sprang up, consisting only of a single sheet of paper, on which were printed detached and miscellaneous scraps of news.

It was not until half a century later that newspapers began to assume the form by which we recognize them to-day. Strangely enough, the turmoil of the Civil wars of Charles I. and Cromwell engendered the desire for news, and at the same time provoked the leaders of the various factions to publish partisan organs to aid their side. The *Dutch Speye, Scots Dove*, the *Parliament Kite, Screetch Owle*, are typical and suggestive names of some. Most of these publications were weekly.

From the outset it was obvious that newspapers and advertising were interdependent. Simply to state the fact that advertisements were inserted in current news publications of the early times gives no adequate idea of the importance of advertising to the newspaper world. Naturally, this dependence was not emphasized at the outset, principally because newspapers had not attained a size of any importance and because very little advertising was being done. In fact, it was not until the approach of the daily paper that the deep-rooted dependence of the newspaper on advertising became fully appreciated; then it was that advertising developed into a business power, overcoming the prejudices of custom and tradition by demonstrating that widespread publicity increased the quantity of sales and profits. So it was quite ordinary to find entire newspapers devoted exclusively to publishing advertisements; in England there was the "Publick Advertiser," founded May 19, 1657, while in France the "Journal d'Affiches" was printed October 14, 1312. The printed sheets whose chief function was announcedly the dissemination of news, found it to their advantage financially, in order to arouse a larger interest among their readers, to allow considerable space for advertising. Frequently more advertisements than news items were to be seen on the front page. Moreover the fluctuating fortunes of the newspapers themselves were to some degree modified by the factors affecting advertising. With advertisements bearing an exorbitant tax, the advertising revenue of the newspaper was curtailed, and the news interest appertaining to the advertisement likewise decreased.

About 1600 printed advertisements were concerned chiefly with the exploitation of books or of articles kindred to the publishers' business. Indeed as far back as 1591, in a German newsbook the title of which is unknown, there appeared a paragraph approaching the nature of an advertisement, which advised the purchase of a Dr. Laster's monograph explaining the secret medicinal properties of a newly discovered plant. To Nathaniel Butler, however, is to be attributed the first genuine newspaper advertisement, the subject-matter being books. The commencement of miscellaneous newspaper advertisements dates from November 21, 1626, when a collection of them occurred in a Dutch black-letter newspaper.

Certain personalities stand out pre-eminently in the early advertising world. Sir Roger L'Estrange was the first man who attempted systematically to convince the public of the vast possibilities of advertising. His genius created three publications: the "Intelligencer," started August 1, 1663; the "Newes," September 3, 1663; and the "Mercury, or Advertisements Concerning Trade," 1668. Nearly twenty years later, in 1682, the astute, shrewd John Houghton founded a weekly paper entitled, "A Collection for the Improvement of Husbandry and Trade," consisting of mere bulletins and prices current in various trades. This paper is significant for two reasons: first, its columns contained advertisements from a great variety of trades, and secondly, in it the personal recommendation by the editor, of certain advertisers, first came into vogue.

The first daily paper in England was the " Daily Courant," 1702; in the United States, it was the " Boston Newsletter," established 1704. Soon the daily paper was the predominant advertising medium. On account of greater news value, it had the advantage of a wider circulation; the advertisements themselves could be made alive with current opinions; and continual repetition had an effective opportunity. Patent medicine vendors, and those to whom dishonest methods seemed justifiable when conducted by indirect and remote means, seized eagerly upon newspaper publicity to further their ends. These constituted the only well-defined group of advertisers until approximately 1850; to-day they are practically extinct. The inadequate transportation facilities limited circulation, and the dubious attitude which most merchants entertained with respect to the ethics of advertising, acted as restraining influences on other businesses. In England there was the added burden of a direct tax on the advertisements, and a stamp tax on newspapers, both of which continued until 1853 and 1855 respectively. Before the Civil War the largest expenditure for an advertisement in the United States amounted to $3,000, and came from E. & T. Fairbanks Company, the standard scales manufacturers.

The decade from 1840 to 1850 was notable for two things. Bill posting had progressed to such a stage that it actually became a public nuisance. Unscrupulous bill-posters insisted on covering every available inch of space with the bills of their particular customers, and the rivalry between competitors resulted in hideous conglomerations of paper and ink. Walls of houses and fences were defaced by the repeated pasting of one bill over another; and so both the advertiser and the public were injured. During this decade, also, the advertising agent came. Without the semblance of the system which characterizes the better agent of to-day, his two-fold function was first, to induce the manufacturers to advertise, and second, to place their advertisements with newspapers. The pioneer agents in the United States were W. B. Palmer, S. M. Pettingill, and George P. Rowell.

As in the case of early newspaper advertising, the magazine during this period contained very little more than announcements of books issued by the publishers. Godey's " Lady Book " and " Peterson's " were the two exceptional magazines which carried back-page advertisements of commercial products. Not until 1864, when J. Walter Thompson entered the field, determined to become a general advertising agent, did magazine advertising, as we know it to-day, really start; and it was not until the decade between 1870 and 1880 that a general use was made of the magazines to advertise miscellaneous trade products. Manufacturers were only beginning to be convinced that advertising was an investment. It was Frank A. Munsey in 1893 who boosted the circulation of his magazine by reducing its price to ten cents. Other magazines copied his example. As a consequence, ten years later it was not an unusual thing for magazines to have a circulation of 500,000. The volume of advertising in the magazines increased proportionately with the circulation. The gradual expansion of the railroads, combined with this wider circulation of the printed medium, made possible the marketing of articles on a national scale. To-day there are 6,000 national advertisers and an approximate estimate of their advertising expenditure is said to be $616,000,000 annually.

At the present day, national advertising has attained gigantic proportions. By reason of its control over the outlay of a tremendous amount of money, it influences, and, in a measure, directs the character and form of advertising media which heretofore were accepted without question in their natural existing state. Magazines, newspapers and bill-boards have responded to the advertiser's persistent efforts to secure neater copy, a more effective arrangement, and in general, to raise the æsthetic standards both of the publication and the advertisements appearing therein. As a consequence, the advertiser and the publisher have profited. Then, too, the incidental effects of these influences have usually reacted favorably to the public. The demand for greater circulation has sent into homes an educational force in the shape of magazines and newspapers; the insistence on variety and nicety in typography, and attractive illustrations, has created to some degree criterions in artistic taste.

The future of advertising is an unknown quantity. But this much is certain: judged by the tendencies which it has exhibited within the past two decades, the advertising of to-morrow will be a decisive factor in the moulding of more things than desires and in the creation of things more fundamental to our civic and economic life than a vogue. The chief reason for this is the change in the attitude of the advertiser toward his profession. Equivocal and dishonest methods have been eliminated, and in their stead has arisen the significant motto, inscribed on the shields at the national convention of advertisers, "Truth." With such a point of view as a foundation, the possibilities for the promotion of the general good are manifold. Thru delicately adjusted publicity the conspicuous antagonism between capital and labor may be mitigated; by means of a fair-minded receptivity and an honest, candid-printed-word, may be destroyed the public's misunderstanding and misinterpretation of corporations' methods; the investment field may be widened; and the growth of communities balanced. Advertising is the inspiration of the future.

QUESTIONS

1. How old is advertising? In what form did it first manifest itself? What economic change necessitated advertising?
2. What are the successive stages thru which advertising has developed? Was there any strong need of advertising in primitive times?
3. Was there any relationship between advertising and the government in early civilization? Name some of the advertising media during this development.
4. When did the second cycle of evolution in advertising come? What has it produced?
5. To what purpose did the *rebus* serve? Discuss the relation between *siquis* and the bill posting of to-day.
6. Mention the factors that retarded early newspaper development? Did the discovery of printing give immediate rise to the newspaper?
7. When did the value of advertising become fully appreciated?
8. Why is the advertising world indebted to Nathaniel Butler and John Houghton? During what period was the advertising agent born?

COLLATERAL READINGS

HISTORY OF ADVERTISING, HENRY SAMPSON.
MODERN ADVERTISING, CALKINS AND HOLDEN, Chapter ii, page 13.
TYPOGRAPHY OF ADVERTISEMENTS. TREZISE, Chapter i.
SELLING FORCES, CURTIS PUBLISHING CO., Part I, Chapter ii.

CHAPTER I

THE ADVERTISER, HIS ARTICLE AND PEOPLE

Desire.—If there be one word which accurately suggests the significance of human nature in its conquest of things, that word is desire. From the cradle to the grave our lives are ever reaching out trying to absorb, to possess, to regulate, to suppress, to attain, to feel; all these, and more, based on the desires of life born out of manifold experiences. If we stop to analyse the function of selling, an economic factor in life's experience, we find it to be based primarily on our desire to possess things. Even though a man be a miser caring for gold for gold's sake, this is a desire. The majority of mankind desires automobiles, vacations, stylish clothing, homes, travel and whatsoever else seems to be found harmlessly pleasurable by others. And it is here that desires become dangerous to society, for we often wish for those things or those conditions that put us into debt to others, and from whose toil there is no means of escape. Now advertising and salesmanship are intimately and directly related to our desire for things. And if the advertiser and the salesman is persuaded that the world is to be made happier, or a more convenient place in which to live, or more beautiful because of the possession of his article or proposition, then, it naturally follows that his goods should be distributed under such economic conditions as will permit all worthy people to enjoy these manifold experiences. In so far as our selling system retards distribution to worthy people, just to that extent is it the seller's duty to take his part in a struggle for a new economic system.

Thus I would characterize the work of the advertiser as twofold: first, to create desire on the part of the class or classes for which his object or proposition is intended; second, to consider himself a factor in the changing of our economic system so that all who would be really benefited should have the opportunity of rightly buying what he has to sell.

Advertising and Salesmanship Compared.—This analysis recognizes the fact that advertising creates desire. In selling under our present economic system, it is necessary to create desire

on the part of thousands of people. When, however, desire
or the vogue for an article has become fixed, and we have competition for the sale of Uneeda Biscuit as against the Educator
Cracker, salesmanship has entered. Advertising is educating
those to whom it is possible to sell but who have not had desire
aroused. To create a favorable impression on the mind of the
mass, previously indisposed, is to create a vogue. It may be
that educating a woman who has never had a carpet sweeper
called to her attention might result in an immediate sale simply
because she does not realize that other machines are in the
market. A man who has never been convinced that a life
insurance policy is a good thing, should not be talked to regarding the payments of a specific policy. He needs to be
educated regarding life insurance in general. This is advertising. For a long time I had been persuaded that a talking
machine was a good pleasure investment, but it was the
best salesman in competition with others that convinced me of
the merits of one machine over another. This is salesmanship.
When the Angelus Company's booklet proves conclusively that
the mechanical piano dexterously played cannot be discriminated
from the work done by an artist, I am immediately convinced
that the piano player is a good thing. My desire for one has been
aroused. When general sentiment is in favor of player-pianos,
a vogue has been created. We may, however, each buy a much
cheaper instrument than the Angelus. At any rate when a vogue
has been established, advertising tends to cease and salesmanship
has begun. Thus, the advertiser changes from advertising to
salesmanship according to the form of his message. His message, either spoken or written, is changed to meet the notions
of the crowd which at one time asks to be told about the thing
in general, and at another, to be told of the merits of this particular thing in competition with others.

With the previously suggested thoughts each advertiser
should learn to discriminate: first, whether he is attempting
to employ the principles of advertising or salesmanship in relation to desire; second, whether he is handling a proposition,
abstract in nature, as a life insurance policy, a bond investment,
or a concrete thing, as a safety razor.

The advertiser's real work, then, is to create a vogue for a particular article or proposition; the salesman's work is to sell his goods, usually in competition with others. Creating a vogue implies an intensive study of human nature. While there are certain characteristics common to all of us as human beings, nevertheless there are attitudes of mind peculiar to the class of society which we represent. Not all people are buying automobiles. Certain classes are buying them. Different machines are being sold to different classes; the Ford machine will usually reach a different class than the Chalmers or the Packard machine.

In what class or classes of people am I to arouse desire for my article? What percentage of the different classes are likely to be susceptible to my appeal? What class or classes can I entirely eliminate? These are among the immediate questions to be asked by an advertiser in connection with the vogue leading to the sale of his article.

The Advertiser's Qualities.—The most successful advertiser, moreover, must be somewhat of a prophet. He must be able to sense, in part, what the effects of new laws, changes of business policy, deaths, public calamities, new discoveries or inventions are likely to be in the distribution of his own goods. It is the ability to think in terms of these larger events that will determine the ultimate success of a proposition. Many advertisers are prone to copy or to imitate. While it is true that it is difficult to find anything new under the sun, nevertheless, that man is likely to prove most efficient whose work and efforts bear the stamp of his personality. Individuality in one's work, if efficiently done, soon stamps the doer as a leader in his particular field.

When John Wanamaker began his present unique form of newspaper copy, it is related that many doubted its effectiveness, yet all other kind of newspaper department store copy became ordinary in comparison. John Wanamaker is establishing a vogue which many others are somewhat hesitatingly accepting, not because they any longer doubt its wisdom, but because it would seem to be stealing another's form. Up until Mr. Wanamaker's time, department store copy had been most ordinary and rigid in form. It was his idea to change, and he did. It is this spirit which characterizes successful men in our age—men who think in terms of changing events; not those who think of the universe and people as fixed in form. When the newspapers began their discussions of the Post Impressionists' and the Futuristes' schools of art, Wanamaker's newspaper advertising was quick to commercialize the idea in advertising copy.

To be alert, to analyze quickly, to see methods of relating the public mind with your article,—these are qualities necessary for the success of the advertiser. Optimism, which believes in the good that is to come; an idea, the result of careful thinking or experiences; energy to carry one's ideas into effect, which often necessitates struggles against the disbelief of others or battles against traditions and precedent;—these are the trio of forces vieing for the complete expression of an advertiser's personality.

The Value of a Good Article or Proposition.—But the modern advertiser is hopeless in his conquest unless he has the goods which will eventually satisfy or meet public demand. Effort resulting in sales, the goods of which afterward prove disappointing to the consumer, while bringing in money at the present time, will ultimately meet with failure. A skilful advertiser may succeed in a given community for a while with a bad article, but his influence will be of short duration. People will soon sense him. If he wishes to continue his artificial success, it will be necessary for him to move from town to town across the country. The death knell of false advertising in connection with an unsatisfactory article has been rung. Severe competition has resulted in a demand for uprightness on the part of honest advertisers; the consumer has felt the need of honesty in buying, and so he approves the passage of such laws as will compel truth concerning his purchases. Thus each article is pleading for a creation that will satisfy a wholesome desire; each consumer is insisting that he be not lied unto; each advertiser is insisting that the other man tell the truth, the whole truth and nothing but the truth.

Let us ask then, what constitutes a good article or a good proposition commercially? Everything in the universe seems to have its place. And when a thing is in its place it is looked upon favorably and recognized as a necessity. When a thing is out of place, it soon comes to be looked upon as valueless and even a nuisance. There are those individuals, however, whose historical sense is strong and who likewise consider the education of coming generations. In their desire to save they establish museums and there preserve those things which have ever been, during the world's history, of service to mankind. Thus the history of the steam engine in its evolution is to be seen in the museum where each timely cast-away invention has been reclaimed to tell to posterity its various stages of progress. Or, again, certain articles pass thru a useful stage later to become ornamental in service. The candle-stick which adorns our banquet table or the mantel-piece, was once merely useful in its function; but the artist has given it a new touch, and it has now become decorative in nature.

Factors Involved in the Birth of "Things."—There are certain factors, then, which culminate in the birth of a thing. One might be termed its utilitarian value. An article should have relation to mankind in the service which it performs. If an object is found functioning in the service of man, a second factor, or environment, has entered into a discussion of its birth.

A given environment contains a working of factors which create, in the mind of some one, a feeling of need. This need is expressed in the form of an idea which, made practical, results in a concrete thing. Thus environment has aroused a feeling of need on the part of some one who satisfies this need by creating what he calls a useful thing.

But still another factor seems to control our appreciation of a "thing" world. This is emotion. Not only do we like an adjustment to our need, but we wish a nicety of adjustment. We wish to be pleased. We have come to regard mere creation as the first step; we speak of it as necessity. We now regard the added emotional pleasure which pleasing form, color, weight and right placement give, as the final test of its *raison d'être*.

The three factors—environment, utility and emotion—are to be found vying with each other for equilibrium in the birth of an object or article. When their relationship is properly adjusted, the particular class for whom the article serves is satisfied, and those thus served come to look upon it not only as a part of the environment, but as needful and emotionally pleasing.

2

This law of adjustment pertaining to the birth of a thing is ever working. The Stetson Hat Company sells different hats in the West than in the East. The cow-boy hat of the Western plains is not that worn by a New Yorker. The clothes worn at a picnic are likely to differ from those worn at a White House reception. The Limousine car has its place quite as much as a little Ford that climbs the veriest hill. Lawn tennis has developed a suit popular unto itself as has the game of base-ball or of foot-ball. In all the instances cited and in any article named, need, environment, and emotion are found harmonizing themselves into the creation of a thing.

Competition between things serving a similar purpose is often based on the emotional factor or, again, on the superiority of utilitarian adjustment to the felt need. The interpretation of the environment out of which an article has come might have resulted in a better emotional appeal by one concern in competition with another. For an article born into the thing realm cannot be separated from the classes of humanity which it is to serve. The increase of intelligence on the part of mankind has meant the increase of things. When a thing first comes into use, it often seems a luxury in nature but with the passing of time these luxuries become necessities. Thus the mind of the world is constantly changing and readjusting itself toward the things of its environment. It is the work of the advertiser to study these changes of opinion as well as to create opinion, always bearing in mind that he is to adjust and so to regulate and so to change his particular article, or the public mind, or the conditions of environment, or all three, that in an exchange of human values money is turned into the cash register at a profit. What constitutes a fair profit or why the profits on different articles should vary from time to time, or the extent to which competition has a right to begin to co-operate in selling in order that all might be benefited, for instance, consumer, seller, and community,—all these are questions vital in the life of successful advertisers. To preserve one's equilibrium and yet to change in order to meet new conditions, is the law to be observed by those who recognize the necessity of self-preservation in a progressive or even a declining economic realm.

That advertiser who is quick to sense the tendencies of his times and to adjust himself accordingly is he who is to be sought after by successful interests.

The People.—It is conceivable that David Harum, away back in the country, could invent a new apparatus for drawing water from his well, without considering it worth while to others. But the economic man would immediately imagine the whole universe using that newer method of drawing water. He would become more and more possessed with the idea that the world ought to use his method. After convincing himself that the method was superior, he would perhaps have the idea patented. After due process of time he would begin manufacturing the apparatus. With smiling countenance and hope, he steps forth to sell.

Presto! Alas! What is the matter? Somehow, humanity does not rush forward to call him blessed. It stands back. Some admit that it looks good; others seem to doubt its efficiency; there are still others who scorn it; yes, there are even those who declare that they would not take it were it given to them. What is he to do? To continue? Of course! Humanity was ever so.

It is related that the first man to create the silk hat met with great difficulties. One bright morning our hero appeared upon the streets in his new headgear and the populace of his particular district became shocked to find him so regardless of precedent. The children from the street and the women from their work soon surrounded him and began to pelt rocks. A general street brawl ensued. Mangled and irritated, he was led into court where he was fined for disturbing the peace and inciting to riot. Not a very kind reception for an article of attire that has crowned civilization's grandest *fêtes!*

Indeed, the first Englishman who suggested laying gas pipes was hooted to scorn. " The idea! The idea! Think of it, lighting the city with smoke sent through pipes laid in the streets! " But the pipes have burned their smoke.

Once more, think of Fulton and his steamboat. The assembled mob actually trembled with fear instead of with joy, that the laws of nature had again been made to co-operate with man.

The Seller and the Crowd.—That selling means force is

generally admitted. The seller stands on one side of an imaginary line, the crowd on the other. The seller is trying to get the crowd to give money for his article, but humanity often will not buy with the mere display. Then it is that the advertiser begins to study this mass of humanity. What does he find? First, that men, women, and children are subject to varied expressions, but their expression is always according to fixed law. He analyses closely enough and names their ways of acting—habits and instincts. Custom, tradition, and precedent vie with other qualities in an attempt to keep the crowd from recognizing his proposition. But he also discovers that these same people are plastic by nature. The young are more susceptible to influence than the old. Constant repetition and reference to the past, with persuasion and reason at work, seem to affect the old. Appealing to the fanciful, the novel, the unique, and feeling in general, as, love, grandeur, reverence, sublimity, serenity, humor, pathos and the beautiful—these are means of getting the youth. And each class of society can be appealed to differently. With a study of this crowd, behold billboards, magazine advertisements, letters, street car advertisements, newspaper advertisements, show windows, demonstrations, trade papers, electric signs, circulars, booklets, posters, unique and novelty advertising to appear! Soon big business means national and even world-wide advertising, and the end is not yet.

Hardly have these forms been thrust among us, when the student of human nature appears. Then he points out three great mind principles at work in order to produce these changes in the life of humanity. The first is that of suggestion. Some of the crowd, approached in the right manner, seem directly impressionable; but—there must be " the right manner." If these are once persuaded, behold, a second group develops for consideration. These are they who imitate. Too timid to venture where others have not gone, they are the first to follow a leader. There remains, however, the vast mass of humanity who will slowly come to recognize this newer vogue and will finally be tempted to buy. The lack of money, conservatism, self-preservation, and a multitude of forces are at work to retard the advertiser's progress, but it is just because of this slowness to accept that the position of advertiser and salesman has been created in our economic system. It is his work ever to educate and then to get the will of humanity in the act of a purchase. He must create the world anew with his article, and all the world must hear as well as take heed unto his cry. The will of humanity is to be his will, as his will is to be the will of humanity.

Summary.—Thus in beginning the study of advertising the student is to become a student of himself, a disciplinarian of himself, a man of personality who has the power to breathe the life of individuality into his article or proposition; his article is to be a well-born article in that it comes forth from an environment which it serves usefully and pleasingly in making the life of humanity progressive; his mind must ever be alert to study the whims, fancies and mind tendencies of people in order that the will of humanity might declare, " I like your article or proposition; you seem just; I am willing to pay you a fair profit."

Such an advertiser is a teacher. He is a teacher regarding the things which humanity needs in order to be happier and better. As invention permits of increased production, and as humanity seeks more and more to enjoy the blessings of intelligence, competition shall give way to co-operation; and injustice shall bow low before the justice that distributes to the needs of all who are worthy to take part in the procession of economic progress. Such is the noble work of the advertiser.

QUESTIONS

1. What is the twofold characteristic possessed by every efficient advertiser ? Name some of his chief qualifications.
2. Where does the threshold of demarcation begin between the advertiser and salesman ?
3. Name the three essential factors that determine the birth and purpose of any article.
4. Discuss the importance of plasticity to the advertiser.
5. State some of the methods the advertiser should employ to cross the imaginary boundary separating the buyer and the seller?
6. To what advantage may the student of human nature harness the three great mind principles of the power of suggestion, imitation, and reason?

PROBLEMS

1. What principles in advertising and salesmanship are involved in the two following *Public Ledger* advertisements (Figs. 1 and 2) ?
2. A store has show windows facing both on a fashionable street and on a commercial one. Display the same commodities to both classes.

3. Combine the three factors: utilitarian, emotional, and environmental, in an advertisement.
4. Given—an article formerly possessing utility, now *passé*. How would you dispose of the commodity?

Get the Ledger Habit

The Public Ledger daily and Sunday is the same newspaper. It is written by the same writers, edited by the same editors, printed on the same presses with the same facilities and skill that make it such a great newspaper always.

When you read the daily Public Ledger it becomes a vital part of your everyday life. It becomes a habit you wouldn't shake off if you could. It informs and amuses on terms that enable you to respect it and yourself.

Reading the Public Ledger daily is the most satisfying habit you could form. And for such a small amount! Ten cents a week—*first thing in the morning since 1836.*

Fig. 1.—Which? Advertising or Salesmanship?

5. In a community where two business houses represent their product, one according to sound business principles, the other by false standards, the latter firm seems to enjoy the greater success. What kind of an advertising campaign would you employ to present to the people the fair article's true worth? Illustrate.
6. Construct a pure advertising advertisement and contrast same with one involving salesmanship principles.

COLLATERAL READINGS

PUBLICITY AS A CREATIVE FORCE IN BUSINESS, E. ST. ELMO LEWIS (Booklet).
THE SCIENCE OF ADVERTISING, EDWIN BALMER.
ADVERTISING AND SALESMANSHIP, HUGH CHALMERS (Booklet).
MODERN ADVERTISING, CALKINS AND HOLDEN, Chapter i.
ADVERTISING FRENCH, Chapter i.

Does Advertising Minimize the Salesman?

Deep down in many a salesman's heart is an antagonism to advertising, because he believes that advertising would rob him of his highest value. If advertising sells the goods doesn't it reduce the salesman to an automaton? Doesn't it make it possible to use lower-priced men? *Quite the opposite.*

Without doubt, advertising does minimize the ability required to sell *a given amount of goods.* But that is in no sense its function. The purpose of advertising is to sell ten packages or yards or pounds where one was sold before.

Advertising, therefore, means dealing with larger quantities and larger problems. It changes the salesman from a plodder to an executive. It enables him to sell his ability and experience on a constantly rising market. The highest priced salesmen in demand today are those who can make the most of the opportunities created by advertising. The only salesman who has anything to fear from advertising is the man who cannot rise to these higher requirements.

Again, successful advertising not only means better salesmen, but *more* salesmen. And more salesmen mean more pace-makers, more supervision. So we find everywhere that the successful salesmen of the concerns which began to advertise yesterday are the branch managers, the territorial managers, the general sales managers of today.

For no class of business men has modern advertising a more inspiring message than for the able and ambitious salesman. He is advertising's natural ally.

THE CURTIS PUBLISHING COMPANY
Independence Square, Philadelphia

Fig. 2.— Which? Advertising or Salesmanship?

CHAPTER II

THE FUNCTION OF SENSE EXPERIENCE IN ADVERTISING

Sense Experiences.—It is a beautiful evening in June away up in the Adirondacks. The sun is just sinking with a red that betokens a fair day for to-morrow. We are seated on a tuft of ground that permits us to view the quickly rushing waters of the creek tumbling smoothly over the man-made dam. Sit with us for a few moments. What happens? A fish leaps up, flashes its silvery belly for a moment and disappears; circle upon circle widens into circle, and the water is at rest again. The tree opposite mirrors itself in the calm blue radiance of the water. Suddenly a cry breaks nature's stillness, a cry of hysterical delight: the little boy, fishing farther up the stream, has caught his first fish. But the fish soon lies quietly upon the ground; its gills move more and more slowly; at last it is dead. A bird is yonder hovering over its nest as it sends forth its evening notes of good-night. The fireflies have sprung up from the grasses all around seemingly to light our path homeward. Night has begun with night's noises.

What is the significance of this description? Merely this, that life primarily consists of sensations. The world is sending to my brain, each moment, a multitude of experiences. Now one holds the attention, now another, while at another time several are working together. It is because of sense experiences that I think. Without sound, light, taste, smell, and all the experiences of sense life, my mind could not say, "What a beautiful night!" The little boy could not proudly exclaim, "My first fish!" Life is thus a process dependent upon sense experience.

Each business is directly related to some one of our sense experiences. The sale of food is dependent upon our appreciation of the taste of things. Coal generates heat in order to satisfy the temperature spots which dot our bodies. Ice saves us from too much heat. Because of the temperature spots, heat and cold, we have the coal business, railroads to carry the coal, refrigerators, ice, metal industries, and thus on thru an endless circle of human activity.

The advertiser's work is largely to create desire where people's senses have not yet been aroused to appreciate his particular article. His mission is to educate people's senses to accept, as either necessary or pleasurable, what has not before been an experience. Or even in the case of an abstract proposition; as, selling fire-insurance, it is the wise advertiser who transforms calamity into a concrete picture containing specific sense experiences.

Each business is more directly related to one sense than to another. The advertiser should see to it that the public is periodically impressed with the quality of sense experience upon which his business is based. There are always groups of people who have not been initiated into the realm of discriminating taste. Yet when they have once come to realize the pleasure involved, the feeling of utility or necessity, the value of your article to satisfy completely, they become regular customers. Years ago there was a very good advertiser of olives who attached to the statement, " I do not like olives," the notion that if one were to eat three, each time, that after several attempts to cultivate a taste, behold,—olives would become a goodly food. That idea will do more to create a taste for and eventually to sell olives to a new group, than any other. And it is quite true that innumerable people have thus acquired a taste which has become as favorably pronounced now as it was formerly disappointing.

Let us analyse the different factors involved in our sense life and make direct application of these principles to the field of advertising. Let the statement, " One advertisement is often more impressive than another, because of a stronger appeal to our senses," be the basis of the discussion.

Touch.—From an evolutionary point of view, touch is probably the first distinctly differentiated sensation. Objects are more important to us when in direct contact. The force of pressure, softness or hardness, roughness or smoothness, are the fundamental experiences. But touch, as in the case of the other senses, is often reinforced by combining it with the others.

Advertisement Fig. 3, with Buster Brown pulling his stocking away from Tige, illustrates our appreciation of durability. "Certainly those stockings wear," is our thought. The statement, "They're made to stand the wear and tear of strenuous play," is re-enforced by Buster's efforts.

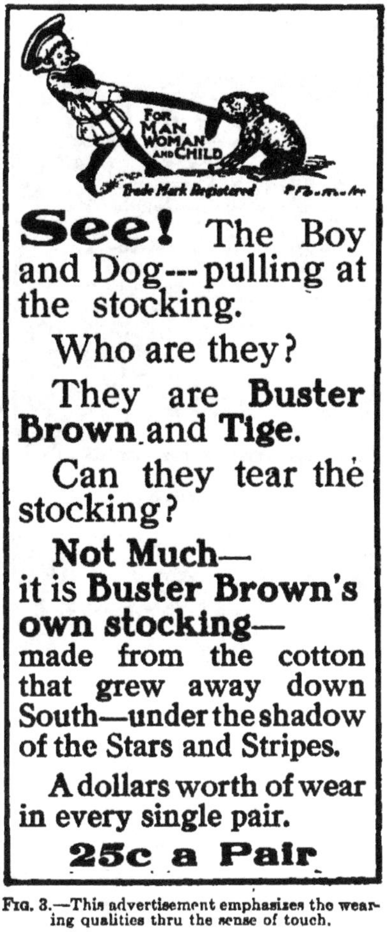

Figs. 4, 5 and 6 are worthy of comparison as illustrations attempting to convince us that each face powder is excellent. Fig. 4 emphasizes complexion powder and presents a type of girl healthy in appearance, so much so, that we begin to wonder why she needs powder at all. Fig. 5 shows the puff actually used in placing the powder, and the girl seems happy enough in its use. We feel sure that she is pleased. In passing judgment upon her as a girl, however, we would be likely to say, Fig. 4 is decidedly more pleasing. Fig. 6 is in decided contrast to the others. It neither impresses us with the powder, nor is the girl particularly thoughtful of it herself. It is a neutral impression which we receive. Could the touch of Fig. 5 be combined with the type of beauty found in Fig. 4, we should have told a story of pleasant touch, a pleased

See! The Boy and Dog --- pulling at the stocking.

Who are they?

They are **Buster Brown** and **Tige**.

Can they tear the stocking?

Not Much— it is **Buster Brown's own stocking—** made from the cotton that grew away down South—under the shadow of the Stars and Stripes.

A dollars worth of wear in every single pair.

25c a Pair

FIG. 3.—This advertisement emphasizes the wearing qualities thru the sense of touch.

and attractive girl, and possibly created a desire to learn more about the powder.

Taste.—Good things to eat are always suggestive of pleasure. Our food companies have been quick to create standards of eating such that the use of their particular goods stamps the user as a discriminating individual. Because of our desire for purer food, bulk goods have given place to those sanitarily packed in boxes and put up in cans. In fact the suggestion of a nicely done up article of food is enough to guarantee its taste to many. But taste, for its complete expression, associates itself readily with the other senses. Smell is aroused as indicated in the steaming

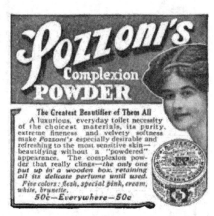

FIG. 4.

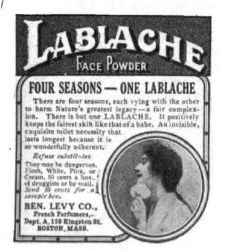

FIG. 5.

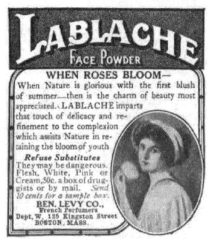

FIG. 6.

FIGS. 4, 5, and 6.—These advertisements illustrate different appeals to sell powder. An improved sense appeal is suggested.

coffee-cup; smoothness is suggested as indicated in the quivering and translucent gelatine; satisfaction, as found in facial expression; tasty food for tasty people as suggested by the table linen, dishes or silverware;—all these are the methods of arousing us to a greater appreciation of the taste of things. Actually to tell how a peach tastes is impossible; but to make it a golden-yellow color in contrast with its bits of dark red in a cut-glass dish with rich cream at hand, is quite enough to suggest pleasure in eating.

Fig. 7 unites touch, color-contrast, our appreciation of beauty, a feeling of skill, and a regard for the conventionalities of the day. Imagine the simple effect created by the appearance of the grape juice alone. Think of the improvement when it is held by graceful hands. How much more suggestive it is of taste and quality by the above complex combination.

Smell.—The sense of smell as related to odor is likewise often accomplished by suggestion. When we experience the odor of a rose, the nostrils are drawn in, the head is inclined to be lifted and the facial expression changes to that of pleasure. Soap may be made desirable to satisfy sense experience in so far as it indicates odor, unless some other quality, as, the " Purity of Ivory Soap," is emphasized. Fig. 8 is similar to many advertisements gotten out by the Jergens Company. Their advertisements always seem to appeal strongly and pleasantly to our appreciation of a perfumed soap. Life Buoy Soap is liked by many because of its carbolic acid odor; it is declared by a few that this suggestion alone recommends it as a cleanly soap and worthy of trial.

It is true that people differ with regard to what is a pleasant odor, but this is often a question of education and the advertiser in calling up pictures of odor must adapt himself to the class with which he is to deal. He must bear in mind that to develop a liking for odor is one thing to accomplish; to satisfy a liking, that is already acquired, is another.

There is in Antwerp a large perfume shop located at a junction of two streets which, uniting, form a single broad street. On either side of the shop's second story are immense gilded urns. Upon *fête* days, when the masses are thronging the streets,

Welch's on grape fruit

—adds to the deliciousness of the grape fruit
—gives you something "different" at breakfast
—makes a snappy appetizer before luncheon
—or a pleasing dessert for dinner.

Nature's best is AT its best in

Welch's
"The National Drink"

Welch's is absolutely pure—it is nothing but the purest juice of choicest selected Concords, pressed when fresh from the vines.

The juice is sterilized and hermetically sealed in glass at once. The exact, sanitary Welch method secures and retains every bit of the fresh-fruity tart-sweetness and healthfulness that Nature puts in the grape.

Use Welch's in making desserts, ices, punches, etc.

*Do more than ask for "Grape Juice"—
say Welch's—and get it!*

If unable to get Welch's of your dealer, we will ship a trial dozen pints for $3, express prepaid, east of Omaha. Sample "Junior" four-ounce bottle, by mail, ten cents.

The Welch
Grape Juice
Company

Westfield,
New York

FIG. 7.—The various factors herein associated with "Grape Juice" tend to emphasize its taste quality.

a most pleasing odor of burning incense whiffs itself within scent of the crowd. A search instinctively begins. There, issuing from the urns of the perfume shop are streams of wind-driven smoke; the crowd is curious and stops; yes, the odor comes from the urns. A good advertisement, unique in character, yet one which tells the story of perfumes.

Sound.—Those who sell musical instruments or telephone systems, those who cry out their wares—these are all dependent upon the sense of hearing to transact business. In selling a talking machine the salesman is exceedingly careful to cater to the hearing notions of his prospective customer. If one needle seems too loud a softer one is immediately adjusted, with an apology for using the wrong needle. Primarily, it is "sound" that the salesman is selling. So in written music advertisements those which emphasize tone and arouse our ap-

FIG. 8.—This pose suggests odor.

preciation of music are most impressive. Professor Walter Dill Scott has shown how the piano business has for years neglected to emphasize tone qualities by means of suggestion. The picture of a piano was all that seemed necessary. Of course a piano in a tastily decorated home is attractive; but a feeling of music should pervade its atmosphere. Both the Victor and Columbia people have succeeded admirably in bringing to the masses a feeling of the power of grand opera music by means of the various stage effects which surround the great singers. There is a constant suggestion of the charm of music; even the musical notes which have sung the phrase of a motif have added to the advertiser's persuasiveness.

The Victor's trade-mark with the slogan "His Master's voice" has a combination of qualities based on tone suggestion that cannot be excelled. See Fig. 9. Figs. 10 and 11 show two different points of view in handling the tone quality of a piano. Fig. 10 sets the mind comparing the Haddorff piano with others. It makes a claim in the state-

FIG. 9.—His very attitude suggests tone.

ment, "The Only 100% Rich Toned Piano," that is difficult to believe. The old gentleman is quite convincing, however, for there is an instructive tendency to hearken when experience and character are associated with old age. Yet how much more pleasing is Fig. 11 with its statement, "200 Years' Search For This Tone." Other pianos are not weakened in our respect, while the Haddorff tone quality is decidedly strengthened. The illustration, Fig. 11, is also suggestive of the evolution of this tone, and we would gladly hearken to it. In Fig. 10 the reader begins to calculate mathematically. In Fig. 11 he is not only delighted with the suggestion of a tone that has demanded so long a study, but he becomes interested immediately in the Haddorff's rich and brilliant tones.

Temperature Sensations.—Just as we possess organs of sound by means of which we become aware of noises in the universe, so we have scattered over the body certain small areas known as temperature spots. Some of these respond to heat, while others respond to cold sensations. If a business is related to our appreciation of hot and cold elements, we should so present these sensations as to force attention to their practical application.

Fig. 12 suggests summer as well as winter. The white-clad peaks recall all the snowy mountains of our experience. It is easy to associate the work of the White Mountain Freezer with ice cream. The icy atmosphere can not fail to impress one with the idea that the freezer freezes, and that the freezer does the work satisfactorily. Notice how summer and winter are advantageously contrasted to emphasize the work of the freezer.

Sight.—Sight is undoubtedly the most important of the

The Only 100% Rich Toned Piano

HERE is a piano which, in just one very important particular, stands at the head of all pianos. It is the one piano that does not have its brilliant notes weakened in richness in order to make them even in power with a number of weaker notes. For there are no weak notes in this piano. Everyone is 100% full, rich and satisfactory.

HADDORFF

The Piano with the "Homo"-Vibrating Sounding Board

The *Haddorff* specially constructed sounding board absolutely assures each note the utmost brilliancy. The result is that the *Haddorff* tone —the "Homo"-tone (from the Greek, meaning "of like, full tone throughout")—has a wonderful quality which you must not miss hearing.

The *Haddorff* tone is recognized as also being notably pure, sweet and of great sustaining power. The materials, workmanship, scale, action, veneers and case designs are of the highest quality known. The "Homo"-tone quality is present in all the *Haddorffs*—uprights, grands and player pianos—and we strongly advise your looking into its merits for whatever style you are interested in.

Write for Free Booklet of the Haddorff Piano and Its Wonderfully Rich Tone

You will surely want to know more about this supreme tone quality. It is all explained very clearly in our tasteful booklet. Send this coupon and become informed on one big point about pianos.

FIG. 10.—This advertisement emphasizes the Haddorff piano in competition with others. Tone is merely suggested

200 Years' Search for This Tone

HERE at last, after piano makers have been seeking for it for 200 years, is the piano that does not have its brilliant notes weakened to get evenness. In this piano every note is 100% rich and brilliant; and the resulting tone — the "Homo"-tone — will yield some of the most charming music you have ever heard.

HADDORFF

The Piano with the "Homo"-Vibrating Sounding Board

No sounding board except that of the HADDORFF assures every note alike the fullest tone richness. We want you to realize the startling nature of our statement, and to become more informed about this most remarkable sounding board.

In scale, materials, workmanship and case designs the HADDORFF will richly satisfy you.

Free Book on the "Homo"-tone

Don't neglect to learn about one of the great piano tones of the world. Send Coupon for book on "Homo"-tone. You'll be glad to secure this information, for it will improve your judgment of pianos. Mail coupon now.

FIG. 11.—Appeals to our common sense or efficiency based upon a pure tone.

senses. By means of sight we experience light and shadow, beauty and ugliness, form and color, height and weight. All the senses inter-relate themselves in order to form a pleasing panorama for the eye. Whatever conforms to the sense of sight intensely enough to impress us, is most important to the advertiser; for he must depend upon what the eye can comprehend in order to get his advertising message to the outside world. Consequently, much of this book is directly related to what the eye comprehends, in co-operation with all of our senses, in order to educate people into an appreciation of whatever goods we have to sell.

In analysing sense life in connection with advertising, em-

The Freezer That Lasts a Lifetime
The enduring quality, ease of operation and quickness in freezing of the
Triple Motion
WHITE MOUNTAIN
Ice Cream Freezer
make ice cream making comparatively easy. The surest way to have pure ice cream is to make it in a White Mountain Freezer. Sold by dealers everywhere.
Write for free booklet, "Frozen Dainties."
The White Mountain Freezer Co., Dept. ?, Nashua, N. H.

Fig. 12.—Intensity and durability are here directly related to the freezer.

phasis has been laid on the necessity of appealing to the elements within the single sense upon which a particular business is to be based. Moreover, other senses are to be used only as they tend to re-enforce the particular sense quality.

Emotional Factors.—But we must immediately recognize that all advertising is not to be reduced to a single sense experience. Other factors are at work. Moods or feelings are being experienced. Humor, pathos, happiness, and even reason are among the suggestions contained in advertisements. And so it becomes necessary to regard advertising in this other sphere of expression.

After we have had many simple experiences, our imagination begins to relate these and to combine them until our minds have

3

created a realm which enjoys combinations of ideas not found in the actual world. Thus the advertiser begins to create pictures and to arouse feeling, mingled with curiosity, in the presentation of his advertisements. He begins to create a new realm. But the advertiser is not merely to amuse or to entertain people; nor is he to reflect back their simple experiences. He is to inject into his advertising picture, be it written or illustrated, an idea of desire on the part of the reader. Constantly advertising, constantly analysing effects, constantly experimenting with the multitudes who read these advertisements, is to result in such judgments regarding his work as to enable the advertiser to get the will of these same people. Getting their will means getting them to purchase.

It is given to literary men to create literature. It is the work of the advertiser, not to create a literary atmosphere in connection with his article or proposition, but to educate people, often by means of literary principles, into an appreciation of the sense quality of the goods which he is attempting to sell. Force which incites one into action is the quality to be set going in the process of reading the advertisements of any campaign.

Where to Study the Crowd.—The careful advertiser is he who studies these human characteristics in their various settings. Wherever crowds gather—in theatre, street, fair, or circus—he should seize with delight upon the expressions of approval, disapproval, or silence as indicative of the receptiveness of the class being studied. Attend the most ordinary theatre and observe how necessary is a direct appeal to the lower senses, as compared with the appeal to the higher feelings, found in the legitimate drama.

Attend the fairs of small places and observe how the day starts with decorum by all, only to end in a mob spirit that revels in storms of confetti, shreds of colored ribbon paper, horns, and cries of hysterical laughter. Then get acquainted with the quiet and sedate in life, the religious and the sorrowful. Fill your own life with the sorrows, hopes, ambitions, and struggles of mankind. Learn to reason and balance the forces of life that are sweeping the world thru experiences,—then act. But put this knowledge on a commercial basis, if you are an advertiser.   This knowledge is to sell your goods.

The Mind and Its Laws.—The mind having had reported a multitude of sense experiences begins to systematize and to arrange these for future use.   It is for the mind that the world is impressing us.   But first of all the mind demands one thing of the world, namely, that its impressions be intense enough. Many of the ordinary street car advertisements illustrate failures on the part of advertisers to regard this demand of the mind. Certain cards need a somewhat stronger tone of color, others are poorly arranged in type form, or the illustration is so ordinary as to be unnoticed.   Such combinations or contrasts should be effected as impress us with sense consciousness; the more pleasing the effect, the better the advertisement.   To satisfy this demand for a positive sense impression, that advertisement has succeeded best which continues itself in consciousness until a feeling of individuality has been aroused.   Should each street car advertisement be individualistic in nature, and properly placed, the reader would be led to scan each card within the eye's glance. Thus the first mind-law to be regarded in judging the merits of any advertisement states: *Each advertisement should consist of an intensity strong enough to force itself into the consciousness.*

When once a given street car advertisement has forced itself into our attention, the mind begins to act upon it.   Perhaps, for the moment interest or even pleasure is experienced, when suddenly, the mind finds itself absorbing with equal interest the next placed advertisement.   Thus we find advertisements vying with each other for attention, and our second law of the mind states: *One sensation tends to modify another when each has an equal chance of forcing itself into consciousness.*   One advertisement tends to modify the effect of the other, however, only in so far as each is excellent and individual in nature.   When this is true there will be a tendency on the part of the mind to read each one thoroughly before passing to another.

Again, in looking at street car advertisements, certain ones placed next to each other begin to associate themselves unpleasantly in the mind.   Dirty saucepans do not associate well with

Campbell's Soups. People prefer pleasant thoughts to unpleas-· ant ones, and if the tendency thru thought experiences is such as to take one's mind thus subtly away from the real thought of the Campbell's advertisements, the purpose of the advertisement has failed. Thus the third mind-law might be stated: *The arrangement of two or more advertisements is often such as to associate themselves unfavorably in consciousness.*

Another mind tendency in connection with advertisements relates itself to that which is new to experience as compared with that which is old. For instance, the mind regards curiously and interestedly that which is new in experience. The old presented in a new form arouses interest, and the interest is likely to be sustained until I have completely associated it with the past. In this manner the new is re-enforced by the past. When there is no past to which the mind can associate its new experience, the novelty of the new effect takes precedence over the real thought. Curiosity, wonder, or distrust will associate itself, often resulting in an unfavorable, rather than a favorable judgment. It is constant repetition which will finally win the mind to a speaking acquaintance.

The Sought-for Advertisement.—Up to this point we have been talking of the mind being acted upon by outside advertisements. There is a state of mind which actually searches for advertisements. Many a woman has eagerly searched the newspaper for a particular department store advertisement. When we go to the classified advertisements of a journal, our own previous interest is determining what we shall or shall not perceive. But even here the necessity of good form, of strong sense appeal, and of thought must be heeded, for there are always advertisements, alike in nature, vying each with the other.

Wherever advertisements are placed in competition with each other for attention, each advertiser has a right to insist that his advertisement be granted such position as will give it greatest force. When this is done, however, the weaker advertisement loses in prestige. The fault often lies in the make-up of the advertisement by a weak advertiser. As suggested before, until each advertisement is individualistic in nature, and is made to harmonize with the laws of the mind, the weaker advertiser has no right to condemn the success of those advertisements which respect the details of these laws.

Summary.—An observance of an intense enough sensation; the fact that one sensation tends to modify another, and, hence, one advertisement is modified by those about it; the tendency of the mind to associate itself pleasantly or unpleasantly with the objects of stimulation; the tendency for the present object of stimulation to be modified by the thought life of the reader:— these are the mind laws which govern the placing of advertisements in relation to each other as well as the text matter which each individually contains.

QUESTIONS

1. What do you suggest was the purpose of the descriptive paragraph at the beginning of the chapter?
2. Are sense impressions necessary to thought? Explain.
3. Summarize the fundamental mind-laws that every advertiser must remember.
4. Can the present object of stimulation be modified by past experience? If so, how would you utilize this modification? How does the factor of age enter?
5. What is the difference between sensation and feeling? Discuss individuality and intensity in advertising.
6. Should sensation value disregard classes? How may advertisers aid in creating a distinctive class? Can taste be cultivated by appealing to the senses?
7. What advertising factors does the good actor possess?

PROBLEMS

1. Yours is one of several advertisements vying for attention. Sensations tend to modify one another. How can you reconstruct your copy to make unity aid you in this competition for attention?
2. Locate an advertisement in which three or more senses are employed.
3. As it is the advertiser's business to create desire thru sense impressions, draw an advertisement illustrating same.
4. Create a new advertising realm by combining simple experience imaginatively.
5. Find a series of individualistic advertisements.
6. Is it better to appeal thru a single sense or a blending of several? Present one that conforms to your opinion.
7. Present six illustrations showing the appeal of each of the senses.
8. Does it pay to double your name space in a directory or telephone book? Discuss.

COLLATERAL READINGS

BRIEFER COURSE IN PSYCHOLOGY, WM. JAMES, Chapter ii: "Sensations in General."

ADVERTISING AND SELLING, HOLLINGWORTH, Chapter ii: "Nervous Basis of Mental Process."

CHAPTER III

INSTINCTS

Significance of Instinctive Appeal.—When we come to analyse humanity *en masse* we find that there are certain situations where each one tends to act in the same manner. For instance, if a steamer is sinking in mid ocean, without time having been given for deliberate action, it takes a powerful mind of reason to subdue the excited people. In their scramble for safety, each disregarding the other, instinct is working; and, in times of great calamity, people almost unconsciously tend to save themselves regardless of others. In fact, under great pressure, people have been known to save themselves without ever having been conscious of what they were doing. An instinct is an hereditary capacity for a co-ordinated complex of reflexes. The tendency on the part of humanity to respond in the same manner, under similar circumstances, whenever a stimulus is presented, is regarded as instinctive. Advertisers have grown to appreciate the significance of instinct in the writing of their advertising copy. If humanity possesses certain instincts in common, with a tendency to respond provided the proper stimulus is presented, then nature herself has already created a condition where great waste can be eliminated. In other words, I do not need to teach the child to play in order to sell my toys, for the child has already been given a feeling of delight in play, and he reaches forth to grasp the red rubber ball. Instinct thus implies a complexity of relation. When the child reaches for his ball, it is not merely to experience the sense of touch, but also to contemplate the ball in terms of its form and in the enjoyment of its various movements. Hence, upon the theory of instinct we find progressive firms like Marshall Field, of Chicago, classifying their toys and playthings as nature would classify them for children. We have six natural periods in the development of the child: first, the chief interests of the baby from birth to 1½ years; second, the instinctive tendencies of later infancy from 1½ to 4 years; third, the kindergarten age from 4 to 7; fourth, the individualistic age from 7 to 10; fifth, the age of cliques, clubs, etc., from 10 to 13; sixth, the age of hero worship from 13 to 15. Each group is found to have play characteristics peculiar to itself and, because nature has thus endowed us with instincts, it is possible that toys and playthings be especially fitted for the different periods of each group.

Again, from time to time throughout our lives, nature changes our appreciation for instincts. For instance, the boy and girl have common interests from the years 1 to 12. From 12 to 16 our boys and girls become self-conscious, and each is inclined to form cliques and clubs, and, at the same time, be hero worshippers. From 16 to 20, there is a tendency for each sex to appreciate the other. And at this time young people are said to care more especially for people than for anything else in the world. After youth has responded to marriage, we find a tendency to regard material possessions as paramount. The possession of things for the increase of human happiness becomes a problem of daily life. The years between marriage at about 21 or 22, and 40, are those filled with trials and experiences which call into play the most heroic of qualities. There are successes balanced by failures. There are almost inexplicable disappointments. The whole universe becomes more and more interesting. Human nature tends to adjust itself to a habit form of expression. The more habitual we become, the freer we leave the higher brain organs to function upon the deeper problems of life. There is a no more miserable or pitiable human being than that one in whom nothing is habitual. Habit thus tends to follow the course of least resistance in the getting of things done, oftentimes, however, at the expense of progress. Yet, living through this period, middle age, with the oncoming of its own posterity, it in turn is forced to recognize anew the needs of a rising generation. Middle age, on thru old age, begins again to be impersonal toward life; it tends to grow more sympathetic and, although fixed in its habits, yet is glad to extend its hand as grandparent to the rising generation. Thus does nature, in her cycle of human events and activities, unite all the periods of life in controlling the necessities of humanity in a common purpose.

It is regarding these instinctive habits and tendencies common to us as human beings that this chapter treats. If the advertiser realizes that the presentation of an advertisement, containing an impulsive or instinctive factor common to humanity during a particular period of time, will bring a response—a response which is natural for every human being—the chance of that advertisement being universally seen is greatly increased. Because human beings are instinctive, the advertiser gains in his control accordingly as he readily adjusts himself to these tendencies of response. But in his analysis he must be careful: first, to realize just the response which he wishes to get; second, from what particular class of people he desires this expression; and finally, take into account the particular period of life.

If the advertiser arouses the instinctive nature in a manner which tends to please the individual, he has taken one of the first steps in the creation of desire. If he can insert an advertisement within the columns of a newspaper or a magazine appealing to those instincts which crave for expression, he may hope for a reaction in favor of the thought which he has presented.

Self-preservation as an Instinct.—The instinct which is most personal is that of self-preservation. Each of us can say, " My hat, my coat, my body, my automobile, my aeroplane—they are mine." We do not like to feel that several families have an automobile together. We rather like to feel that we individually own and possess these things. But to get these things in the possession of humanity has required tremendous energy on the part of those who originally made them. In time, however, people have been taught to appreciate the value of these articles, and so important have they become as a factor in estimating the value of developing personality that to be without the possibility of possessing them has come to be recognized as a plane of living largely inefficient. It becomes hard to differentiate between what we are and what we own. Thus, whenever a new article is presented to the buying public, the advertiser must attempt to make his article desirable for possession. A serviceable article thus presented to the public has the effect, that, to be without it, is to lack progressiveness. To save one's self-respect in the eyes of others, demands possession. Self-preservation requires of each of us that we possess lighting conveniences other than candles. The extreme of this is seen in the general tone of much of the present tobacco advertising. The copy is such that it suggests " non-progressiveness " on the part of those who do not form the habit of its use. To create sentiment in favor of the necessity of a thing, people must be taught to appreciate value where no value has previously existed. When an advertiser succeeds in getting groups of people individually to say, " I want this thing for myself," he has begun to be of real service. To preserve ourselves in the " thing " realm, then, is to possess these things which are not necessary but which can effectively be proven to make each life happier.

The Food Instinct.—The food instinct is perhaps one of the most primitive instincts which the human race possesses. Herbert Spencer has said that, as far as eating is concerned, the average individual will naturally insist upon those things that are helpful for him, take the right amount of exercise and develop his life uniformly, depending upon his instincts. Instinct can thus emphasize the idea of pleasure. Although cultured men and women do not spend hours in a discussion of those things which are palatable, yet a meal well cooked and well served has its place in our daily life. But the mere appearance of food does not tend to arouse the greatest possible desire for it. Our latest advertising reveals the fact that people like an interpretation which consists of associated ideas in connection with food advertising. For instance, if I go into a restaurant which has a dirty cloth laid upon an uneven table, with silver that is tarnished or in quality displeasing, the meal, howsoever well cooked, does not strike my fancy. But if the table has been pleasantly located, with the cloth clean and the waiter exceedingly gracious, howsoever simple the food, I am at least contented in mind. Thus, while food is a necessity and appeals to my self-preservation, nevertheless, the particular manner in which it is presented to me determines my attraction toward it. Fig. 13 is typical

Fig. 13.—Appealing to the *food instinct* through the idea of pleasure.

The Safest Breech-Loading Gun Built!

For ducks, geese, foxes, trap shooting and all long range shooting, use our famous 12 gauge guns as illustrated. For snipe, quail, partridge, woodcock, squirrels, rabbits, etc., our 16 and 20 gauge guns are smaller and lighter—handle quicker and with wonderful precision. You can use 2¾ inch shells and good, stiff loads in the 6-shot 16 or the exquisite new 5-shot 20-gauge repeater.

Marlin

Grade "A"
12 Ga., $22.60
16 or 20 Ga.
$24.00

12-16-20 Gauge
Hammerless
Repeating
Shotguns

They have Solid Top — a thick steel wall of protection that also keeps out rain, snow, dirt, leaves, twigs and sand. Side Ejection (away from your face and eyes). Matted Barrel—a great convenience in quick sighting—costs extra on any other standard grade pump gun. Press-Button Cartridge Release—to remove loaded cartridges quickly from magazine. Double Extractors — they pull any shell. Six quick shots. Take-Down Feature—for convenient carrying and cleaning. Trigger and Hammer Safety—a double guard against accidental firing. Solid Steel Breech — the receiver absolutely solid steel at rear as well as on top.

FIG. 14.—Here the spirit of hunting is emphasized by an appeal to the "right moment" to purchase a gun.

of the principle of association working in the creation of sentiment for " Sunshine " specialties.

The Hunting Instinct.—The most important instinct which associates itself with the masculine type of mind is that known as the hunting instinct. When certain seasons announce themselves, we see groups of Nature's followers getting together appropriate suits, guns and ammunition, fishing tackle and provisions. Nature herself, with breezes fresh enough to urge on, encourages men's actions: but she does not always reward the effort put forth. One chases the deer in the forest; the other sits all day long, waiting patiently for his fish; another tramps for hours thru the dense forest, happy if he but catches the trail of that which seems to be moving. A single shot that brings to earth some shy animal fills its possessor with extreme delight. And, as one writer has put it, when we come to add up the cost of fishing tackle, lines, gun powder, guns, etc., spent each year to satisfy this craving, the expense is enormous. Men's inconsistency in the expenditure of time and energy pursuing game at the beck of this instinct, is shown when they chide their wives for following a " something-for-nothing " impulse thru all the department stores, hunting for a bargain. Back of both impulses, however, is to be found the idea of combat. Let two individuals begin an open fist-fight. The tendency is to make the ring wider and, although not openly, yet secretly, there is often a tendency to encourage the fighters just to see what will happen. The idea of sport itself, apart from painful consequences, becomes exceedingly fascinating. Fig. 14 is an advertisement attempting to lure us on into a purchase of goods thru the arousing of the hunting instinct.

The Clothing Instinct.—Our desire for clothing and ornamental adornment has become instinctive. Our clothes have become a part of life's enjoyment. Moreover, each class of society tends to consider itself in relation to dress. The kind of position which we hold partly determines the kind of dress which we should wear, and a great number of people's effort in realizing greater happiness consists in seriously considering the question of dress. There are two factors which tend to modify all of us in our con-

ADLER-ROCHESTER-OVERCOATS

A Marked Example of Our Leadership

A few years ago the overcoat was just an overcoat; simply a stolid covering to give warmth. Today we have made the overcoat a garment of real beauty, real individuality — real distinction. Under no circumstances neglect the opportunity of seeing the style, the dash, the personality to be found in Adler-Rochester Overcoats this Fall & Winter.

OUR BOOK of MEN'S FASHIONS
This series of drawings from life is now ready

A fashion authority illustrating our Fall & Winter Suit and Overcoat Models $40 to $60. To secure a copy of this book, please send your address at once.

L. ADLER, BROS. & COMPANY
ROCHESTER, N.Y. U.S.A.

A beautiful reproduction, in eight colors, of James Montgomery Flagg's painting shown above will be mailed to you upon receipt of ten cents in stamps. It measures 10x17, and is ideal for framing.

Fig. 15.—The ideal for the social type.

sideration of the clothing problem, namely, that of ornamentation and adaption of style to our particular individuality. At a recent conference of jewelers the statement was made that the well-dressed men and women considered seriously the question of jewelry by way of ornamentation. If we have an article which lends itself to our desire for dress or ornamentation, it becomes necessary to discover the particular class of people who can be taught to appreciate the values which we have to present. Whatever the class to which we belong, there is always the possibility of one particular type of dress which seems to be ideal for that particular class. In other words, we like to picture our ideal self; thus, when an advertisement impresses the reader with the. idea that he himself can be like his ideal, there is a tendency toward immediate response. We all tend to admire our ideal selves. The seller of clothing should then come to realize that his appeal is to a specific class of people, rather than a universal appeal, and that his advertisement is for those to whom a certain ideal is possible. An average business man is not fascinated by the clothing worn by college students, nor does the simplicity of the business garb appeal to the young men. Therefore, an advertisement in its attempt to create desire, must be the ideal for the particular class to be reached. Figs. 15 and 16 give us examples of two different classes of society, each of which is appealed to differently with regard to its ideal.

Something-for-Nothing.—Ingrained in human nature is the desire to get something-for-nothing. Human nature tends to follow the course of least resistance. Our magazines and newspapers a few years ago were filled with advertisements, the copy of which teemed with the spirit of " something-for-nothing." The word " free " became all important. The cheapness of articles had a ready response, but this method of advertising became so detrimental to honest concerns that insistency upon honesty became popular. However, in spite of a tendency for absolute honesty, the masses are still inclined to say, " I am willing to take the chance." If copy emphasizes the idea of getting something-for-nothing, thus concentrating the idea on price

"Well-dressed" for $17

The wide-awake, aggressive American of today demands "good clothes"—clothes that express the best there is in him and give him "individuality". Many men, however, think they can't buy clothes that will do them justice for less than $25.

If you are one of these, Styleplus Clothes $17 will open your eyes; they will give you *style, appearance, comfort* and *long wear* in fullest measure at $3 to $8 less than you have been accustomed to pay for equal qualities in your suits.

We buy more woolens than any other manufacturer and we apply *scientific economy* throughout our vast plant. Into this *one* suit—Styleplus Clothes $17—we throw our tremendous resources—and *you* are the actual gainer to the extent of $3 to $8.

Styleplus Clothes $17

"The same price the world over"

are *genuine, good* values from the bottom up. The skeleton is made with the same minute care as the "parts which show". Fabric all-wool and of exclusive patterns; canvas and tape watershrunk; coats hand-tailored; button-holes all hand-made; linings iron-strong. Try one on and see how well it makes you look for $3 to $8 less. Ask to see some of these!

FIG. 16.—The conservative and saving class is appealed to here.

47

rather than on quality, customers are likely to be deceived into believing that a thing is really better than it is. Now all advertising should be educational in its nature rather than an appeal to mere price, and it is better to train people up to the idea where they can appreciate the quality of things, and where they believe that they are getting actual value, rather than something-for-nothing. Suppose we have a $3.50 shoe. We should not advertise a cheap shoe, but we should rather dwell upon the idea that people are getting a shoe for $3.50 which possesses certain valuable qualities. This is educating people with regard to the value of the goods. It is a recognition of this principle which has changed advertising copy of recent years. However, the "something-for-nothing" idea is still expanded upon and is just as forceful as ever, although its form changes from time to time. The "Premium Offer" is founded on this instinct. When the skilful advertiser wishes to encourage the sale of his tobacco, he creates the picture of a husband smoking his cigar. With an artistic touch the imagination revels in the rising smoke until we see the velvet outline of a chair or a vase, and the wife, thus lured on, believes with every purchase of tobacco that, after all, the smoke-money has not been wasted. She instinctively wants one of the prizes. Nor is this idea confined to a single class of people. Take, for instance, the bargains in dry goods stores. All classes of people are appealed to. Whether or not the premium business is perfectly legitimate, is a question for serious consideration. Nevertheless, I am convinced, after watching numerous folk apply for their premiums in these premium stores, that many people are made happy. These women gather together with their premium stamp books in hand, and with a look of anticipation pick out what seems to them an appropriate gift. Lured on by the instinct of something-for-nothing, the actual possession of the goods makes them happy. Again, it might be said that the life insurance business is partly based on this instinct of something-for-nothing, as well as self-preservation. To be told that if you pay your premium for three years, not costing more than $75, with a possibility of your relatives collecting $1000,—it somehow appeals to the imagination of many people.

Youth is particularly impressed with the idea of something-for-nothing. When rattlers or balloons are given away during appropriate festivities or seasons, youth is struck in its fancy. The giving of a single piece of candy by a barber as the little boy leaves his chair, is enough to insure long friendship between the two. It is not that the " something-for-nothing " idea should be eliminated from our advertising, even though there are actual circumstances, as in the case of the premium system, where multitudes of people, in many instances, pay for their prizes. Indeed, without the premiums many would not be willing to purchase the same article. Yet with premiums they do not feel the burden of the cost, but are thus encouraged indirectly to save; and it is to them, from all practical standpoints, the receiving of " something-for-nothing." However, when this free idea is featured in a way to deceive people with respect to the actual value of the goods, or where there is not good value given, whatever the circumstances, we have a question which should demand ethical consideration.

The Hoarding Instinct.—Then there is the hoarding instinct. Even our animals respond readily to the feeling associated with the idea of saving. Sit in the woods some day and watch the squirrels gather nuts. You cannot help but ask yourself—Do they really know where they are putting them, and will they be able to recover them when they are hungry next winter? Again, the honey bee lures us on to encourage this instinct: it goes out to gather its honey, instinctively to return to the home of its increasing honeycomb. And when the lad of fifteen years finds himself collecting stamps, old coins, stones, birds' eggs, and even animals, he is obeying the collective instinct which is based on the hoarding instinct. The hoarding instinct, too, is what fills our family garrets. Instead of throwing away those things which have passed out of our existence as needful, there is ever a tendency to put them away, in order that whenever the need arises it shall not find us unaware. Our banking institutions and life insurance companies are partly dominated by this hoarding and cautious tendency of people.

The Constructive Instinct.—Just as birds are possessed in

4

early springtime with a desire to build for themselves a home, so does man have the constructive instinct. All progressive people are found desiring to construct in some form. When marriage has channeled the human feelings of a couple, the desire to construct arises. They wish to build and to possess a home. But the mere building of a home does not entirely satisfy. Hardly has it been put up than a new room is suggested or a different kind of roof is desired. There is the element of change ever present in the midst of that which seems to be fixed. Another story to the house is wanted; or, the introduction of electricity in some form suggests a re-arrangement of the general plan. Thus, human nature would re-make the earth.

The Parental Instinct.—The parental instinct shows itself in the mother when she surrenders her life in love to the rearing of her child. The passionate instinctive devotion of a mother—ill herself perhaps—to a sick or dying child is a typical manifestation. Contemplating every danger, triumphing over every difficulty, outlasting all fatigue, woman's love is here triumphant over her own feelings in the care of her children. The mother cares for and loves the child, it seems more to her than her life. Her concern gives pleasure and enjoyment. In the father the same instinct is shown when, in his regard, he is willing to fight and struggle in order to preserve the physical well-being of his offspring. The regard for this instinct in its relation to personal development is noticed in the instance where a young man said: " I never noticed Mellin's baby food advertising until I had a child of my own." Thus it is that there are innumerable advertisements constantly being presented before the people which have no appeal, simply because the background of individual experience is not such as to force cognition of that particular thing. On the other hand, when a new human experience enters a life, things which were before entirely disregarded in daily contact now become of utmost importance.

Beauty.—Another instinct is that of beauty. Beauty fascinates us from the earliest days of childhood. All other factors being equal, if two articles are presented to an individual, one of which adheres to the laws of beauty, the other violating them, the tendency for the majority of people will be to accept that which is more beautiful. When the price of a thing is insisted upon over and above the beauty of the thing itself, in competition with that which appeals to mere beauty, an element has been introduced which, from the artistic viewpoint, tends to diminish the possible sale of that article whose appeal is to the mere cost. Our emotional nature should be made to feel the value of a thing in its beauty-interpretation quite as much as the insistency upon a mere price. A hook and eye manufacturer remarked that he always made it a rule to criticize his advertising with the idea of improving upon the appeal to beauty. His was the first street car advertising ever introduced to the public and the results were most profitable. It must be admitted, however, that there are certain dangers in connection with the presentation of that which is beautiful. We are likely to become so absorbed in the beauty that there is not even suggested the idea of self-possession, and howsoever beautiful an article may be to look upon from a distance, from the seller's standpoint, his article must be sought after in purchase.

Curiosity.—During all periods of life people are prone to be curious. The advertiser has employed this instinct in the creation of puzzle and novelty advertisements. Whenever the element of chance is employed enough to suggest the curious, we have the basis for concentrated attention on the part of a given group of people. For instance, a prominent shoe company had in its show window a large jar filled with water, in which had been placed a half dozen miniature rubber babies of different nationalities. The display was so mechanically arranged that the babies would start at the bottom of the jar, rise to the surface, apparently breathe, and then descend. Thus there happened a continuous race between the babies of different nations. Strange to say, men seemed to be most fascinated by this display. In fact, the interest became so intense that even betting was engaged in. The Lion brand collar concern once placed on the bill boards of a large city their trade-mark, consisting of a lion without the name. This was before the trade-mark name had become common knowledge. The work had been uniquely done and attracted

considerable attention, but they delayed so long in attaching
their own name to the earlier display that, when it was placed,
the public had about forgotten their previous curiosity. On the
other hand, a laundry company in the same city startled the citizens by writing across bill boards in various sections, on the same
day, " Stopyourkickin." Curiosity was aroused and this advertising became the subject of all conversations. Before curiosity
had waned, the name of a prominent laundry appeared which
advertised the fact that every article would be properly mended,
if torn ; new buttons sewed on ; and, in fact, the laundry of each
customer would be kept constantly ready for wear. The returns
from this advertisement were enormous. Thus, in considering
curiosity, we should remember that there is that which is known
as the psychological moment. When curiosity, then, is oppor-
tunely satisfied, the desired effect is likely to be obtained.

The Sex Instinct.—The part that sex plays in advertising
is not to be under-estimated. Many advertisements " get their
message over," partly because of the unique effect obtained by
introducing a type of individual appealing to a given class of
people. A certain New York clothing concern has several athletic
fellows wearing nobby clothing, but the group is always accompanied by one girl. The effect of this on a certain part of the
public is indicated when a young man states : " I always look at
X's advertisement to see whether or not she is pretty and what
type of girl will next appear." With respect to sex appeal,
however, there are certain dangers to be noticed. One should
be very careful in selecting that type of character which best
adapts itself to the article advertised. For instance, if articles
practical in nature are to be sold, where the efficiency idea or
mechanical adjustment is necessary, a type of woman with angular features and neat mathematical appearance is to be preferred over and above the type which is represented by mere
society. On the other hand, if an elaborate automobile is to be
sold, and one of the talking points involves a social interpretation, that type of beauty should be introduced which will appeal
to this specific class. Here mere beauty of form rather than
efficiency may serve as a convincing talking point.

Again, to introduce a sex appeal, upon all occasions, is not desirable. Many calendars become nonsensical in their purpose merely because they appeal to vanity and not to deeper or more settled inclinations of people. The superficial is to give way to that which is more sincere.

QUESTIONS

1. Mention several instincts which are characteristic of each of the six natural transitory stages in the development of the child.
2. What is your definition of instinct? How does it differ from habit? Illustrate each.
3. How may the efficient advertiser utilize the different instincts to create desire.
4. Upon arriving at the age of young manhood and womanhood, mention the instincts the advertiser should appeal to.
5. Give specific examples wherein the advertiser's appeal to the instincts has been overdone. Illustrate.
6. What articles would be likely to be purchased by college men based on an instinctive appeal?
7. Name ten different articles or propositions based on the various instincts.

PROBLEMS

1. Select four different advertisements appealing to the same instinct.
2. Select two different advertisements of the same company appealing to the same instinct.
3. Create five advertisements appealing to three different instincts.
4. Prove by four examples of selected illustrations that different instinct appeals are made at different seasons of the year.
5. Christmas window display of toilet articles—what instinct?

COLLATERAL READINGS

BRIEFER COURSE IN PSYCHOLOGY, WM. JAMES, Chapter xxv.
THE PSYCHOLOGY OF ADVERTISING, WALTER DILL SCOTT, Chapter v.

CHAPTER IV

IMAGINATION

Effect of Imagination on Economic Progress.—Imagination is a quality of mind common to all good advertisers. It is one of the fundamental factors in his progress. It is because of imagination that the advertiser often disregards the past and the present in order that there may be a future for which to strive. It is the man with imagination who has tunneled the Hudson River; it is he who has dug the Canal at Panama; it is his influence that strives to conquer the air; it is he who would communicate with distant planets; it is *this* one who would become as a god in his conquest of knowledge and in his control of things. The man with imagination is he who has visions of a world to come and whose influence repeoples and builds anew the earth.

But he who allows his imagination to play with the forces of life creatively and persistently is heaping unto himself a multitude of troubles. That which is new to others, is seldom found to be accepted immediately. The history of the Bell Telephone records the business man refusing to accept so impossible, and what seemed so impracticable, an invention. They did not have imagination enough to see its possibilities. Alexander Graham Bell did. Thus, there is the so-called impractical idea associated with the dreamer of dreams. He is looked upon suspiciously. Once let his dream become a reality, however, and the multitudes are quick to change their opinions. That advertiser who has a vision in connection with a campaign is likely to meet with opposition. But it is his duty to overcome this opposition and so to act as to bring about the object of his dreams. Unlimited energy; an ideal as a result of imagination; logic in holding one's balance in the present, often to the point of being politic, are the factors involved in a progressive advertising career. It is the clerk who lacks these qualities: this is why he is a clerk. To do what someone else says, to be insistent upon the letter of the

54

law to the point of destroying the spirit,—this is characteristic of the clerk. He never regards an exception as possible; he distrusts the motives and the difficulties of people not of his position or of his orders. He would never think of acting upon his own initiative, of taking a chance, or suggesting to the firm of which he is a part the possibility of a change that would create more profitable relations.   The lad who drives horses or steers an automobile thru the streets of his city has a better chance for personal development than the above-mentioned clerk because the experience with street cars, hurrying pedestrians, accidents, and the eccentric methods of many people make the adjunct " keep to the right " a factor of secondary consideration, and make him use his own initiation. It takes energy to do the exceptional thing. To have done that thing and to be ready to do new things, implies a nature that has a greater chance of developing individuality than that kind of a position, as in the instance of many clerkships, which cowers the individual in the presence of authority.

The moving picture business illustrates the importance of imagination in a most lucrative field. Those who would be successful in creating that kind of a desire which is to appeal to humanity, must live in a changing realm. The actors who play their parts must be ready to change from prince to pauper, and from youth to old age.

The opening of the Panama Canal has brought the west coast of the southern continent thousands of miles nearer Europe. This means that Europe will redouble her efforts in South America. The imagination of the American manufacturer is beginning to play. This new competition begins to create different pictures for each manufacturer; but, woe to the one who sees no picture.

An article commenting on our trade relations with South America reads as follows: " Another obstacle in South America is the obstinacy with which American manufacturers stick to one method of manufacture. They will not make the same pattern of print two seasons in succession, but they persist in making

their goods the same width year after year. ' The American
manufacturer,' says the Latin-American, ' is pigheaded because
he will not change the pattern of his prints to suit the changing
American market.' The Latin-American has his own ideas
about the *parcine* qualities of the manufacturer in the United
States who will not make goods of a width to suit his
customer. . . .

"Then, too, we are prone to pack too heavily. Importers
in most countries of South America are charged duty on gross
weight of packages. The heavier the packing, the heavier the
duty. South Americans who buy cloth always ask that the
board around which the bolts are wound be taken out. This is
seldom done. The result is extra and unnecessary expense with
the custom officials. Also, some enterprising packer will put
goods in heavy cases, reinforced and strengthened, and remark
complacently: ' I guess that will hold those fellows down there
who handle freight.' If he had used light packing, thoroughly
waterproof, the customer would be saved extra duty and his
goods would have arrived in good shape instead of being ruined
by water.

" A few years back a firm doing a big business in the interior
of Ecuador bought in New York a large consignment of stationery. The order amounted to $16,000 and the customer paid
cash. Specific instructions were given the shipping firm how
the stationery should be packed. It was explained that the merchandise would have to be unloaded by lighters and then shipped
part of the way on railroads and then on pack mules. It was the
rainy season, and it was pointed out that the sudden tropical
storms would play havoc with the papers. The customer asked
that the paper and envelopes be wrapped in heavy paper and then
in light canvas, which should be shellacked in order to turn
water. All these instructions were ignored. When the goods
arrived about two months later, all the envelopes were stuck
together. The loss was $16,000 plus customs, duties and
freight." These instances show remarkable stubbornness on the
part of the American. He fails imaginatively to see the Latin-

American conditions in handling goods, as well as to appreciate that the Latin-American temperament is different from his own.

The Advertiser's Imagination.—It is imagination, the ability to put ourselves in the other man's place and to act accordingly that brings results. It is a fact to be noted that when we ourselves have passed thru any kind of experience our sympathy is all the more extended to those who are passing thru the same thing. It is indeed difficult to see ourselves as others see us, or to appreciate that there are really two sides to every question. The advertiser must develop a mind which can live thru the experiences, in imagination, of all classes and conditions of people, for it is thru this quality of mind that he must make himself adaptable to the needs and desires of mankind.

The Kinds of Imagination.—Professor Halleck has given five classifications of the imagination: first, imagination may be such as to produce an approximately literal image of a thing (No. 17); second, imagination has the power to separate the parts of concrete objects (No. 18); third, imagination has the power of forming simple combinations of separated elements (No. 19); fourth, imagination has the power of diminishing the size of an object (No. 20); fifth, imagination can enlarge (No. 21).

The sixth kind of imagination has the power to select from the elements of past experience to obtain a new rational product. With this type of imagination working, Edison produces his phonograph and electric light bulbs. This is constructive imagination as opposed to other kinds which modify actual appearance in order to make a more vivid impression upon the mind.

Power of Imagination in Literature and Life.—To reemphasize the power of imagination let us turn to the various interests of life. In literature we find characters created whose personality is as impressive and real in influence as that of our relatives. Scrooge and Tiny Tim invariably come in our thoughts at Christmas time. Who can take a trip up the Hudson without finding himself contemplating the happy hours of Rip Van Winkle? Mrs. Wiggs of the Cabbage Patch has a philosophy of life from which we do not wish to escape. And what hours of enjoyment Robinson Crusoe has given us. We think of him often and are always happy to introduce the rising generation to this universal character. These books, based on the possibility of imagination to be swayed and controlled, have made money for their publishers. The names of the characters have come to advertise the books. We have come to say, "Who is this Nicholas Nickleby?" An act of purchase is often the result.

Again, the play of the imagination is found in the scientific realm. We find its power in such books of Jules Verne; as, "Twenty Thousand Leagues Under the Sea" or "Around the World in Eighty Days." When Verne first wrote these works, they seemed a nightmare of dissipated energy to the reading public. We do not dispute the possibility of their realization to-day.

In Moore's Utopia and Plato's Republic we see morality holding before our gaze an ideal form of government.

Recall the fabulous stories as related by Mandeville. In our own time, Cook, with his North Pole dash startled the universe. People's imaginations were fired. Advertisers were quick to seize upon this interesting subject and, if for nothing else, Cook has lived to serve the advertising realm.

Examples of Advertising-Imagination.—In the advertising realm there are equally interesting characters which have interwoven themselves into the fabric of people's minds. There is Phœbe Snow, with her rhyme and metre, telling us of the cleanliness of the Lackawanna Railroad. She is usually attired in spotless white. The engineer, with his soot-begrimed face, is looking down upon her in friendly mien from his cab window. Phœbe is an individuality with a changing identity; for she changes in personal appearance from time to time. Nevertheless, she holds a place among fanciful persons in the advertising realm. On the railroad train, this past summer, a young lady declared her trip East would be incomplete until she had taken a ride on "Aunt Phœbe's road" in order to convince herself regarding the cleanliness of the Lackawanna Railroad.

Sunny Jim startled us with his happy countenance. He was perhaps suggestive of our "before and after" advertisements, which have always been popular. His was a personality so strong and winning that the tendency was to forget the food which made him the man he was. Force, as an article of food, tended to lose its identity. Whether this advertisement was profitable to the company itself, at the time or not, it at least paved the way for subsequent breakfast food advertising, and its effectiveness undoubtedly has been to make all breakfast foods the more popular.

Another advertisement is that of Pear's Soap, entitled "Bubbles." Here the charming boy is represented as blowing bubbles. One has just been cast into the air and the little fellow is looking with wondering eyes as it disappears in the distance. The picture is, of itself, artistic and appealing enough to attract universal attention. Moreover, the blowing of bubbles has something of a charm in it for everybody and we respond to the wonderment of the child.

Appreciation of Advertising Art.—From the story related, had the artist who first sold the picture to the Pears people suspected that his creation was to serve in the advertisement of so ordinary a thing as soap, possibly the transaction would never have taken place; for between the business man and the artist there often seems to exist a gulf. Artists, as a class, hate to see their productions associated with industrial life. "Art for art's sake" is their motto; and we must admit that commercial art is a kind peculiar unto itself, with an appeal other than that of mere beauty or emotion. Yet there is no reason why the artist should not be plastic enough to perform both. Often the advertisements might advertise the work of an artist far more quickly and satisfactorily than art exhibits. Moreover, the real artist operating in the business realm has a chance to raise the standard of art appreciation generally. The business man and the artist should each grow to appreciate the other's point of view and then join in a campaign of conquest.

The true artist's point of view is always that tending toward universality. The average business man is too often engrossed in the details of his business to appreciate the point of view likely to be taken by the outsider in connection with his proposition. The more successful advertising men thus unite those

FIG. 17.—A literal image effectively used.

two forces, that of business detail and artistic generality, in such a manner as to obtain a selling exchange.

It is quite interesting to compare different nations' appreciation of advertising art. Each has developed forms peculiar to its own environment and needs. For instance, the poster is wonderfully productive in Europe as compared with America, the reasons, perhaps, being that the Europeans read fewer newspapers, and their popular magazines are limited in number.

In the advertisement gotten out by the North German Lloyd Company (Fig. 17) we have a simple key so related to the form of the advertisement itself as to produce an effect on the imag-

FIG. 18.—Imagination here tends to suggest the parts of the individuals.

ination. Somehow or other we get into the spirit of what a key actually does. The imagination immediately associates a trip to Europe with the idea expressed in the lower right-hand corner,—" The Key to Europe." In order properly to feel the forcefulness of this key in connection with the advertisement,

Fig. 19.—Imagination used to suggest human feelings and instincts.

try to imagine the same without the key. Thus, by the introduction of a literal image of a thing in connection with any thought necessary to be "gotten over," we have aroused a number of associations such that imagination tends to revel in another world than that of a mere reason.

We have a small advertisement (Fig. 18) containing excellent attention value, not only because the mechanical arrangement is exceedingly pleasing, but in that the mind projects itself back of what is actually seen and tends to complete the picture. The putting on of the " New Skin " allows suggestion for each individual. Likewise the little boy at the top of the advertisement who is pantomiming his sentiment, gives the mind a chance to fill in the picture imaginatively in feeling, if not physically.

The Campbell's Soup advertisement (Fig. 19) is typical of the purely imaginative. Here we have a combination of ideas which are not met with in ordinary life, yet which tend to associate a group of emotions, immediately comprehensible. The effectiveness of this advertisement is readily detected. If we were to conceive of each vegetable crying instead of possessing that pleased appearance, the idea of a good soup would be immediately destroyed and negative ideas would tend to suggest themselves. As it is, happiness is suggested, uniqueness is emphasized, and the complete picture of satisfaction readily associates itself with the idea of excellent soup in the making. Advertisements of this nature are destined to have an effect in any advertising campaign. It is not that all advertisements gotten out should teem with this particular quality of imagination, but it is preferable in advertising any article that this kind should be introduced occasionally to break the monotony and allow individuals to revel in the purely imaginative. Attention to human interest is thus concen-

FIG. 20.—Diminution of the size of an object used with a playful and pleasing effect.

IvorySoap—it keeps the nation clean

Every minute of the day and night, Ivory Soap is being used somewhere, some way, to keep our nation clean.

In city, village and on the farm, millions of people start the day with Ivory Soap; use it for the toilet and bath; use it in the nursery and for fine laundry purposes; and end the day with it in the warm, evening bath.

Throughout the country, it is recognized that Ivory Soap does exactly what a soap should do. It lathers freely, cleanses perfectly, then rinses readily—and it is pure—harmless to skin and fabric.

IVORY SOAP .... 99$\frac{44}{100}$% PURE

Fig. 21.—Imagination here both enlarges and reduces the things of ordinary life.

trated, a factor which results in a broader interpretation of a specific thing.

Morse's Chocolate advertisement (Fig. 20) is one quick to catch our imagination. The ability of a soldier so to diminish himself in size as to be able to balance himself upon a chocolate, does not tend to discount the value of the chocolate, but playfully to associate the chocolate with our past knowledge of a play known as "The Chocolate Soldier." The ideas of our past are thus called into an imaginative, composite picture of Morse's chocolate.

The Ivory Soap advertisement (Fig. 21) teems with largeness of view. There is that which is positively fascinating when one contemplates the entire world. As the hand projects itself from the dark distance toward the earth, containing therein an enormous cake of Ivory soap, suggested cleanliness covers the entire continent. We are filled with varied thoughts, each one of which tends ever to associate itself about the desirable use of Ivory soap. This advertisement is really a combination of the power of the imagination to separate parts of concrete objects as well as to enlarge the size of an object.

QUESTIONS

1. What qualifications are essential in the progressive advertiser's career? Does plasticity co-operate with these factors?
2. How can the imaginative advertiser educate and bring into closer harmony people of different natures, countries, and environment?
3. Name the powers of imagination. To what classification does the utilizer of past experience belong?
4. When can the power of imagination destroy identity? Illustrate.
5. Discuss the advertiser vs. the artist. Suggest an equitable solution to their existing animosity.
6. Can you mention any great achievement or any great man who did not possess the powers of imagination?

PROBLEMS

1. Do you consider it a wise policy to introduce imaginative characteristics in the advertisements of a firm whose policy has always been prone to stick to the practical features of advertising? Discuss.
2. Outline a brief advertising campaign wherein you have created an individual with a changing identity.
3. Present five illustrations where the powers of imagination have entered into the several different fields of business.
4. Do you think the American advertiser takes his work too seriously? Compare typical foreign advertisements with ours for the purpose of determining imaginative qualities.
5. Draw a concrete imaginative advertisement which will be universal in its appeal.

COLLATERAL READINGS

BRIEFER COURSE IN PSYCHOLOGY, HALLECK, Chapter vii.
IMAGINATION IN BUSINESS, L. F. DELAND.

5

CHAPTER V

PRINCIPLES OF MEMORY

Memory as an Element of Success.—The mind is constantly receiving impressions from the outside world through the senses. These sensations tend to modify the structure of the brain in the creation of what we call brain-paths. Just as a paper that is folded retains an impression of the crease, so the brain is marked by every impression which is made upon it. However, we are ever conscious of the fact that it is not possible, upon every occasion, to recall to mind the past. Try as we might, there are times when our memory defies a recall; therefore we have come to say that he who can bring up his past experience whenever necessity demands, has a good memory. He who is caught in the throes of forgetfulness has a poor memory. Intelligence always craves for the complete expression of this ability to recall, known as memory.

Significance of Memory in Advertising.—The advertiser, in the writing of his copy, should always consider the campaign which he is about to put forth in connection with the possible play of the memory in emphasizing need for his goods. When first impressions of an advertisement have been created such that the reader feels himself controlled by the force of an advertisement, there should be such elements introduced into the text of succeeding make-ups as to remind the observer of the past advertisements. A campaign which is properly analysed from the memory standpoint should show the effect of the past to control men's actions even when the printed page is not before them. For instance, a young married woman has entered a grocery store for her first household purchases. She has never before seriously considered the possible different brands of goods. When the clerk asks what kind of breakfast food she desires, the chances are that Cream of Wheat will be one which she remembers as having definite qualities. She has become acquainted with the name "Cream of Wheat" through advertising, and at this particular moment of need her mind tends to reflect back to the past. There is a certain drug store which depends upon memory to assist in

66

many sales. For instance, when a purchaser enters the store and asks for tooth powder, the clerk is instructed to say, "What brand or make?" This druggist maintains that people naturally do not like to appear ignorant regarding a proposition and that the usual tendency is, immediately, to name the brand with which they are best acquainted. If the business world would take time and patience to test the public in its purchases, to find what names cling in the minds of particular groups, we should be in a position to judge somewhat regarding the thoughts of the multitudes as formulated by extensive advertising.

Maximum Memory Value.—Any persistent advertisement may at some stage be said to have reached its maximum memory value in its various kinds of appeal. When your advertisement, above all competitors, tends to come quickest to the mind of a given group in the choice of a particular brand of goods, this stage has been reached. The question, therefore, which each advertiser should ask, in reviewing the copy which he has written, is: *Do I have those elements within my copy which help people better to remember my goods?*

Wide Scope of Memory.—The subject of memory involves all the qualities of the human mind. If an advertising stimulus is presented which can call up many pictures, each of which tends to enforce the argument desired to be impressed upon a given group, that advertisement has within it real memory quality. It is readily seen that a single advertisement presented may have within it the possibility of continuing, for some time, the thought of an individual. Take, for instance, the famous Ben Hur electric light sign advertisement once presented in New York City. Here we have recalled the picturesque events of Roman days,—a form of enjoyment and a kind of life which appeals vividly to the imagination. We find ourselves unconsciously reviewing all of the past history we have ever possessed. Certainly, many an individual, if he has never read Ben Hur, must in a measure be inclined to get at the source of so great and effective an allusion.

Essential Factors of Memory.—In considering the question of memory there are the following six factors which, persistently used, cannot fail to impress one with the continuity of an advertising campaign: repetition, poetry, intensity, association, ingenuity, imagery.

Repetition—Identity.—First there is repetition. Constant repetition cannot fail to force itself into final conscious recognition. The world about us is filled with a multitude of factors which to many, during certain periods of life, have no recognition as existing. Yet these same things are recognized by many others. However, occupying a persistent place, though insignificant, the mere fact of their *being* must finally react upon the human mind for recognition. But the advertiser who wishes quick returns is not satisfied with modest copy and seeks to introduce such elements into the make-up as will force recognition. Repetition, as intimated above, depends upon the past to enforce the present; consequently, when advertisements appear successively by a single concern, howsoever small, there should be an element of identity common to all of the advertisements. A common identity is the bond which unites the entire campaign and at the same time enforces memory. Again, by way of intensive analysis, it must be stated that whenever that which is obscure does come to one's attention, the chances are that it will be remembered afterwards. There are many small advertisements in every magazine whose appeal to the eye is, at first glance, lost by hundreds of people. It may be that six months go by until, by some peculiar combination of circumstances, that particular announcement is most vividly brought into recognition. When this happens, the reader is conscious of the fact that he has in a certain hazy manner already become familiar with its contents, yet has not consciously related himself to its existence. I should say that the poorest kind of advertising, if used persistently with a common identity running throughout the entire campaign, would at least bring uniformity of replies. On the other hand, a campaign poor in make-up, in that there is not a common identity, would be rather spasmodic in its returns. It would seem that the old maxim, " If at first you don't succeed, try, try again," is true regarding the poorest repetition. This of course only means that it is better to do even a small amount of poor advertising than not to advertise.

Identity which forces memory is to be seen in such advertisements as " Gold Dust," " Sapolio," " Ivory Soap," " Fairy Soap," " Quaker Oats," " Cream of Wheat," and so on down the list.   When the " Sapolio " advertisements picturing " Spotless Town " were thrust before the attention of the public, they fascinated because of their uniqueness.   When, however, the public had apparently become accustomed to the copy, the company withdrew the advertising matter.   There was then a lapse of several years before its reappearance.   Personally, I had never forgotten the first " Spotless Town " copy and I found myself wondering if it would again be used.   This excellently illustrates how a remarkable idea used periodically, even including the idea of years in its presentation, can form a continuous effective thought for humanity.   A new generation comes into consciousness every so often and, upon this theory, this newer generation is introduced to a new idea, while those who have been pleased in the past are glad to greet it again as an old acquaintance.   It is said that the skating-rink craze can be depended upon to bring a good livelihood to its promoters if they periodically, every seven years, introduce roller skating to the community or the country.

Repetition Engenders the Idea of Success.—Again, repetition tends to engender in the mind the idea of success.   Whatever is consciously repeated seems to be holding its own in the world.   When campaigns have been pursued persistently and are then dropped out of the public mind, there is immediately a question as to whether or not failure has been encountered.   If, however, at the psychological moment, a new advertising campaign is suddenly and effectively thrust before the public, to be followed by conservative and regular advertisements, the public is at least interested.   On the other hand, if the campaign disappears entirely, non-success is often the interpretation of what has happened; and such associated ideas are inhibitive factors not desirable in connection with any advertising picture.

It is said that a certain physician in a country community had not been as successful as he wished.   He conceived the idea of placing himself in attention before the people of his particular section, so he began to take drives in all directions.   The farmers, seeing him continuously on the move, began to draw conclusions. They said, "Doctor X. must be in great demand, for he seems ever to be hastening to see some one. However, we do not hear of deaths." It being, too, a time when the telephone service was not in vogue, he was exceptionally fortunate. As no complaints were ever centered against Doctor X., it therefore became a conviction that he must be a good physician. The effect of this was to consider the passing of Doctor X. as an appropriate time when advice might be sought regarding minor sicknesses. It is said that Doctor X.'s practice soon grew. This instance illustrates the maxim, "Nothing succeeds like success," and somehow or other success often depends upon repetition. To get a recognized standard into the public mind should, in its first steps, be the object of advertising. The business world can tell innumerable stories of concerns which have won the public mind through advertising and whose popularity began to wane upon the withdrawal of advertising. Competition is what keeps things moving. Competition is emphasized through repetition. When once this fact is lost sight of by an unguarded merchant, his competitor has had a chance to gain a hearing and possibly has won the day. Water allowed to drop regularly upon a rock, howsoever small the drop, soon wears away the stone. The first drop is not so powerful, but the added drops bring to pass the seemingly impossible.

Comparison of Daily, Weekly and Monthly Repetitions of Advertisements.—Let us, on the basis of the theory derived from a close analysis of general conditions, discuss the subject of daily, weekly and monthly repetitions of advertisements. This discussion at least furnishes material with which to get at the truth. It is not to be considered at all final, but is a suggestion. Suppose you wish to select eighteen days during a particular period of the spring in which to sell motorcycles. The question is asked: Would it be better to run the advertisement continuously for eighteen days or every other day? Again, with the expense the same, would you rather have an advertisement, twice the contemplated size for daily use, every other day? Carrying out the theory of repetition, the same page position should preferably be used in either event. Once seen on a certain page the fact of its being repeated emphasizes further its importance. People unconsciously expect it to be there. Constant repetition should in time force recognition of its being there. But if doubling the size of the advertisement gives decided attention qualities, making positive what already tended toward indefiniteness, then the " every-other-day " program would be better. In this case repetition has been emphasized, and, by reason of the added stimulation thru the increase in size, has increased its memory-value. On the other hand, given copy which, although small, is decidedly individualistic, its constant repetition should also be effective. Money limitations, of course, check all advertisers in their desires. Whatever the limitations, this theory is suggested: *Any advertisement possessing qualities which gain the attention should be repeated not so much constantly as continuously, with such lapses as would tend to reinforce memory with the idea of success, rather than even the slightest positive suggestion of failure.* We must remember that many two-inch advertisements have the quality of getting results, whose cumulative effect is based upon repetition and certain preperceptive elements of human nature, rather than excellency of display or emphatic copy. Again, some kinds of enterprises need larger spaces than others to give required information. Human nature is related to a dignity interpretation of itself. It wishes a nicety of adjustment; therefore, repetition, which tends to affect one with dignity, tends to assist in creating a vogue.

Repetition Differentiated from Sameness.—We must remember, however, that repetition is not sameness. If at this moment you were to walk into my office, you who entered a year ago, the chances are that you would have a different suit, hat, and even a changed expression on your face. Nevertheless, whatever changes have been wrought by passing events, there would still be enough of you to gain immediate recognition. The advertiser must try to keep an identity in the minds of the public, preferably an identity which does not confuse itself with a competitor.

"A.B.A" American Bankers Association Cheques

The sale of "A. B. A." Cheques *for use throughout the United States continues as usual*, and the cheques are affording to travelers in "the S'tates" their customary service of protection and convenience in respect to money matters.

The sale of "A. B. A." Cheques *for foreign use has been discontinued temporarily*, it being impossible to give positive assurance to tourists that travelers' credits will be uniformly honored abroad at all places under conditions which change from day to day.

Through the co-operation of the Officers of the United States Government, Committees of Bankers in New York, London and Paris were enabled in a very short time to perfect arrangements for protecting all forms of travelers' credits issued by American institutions and firms; and holders of travelers' cheques and letters of credit have been by this means relieved from the serious consequences of the sudden paralysis of customary banking facilities abroad.

As soon as conditions warrant, the sale of "A. B. A." Cheques *for use abroad* will be resumed.

BANKERS TRUST COMPANY, Trustee
New York City

Fig. 22.—The repetition of increasing note values herein impresses the memory.

Poetry.—Another impressive form of repetition is to be found in the use of poetry. Human nature has a tendency to respond to the rhyme and the rhythm of words. The bards of Homeric times sang their stories of bravery and valor in rhyme, and they were hearkened to by peasant and by noble-man. Many advertisers have employed this tendency advantageously, until through the "Mother Goose" rhymes of our childhood, we have become acquainted with different brands of goods. The idea of poetry cannot be disassociated with beauty. While a rhyme cannot be said to be beautiful, yet it does possess the idea of harmony. Street car cards have employed this method profitably to instruct the public. A rhyme skilfully made tends to give a touch which indicates quality. In discussing rhyme, poetry, written in a form like prose, is not so effective. Poetry, to be most impressive, should retain its poetic form. Whether we are conscious of it or not, the form in which poetry expresses itself is quite as necessary as the rhyme, rhythm, and thought. Fig. 22 is an example where repetition within a single advertisement, once catching the eye, tends most effectively to direct our after-memory processes.

Intensity.—The second factor in memory is intensity. The degree of intensity decides the depth of the impression made and accordingly tends to fix its hold on the memory. We have already learned that for advertising there is need for attention elements. Everyone, to get at the greatest intensity, should seek for the superlative degree of these attention elements. Intensity should be considered with respect to the following: first, color effects, contrast, and harmony within the advertisement itself; second, contrast and harmony on the particular page; third, styles of type, and the presentation of the goods.

We should remember, with respect to our experiences in life, that there are three natures which are met with in human experience. One is the physical, another that of feeling or sentiment, and last, that of the intellectual. Or, again, we may appeal to factors relating respectively to body, mind and soul. Consequently, the subject of intensity, in connection with its interpretation of any one of these phases of human experience, should try to emphasize the quality desired. Fig. 23 is an example of intensity.

Association.—The third factor involved in memory is association. People remember the past partly because of associations which the advertisement calls up. Association on the part of a stimulus is determined by the following factors: habit, recency, vividness, emotional congruity, comedy and tragedy, pleasure and pain. When Frederick Cook declared himself the finder of the North Pole, innumerable goods were associated with this recent experience of an adventurer. When a life insurance company, after a disastrous train wreck, inserts an advertisement which associates the necessity of a policy with the disaster, recency tends to combine with the present stimulus in the making of such memory processes as are fundamental for the insurance business. Here we would have pleasure and pain,—two opposite forces vying with each other for a memory impression which might result in commercial gain. With life insurance, pictures of misery might prove convincing; while with other kinds of trade, suffering becomes repulsive. For example, perhaps few people would be pleased with an association of an accident and the advertisement of an undertaker. To advertise a competitor's canoe by means of an illustration showing a drowning man, with copy that tended to enforce the merits of your canoe, guaranteed not to do this particular thing, might be somewhat effective for memory. But how much better it would be to emphasize the idea of absolute safety, the pleasures and peace of mind aroused with the thought of safety and a happy environment, rather than emphasize, at your competitor's expense, the disastrous.

Association: Desirability of Emotional Congruity.—Emotional congruity, meaning that the setting in connection with its appropriate emotion be brought out, emphasizes memory. For instance, at the present time a Chicago firm is attempting to sell small farms in Florida. The associations aroused regarding Florida are: the ease with which things are grown, the many crops within a single year and, consequently, the idea of profit. But the promoter is not satisfied with the argument for he emphasizes the delightful climate, the exhilarating benefits, and his absolute guarantee of success,—all of which not only pleases us economically, but gives to us a complete emotional expectation of satisfaction.

Association Should Arouse a Definite State of Mind.— After all, association as effecting memory consists in keeping that combination of elements which arouses a definite state of mind, afterwards susceptible to recall. Even though an advertisement first impresses one unfavorably, it is a decided im-

EDISON MAZDA

Fig. 23.—Not only is the memory impressed by the intensity of the Mazda light itself but also by the character found in the hand.

provement over the one which does not attract at all. It is rather remarkable in connection with the teaching of advertising to find so many students constantly bringing certain advertisements of apparently successful companies, remarking on their poor execution of an advertising idea. If an occasional student brought this, it would not be so remarkable; but invariably, in connection with certain firms' advertising, several students will bring the same copy. Their criticism is that the advertising is poor. I am led to believe, however, that this copy, howsoever poor the impression, is good from an advertising standpoint in that the message is inevitably gotten over. It has within it a quality which impresses the memory. Now, if a company recognizing this poor impression with respect to memory, were to institute from time to time such a campaign as would create exceedingly favorable impressions, it would seem that the campaign would in the long run be doubly effective.

Wrong Association Should be Destroyed.—Every advertiser should at times take pains to destroy whatever wrong associations have been connected with his copy. I have in mind a certain razor company which doubled the price of its blades; the announcement was intense enough to cause widespread discontent. The writer at this time was entering a complaint regarding certain poor blades. He chanced in the store when a representative of the razor company had been sent to adjust a universal complaint of poor blades in that particular community. The fact of his presence had been advertised, and before long the store became crowded with those who had complaints to make. He was most dexterous in his handling of the crowd. First he told how the change from the old process to the new one necessitated a peculiar manipulation of machinery to which the workingman had not been previously accustomed. This accounted for the poor blades. As to price, why, the cost of getting out these blades on the new process would be much greater. Then he proceeded to picture the most expert men in the land examining those blades at an enormous salary. Well, he changed the ill-will of people to acceptance of the proposition at least. As for that particular razor at the present time, the associations of the majority with respect to the exorbitant high price and many unsatisfactory blades are not such as to make a man rejoice in its possession. That it is good, is indisputable. That it is not handled with regard to a consideration of a decent price and a fair deal for all interests, is the feeling of association many have regarding it. We detest

being imposed upon.   People cannot be eternally changing from one thing to another.   Every dealer should conduct
his business on a basis which keeps the consumer satisfied.   A
recognition of the worth of an article is one factor.   Its satisfactory marketing and use, arousing favorable associations in
the mind of the people, is another.   Advertisers reap the greatest
results by combining those elements so that the customer's
association-attitude toward the goods is a pleasant one.

Fig. 24 is an example of memory probably strengthened by
the pleasant associations aroused.

Ingenuity.—A fourth factor which exists in establishing a
memory process is that of ingenuity.   The stimulation of memory by employing a mechanical adjustment of things to assist
the recollection, is known as the ingenious method.   By manipulation, dates and numbers are thus arranged, and, because of
the nearness to certain fixed ideas, are forced into the memory.
" Thirty days has September, April, June and November," is
one of the most common examples.

The use of the word " Uneeda " is really a phase of this kind
of memory.   " Iwanta " was not permitted but was similar in
contents.   A street car advertising sign is now appearing which
consists in an entire broken mass of material to be united in
a puzzle.   Curiosity is aroused.   Day by day the public is looking for the union of the pieces.   Here we have repetition in its
constant, individual, yet varying presentation; association is
appealed to as a problem, for every one is trying to associate
the past to anticipate the putting together of the parts.   The
ingenuity of presentation will impress the advertisement upon
thousands of minds, and because it was so ingeniously presented
it will tend to be remembered.   Thus the method of presentation
becomes as great a factor as the thing presented.   Fig. 25 is an
effective, unique method of helping the memory processes.

Imagery.—Another factor to be considered in connection with
memory is that of imagery.   Those advertisements which bring
to mind past experiences do it through a recall of certain
sense impressions we have had in the past.   It is interesting
to know that we all do not remember things in the same way.

FIG. 24.—Here the delights of mountain scenery are suggested along with travel.

For instance, if asked to visualize the breakfast table of this morning, some people would not be able to call up the picture, but would have to depend on thought regarding each article. To many the picture of one seated at the piano would associate itself with some melody. The melody would surely come if a familiar tune were suggested. A street car advertisement consists of a group of young fellows about a table drinking. The words " And there's always fair weather, When good fellows get together,"

are so placed as to command attention at first glance. Almost immediately the motif of the song comes to mind and you continue on to the close. The words of a song unknown or inappropriate would detract considerably from the illustration. The words " Dropping, dropping, hear the pennies fall " come to mind. It is readily recognized as an ancient Sunday-School hymn. We can also hear the pennies fall into the box and the clink of the coin as it is passed about the class. This is known as auditory imagery or the ability to remember sounds. We also have visual imagery to recall the appearance of things; muscular imagery to recall the

Fig. 25.—Ingenuity of arrangement forces particular attention involving the memory process.

sensations of weight or pressure; gustatory imagery, which is calling up our taste sensations; olfactory imagery to bring up our past experience of smell.

Knowing that whole classes of people find it impossible to recall the past with respect to the images of any given sense experience, the advertiser should constantly change his method of appeal. " Be all things to all men " when the history of a particular advertising campaign is written.

QUESTIONS

1. What relation exists between past experience and recall?
2. What is an essential qualification of intelligence? Explain.
3. When has an advertisement reached its maximum memory value?
4. Name six factors which, when persistently employed, determine the continuity of a campaign.
5. Name the bond which unites the entire campaign and at the same time enforces memory.
6. What part does "affecting one with dignity" play in creating a vogue?
7. Differentiate between repetition, sameness, and identity. What is the value of a common identity in advertising?
8. What form of poetry is most effective in advertising?
9. Into what three natures can the bulk of mankind be catalogued?
10. Association, on the part of a stimulus, is determined by what factors?
11. Is it ever permissible to employ advertising copy that impresses unfavorably?
12. Relate the different forms of imagery.

PROBLEMS

1. After force has gained the public's initial attention, discuss what elements should be introduced in succeeding make-ups.
2. Analyse some current campaign from the memory standpoint; show by illustration, how the effect of past experience controls men's actions.
3. If repetition depends upon the past to enforce the present, explain how this best can be obtained in an advertising campaign.
4. Discuss: "It is better to do a small amount of poor advertising than not to advertise."
5. When a new generation is born into consciousness, how should the efficient advertiser construct his copy so as to solicit the interest of the new generation, and at the same time, please the old?
6. From the standpoint of the advertiser, interpret the following Attention Triangle in terms of memory perception.

Perception
C

ATTENTION /\ TRIANGLE

Stimulus → B Past
A   Experience

7. Which profits the advertiser more, competition or co-operation? Why?
8. Discuss "constantly" vs. "continually" as regards repetition in an advertising campaign.
9. Debate the question: Advantages of favorable and unfavorable impressions created by copy.
10. Discuss ingenuity and create an ingenious factor for a campaign.
11. Determine whether there is any connection between imagery and the senses.
12. As perceptions are not interpreted in the same way by all people, discuss the significance of the advertisers being, "all things to all people." Is this plasticity?
13. Create a series of breakfast-food street car cards to be placed in New York City which regard memory. Analyse the following factors:
    1. Number of cards; 2. Number of street cars in which to be placed; 3. Time to be run.
14. You are about to create a minimum series of cards for an imaginary liniment to be run for six months of the year in New York street cars. This series is to be based on memory appeal. Analyse the factors involved in the process.

COLLATERAL READINGS

BRIEFER COURSE IN PSYCHOLOGY, WM. JAMES, Chapter xviii.
THE THEORY OF ADVERTISING, WALTER DILL SCOTT, Chapter xiii.

CHAPTER VI

ATTENTION

Attention: Fundamental Factor in Successful Advertising.—The fundamental mind factor in all successful advertising has been explained, when we say that the manufacturer or merchant under discussion has gotten the attention of his crowd. On the other hand, it is conceivable that a given business gets the attention of a crowd without being successful financially. That attention is gotten at all, is the significant factor. It means that there is recognition of the existence of a thing. To the average person, the multitude of tiny insects that are running thru the meadow grasses are unknown. If you were to stretch yourself upon the ground, fixing your eyes upon the grass, a procession of life never before realized would soon begin to troop before your gaze. As your interest continued, some one species, because of form oddity, peculiar color, or curious performance, would hold your attention. In the same way people are born into the appreciation of an advertising realm. Advertisements appear upon every hand; yet it is astounding the comparatively few which gain concentrated attention. To the student of advertising it is quite appalling to contemplate the millions of dollars used to tell people about products without gaining the courteous attention of more than a few. No wonder that the average business man looks with reverence at an advertiser who comes into his establishment and triples the sales within a year's time. Such an advertiser is often regarded as possessing a Heaven-sent wand which thus opens the door of commercial opportunity.

Analysis of an Advertisement from Attention Standpoint.—A scientific analysis of any advertisement must begin with the questions, " Is my advertisement of such a nature that people are reading it? Are they having impressed upon them the fact of the existence of my article? Are they inclined to reject or to accept it?" If these three questions are answered in the affirmative, complete attention value may be said to have been attained. *If people are not purchasing, yet the advertisement is well known, at least the attention value is not to be*

condemned, and the advertiser must search elsewhere for the .
difficulty.

Relation of Attention to Sensations and Association of Ideas.—Attention relates itself to two sets of experiences. The possibility of paying attention to anything at all is immediately due to the fact that a sense organ is acting. Without a sense organ we should not have the means of becoming conscious of a thing. Hence a study of sensation in connection with our appreciation of any advertisement is vital. But the sense of sight is the means by which the greater amount of advertising is brought to our attention. Thus an intensive study of the laws which govern sight becomes a necessity. The eye itself, in its various movements, should be analysed in connection with any advertisement to find out whether the make-up of that advertisement is such as to encourage or to discourage attention. So attention, on the one hand, must consider the question of eye adjustment to the advertisement. A second factor which enters into the experience of continued attention is mental in nature. As soon as the eye comprehends the form of a thing by means of eye movement, ideas begin to associate themselves. If this association of ideas is such as to please, then my mental as well as my physical attention is likely to continue.

Facility of Eye Adjustment.—Mental pleasure, however, is not the only experience in our perception of an advertisement. Eye movement in its comprehension of the form or content arrangement of an advertisement is also capable of producing a pleasant feeling. The stroking of a dog gives a pleasing sensation to the sense of touch quite as pronounced as the idea of affection and friendship indicated by his wagging tail. Thus it would seem that, that advertisement which easily adjusts itself to the sense of sight mechanically, is most pleasing. At the same time if it arouses thoughts happy in nature, or relatively so, in connection with the intended message, the greatest attention value has been created.

Factors Aiding an Appreciation of Mechanical Make-up: Distance.—Let us proceed to analyse those factors of eye experience which assist in our appreciation of the mechanical make-up of advertisements.   The distance at which an advertisement is placed from me decides whether or not I shall be able to get its message.   Many street car cards have a lettering either so large or so small that the eye moves quickly on to another advertisement whose reading matter can be more easily comprehended.   Curiosity, alone, which in some manner may have been aroused, will often help to overcome the physical difficulty in reading.   Not a few electric signs are made which flash their messages all too quickly for the average passer-by.   The distance at which an advertisement is to be read by the average person should be the first factor considered in the make-up of an advertisement.   The type size should then be adjusted to this distance.

Style of Letters and Form of Make-up.—Moreover, the style of letters should be distinct and easily comprehended.   The moment the reader begins to consider the style of type, before he has fully comprehended the thought of the advertisement, possible superlative attention value has been reduced.   Rather should the make-up of an advertisement be so related that the emotional or feeling element is also regarded.   For instance, after having read one of the " Campbell Soup Kid " advertisements, I am often compelled to examine the means by which so pleasant an effect was created.   But it must be admitted that attention can be favorably obtained otherwise.   Should ingenuity employ the method just opposite to this, or where the mechanical form is displeasing, yet which forces us to the thought of the make-up, we must admit that attention has been gained and possibly our sale accomplished.   A misspelled word will often gain the attention where its correct spelling would not.   Yet how much more forceful is that advertisement which gets the attention with the same word correctly spelled!   Eye adjustment and consciousness of pleasure which pass into favorable thought, is the regular method.   Howsoever we disregard regularity, we should aim to get concentrated attention.   Complete attention means that the entire mechanical make-up of the advertisement has not, in the least, conflicted with the comprehension of the message.

Making Thought Paramount.—Many advertisements are so constructed that the thought is paramount. We are not conscious of the make-up. If such a message "gets over" to all for whom intended, it is good. It may be, however, that the

Fig. 26.

VIRGINIA COLLEGE
FOR WOMEN   (JUNIOR)   ROANOKE, VA.
One of the leading Schools in the South. Modern buildings. Extensive campus. Located in the Valley of Virginia, famed for health and beauty of scenery.

Elective, Preparatory and College Courses, Music, Art, Expression, Domestic Science. Supervised athletics. Students from 32 States. For catalog address

**MATTIE P. HARRIS, President, Roanoke, Va.
Mrs. Gertrude Harris Boatwright, Vice-President**

Fig. 27.

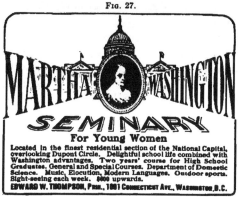

SEMINARY
For Young Women
Located in the finest residential section of the National Capital, overlooking Dupont Circle. Delightful school life combined with Washington advantages. Two years' course for High School Graduates. General and Special Courses. Department of Domestic Science. Music, Elocution, Modern Languages. Outdoor sports. Sight-seeing each week. $800 upwards.
EDWARD W. THOMPSON, Prin., 1601 Connecticut Ave., Washington, D.C.

FIGS. 26 and 27.—These advertisements illustrate the value of focal point and eye movement in gaining immediate attention. Consider the different associated ideas.

touch which gives a feeling of quality would give still greater satisfaction. It is an intensive regard for these details which help considerably in producing individuality, and at the same time result in added attention value. Figs. 26 and 27 excellently illustrate these laws of distance and emotional stimulation in connection with eye adjustment: first, the eye is not so well pleased in the comprehension of Fig. 26 as of Fig. 27 because the type of the former is less fortunately arranged for a pleasing eye adjustment; second, the thought associated with Fig. 27 would be much more effective in its appeal, provided the idea of " city " is the preperceptive factor.

Fancy Type.—Styles of fancy type not easily readable, are to be discouraged, unless the advertiser intends to make his appeal over a long period of time and wishes through constant repetition thus to individualize his work.   Tiffany & Company and The Gorham Company, both dealers in silverware, owe their advertising individuality partly to the style of type employed. Taste should govern the selection of type in all cases.   The thing to be sold should be told in a type garb which is neither over dressy nor slovenly in appearance.   A dignified announcement regarding an article of luxury demands dignity down to the minutest factor of its make-up.   A mechanical journal should not be characterized by fancy types, but by that style which suggests strength and regularity.

Focal Point and Eye Adjustment.—But directly related to the idea of eye adjustment with respect to size of type, ease of comprehension, and its consequent pleasure, is the fact that attention always selects some one point as a beginning.   Generally this point is determined by the ease with which the eye can adjust itself in competition with other points in a particular field of vision.   Every good advertisement will, therefore, have what is known as an *initial* or *focal* point which demands immediate eye adjustment.   Other parts of the advertisement should then be so arranged and related that the eye is mechanically, and preferably unconsciously, forced into a reading of the entire advertisement.   If the advertisement is so arranged that the eye spreads itself in attempting to begin the reading, only to be caught by another advertisement whose focal point seizes upon its restlessness, the effect is a non-attentive yet a possible reader. Fig. 28 consists of two advertisements the arrangement of which is entirely different, but with attention favoring that of F. B. Pierdon.   His trade-mark focuses attention immediately, the eye then travels either to the left or the right and finally completes the reading. That of A. A. Lupien is smaller in size, has good arrangement, and correct sized type as far as eye adjustment is concerned; but in competition for attention, it loses considerably when brought next to one which regards the idea of a focal point and the logical arrangement of parts.

Unitary Effects in Advertising.—This brings us to a discussion of those advertisements, a passing glance at which impresses us as simple or complex in nature. *Whenever an adver-*

Fig. 28.—These two advertisements differ in that one considers the mechanical make-up to force attention while the other emphasizes thought.

tisement is thought of as a unit and cannot be easily divided into parts, the effect may be said to be simple. Figs. 29, 30, and 31 show the development of arrangement by the printer in his attempt to harmonize the principle of eye adjustment to a focal point and to eye movement that is pleasing in effect. Fig. 29 is old fashioned in effect; it is without a border, thus destroying the sense of unity; there are too many factors emphasized and not enough regard for an initial point for eye attack. Fig. 30 is still without a border, but it attempts to unify by means of the fancy lines about the word " Craftsman." The new arrangement gives more regard to varied focal interests, but altogether

THE CRAFTSMAN

FOR

APRIL

WILL CONTAIN

ILLUSTRATED ARTICLES

UPON

LANDSCAPE GARDENING
INTERIOR DECORATION
AND
THE ART HANDICRAFTS

Also, a study upon Two Lives of William Morris, Art Notes, and Reviews of Recent Books dealing with Artistic and Economic Subjects

The Craftsman : Syracuse, New York

ON SALE HERE

Fig. 29.—The sense of unity is lacking.

THE
CRAFTSMAN
For April

Will contain Illustrated Articles upon

LANDSCAPE GARDENING
INTERIOR DECORATION
THE ART HANDICRAFTS

Also, a Study upon Two Lives of William Morris, Art Notes and Reviews of Recent Books dealing with Artistic and Economic Subjects ❧ ❧ ❧ ❧

THE CRAFTSMAN
SYRACUSE, NEW YORK   On Sale Here

Fig. 30.—The attention is here centered, but the general effect is still unsatisfactory.

is rather ornate, and hence detracts from the message intended. Fig. 31 has been given a dignified border, has emphasized the important thought by heavy type, has made secondary the unimportant thought by reducing attention value, and has observed eye movement. It is simple and dignified. Thought and arrangement are thus brought into harmony. These advertise-

. THE .
CRAFTSMAN
For April

Will contain Illustrated Articles upon

Landscape Gardening
Interior Decoration
. . . . . *And* . . . .
The Art Handicrafts

Also, a Study upon Two Lives of William Morris, Art Notes and Reviews of Recent Books dealing with Artistic and Economic Subjects : : : : : :

THE CRAFTSMAN : SYRACUSE, NEW YORK
ON SALE HERE

FIG. 31.—A sense of unity and the centering of attention has been realised.

ments are typical of the process necessary to produce the best effects, and every advertisement should be arranged and re-arranged until a feeling of harmony results.

Principles of Grouping.—It will be observed that the eye readily adjusts itself to groups of two's and three's. Three seems to be the more pleasing, while a grouping of four is not so easily comprehended. The effectiveness of many advertisements is destroyed by a lack of observance of these principles of group-

Tank Cars

Center Anchored Type

Six, Eight and Ten Thousand Gallon Capacities in Stock for Prompt Shipment

American Car and Foundry Co.

New York   Chicago   St. Louis

U. S. A.

Fig. 32.—The arrangement does not permit of immediate eye adjustment.

TANK CARS

CENTER
ANCHORED
TYPE

SIX, EIGHT AND TEN THOU-
SAND GALLON CAPACITIES
FOR PROMPT SHIPMENT

AMERICAN
CAR AND FOUNDRY
COMPANY

NEW YORK   CHICAGO   ST. LOUIS
U. S. A.

Fig. 33.—The effect is simple and conforms to eye adjustment

ing. The balance of white space and text is also an important factor. Too little white space tends to lessen the possibility of eye adjustment and eye movement. The eye is compelled to search about instead of easily and naturally adapting itself to the mechanical parts of the advertisement. Many merchants are appalled by the appearance of white space. To them it signifies a lost opportunity. To the careful advertiser, however, it more often typifies a sure-to-be-seen advertisement.

Figs. 32 and 33 excellently illustrate what a good printer accomplishes by strict adherence to these principles of arrangement. Fig. 32 has an entirely too scattered effect: it is difficult for the eye to seize upon the focal point in its comprehension of the entire advertisement. The moment we begin to read the improved form, Fig. 33, however, attention sweeps us into recognition of the entire page. The partial border of Fig. 32 is of no use, but creates the impression that the advertising message is bursting out the sides. Fig. 33 shows the border effect changed and yet so in harmony with the text as to create dignity and emphasis.

Disintegration: Complex Advertisements.—*Advertisements can be broken up into parts such that the reader passes from one division to the other.* These advertisements may then be said to be complex in nature.

Fig. 34 carries out the idea of a complex advertisement. The illustration part, in the form of a letter F, the rectangle containing the price, the blocked-off descriptive material, and the trade-mark—all these combine to give us a complete description of Fairy Soap. The smaller projection of the letter F may serve to force the attention to the price, or we may begin to read the description, or we may begin most anywhere and find ourselves led on from part to part until the entire advertisement is comprehended. Each division contains its message, which we interestedly read, and each division likewise mechanically forces us into an appreciation of the other division. A complex advertisement, however, has its dangers. If its divisions are not such as to lead from one part to the other, or, if one part tends to send the eye movement to another advertisement, in both instances failing to give us a unitary feeling, then the advertisement loses

FIG. 34.—Carrying out the idea of a complex advertisement.

CORTLAND MOTOR WAGONS

BUILT BY

CORTLAND WAGON CO.

BACKED BY
FIFTY YEARS'
EXPERIENCE

1911

CORTLAND MOTOR WAGON CO.
CORTLAND, NEW YORK

FIG. 35.—A complex advertisement which needs to be simplified.

Cortland Motor Wagons

Built by Cortland Wagon Company
Backed by Fifty Years experience

1911

Cortland Motor Wagon Company, Cortland, New York

FIG. 36.—The printer's form reduced to simplicity.

in effectiveness. The simple advertisement, if the unitary effect is decided and forceful in its thought appeal, is not thus endangered, for it has no divisions. Fig. 35 is an example of a complex advertisement. The message is simple, yet the original writer has tried to tell his story by a most complex arrange-

ment. Fig. 36 is the printer's form reduced to simplicity.
The latter's unitary effect is decidedly an improvement, and in
its simplicity and pleasing arrangement produces a much better
impression than the needless complex repetition of Fig. 35.
A complex advertisement, generally, should have its parts so

FIG. 37.—Without borders.

related as to produce interest in every other part. But where
the parts are telling the same story, as in Fig. 35, we have affectation entering.

All things being equal, if a complex advertisement can hold
the eye and the mind in a perusal of its several parts, in comparison with a simple advertisement, the former undoubtedly
has the better chance of arousing a greater number of associa-

tions in the mind. Each, however, has its advantage. The simple advertisement depends upon thought expression in a unitary mechanical form; the complex advertisement depends

FIG. 38.—Clearly defined border limits.

on two or more divisions of itself to lead to a unitary effect.

Principles Governing the Use of Borders.—A feeling of unity is usually realized by means of a border. A border keeps the eye from wandering to other parts of the page and tends to force the eye within its enclosure. It has the possibility of giving individuality as well as a sense of unity to the text. It becomes the factor which gives form to an advertisement and often has the effect either to draw or repel attention. Two advertisements, side by side, one with and the other without a border, are vying for attention. The bordered one will usually win. The border, however, should always be made subservient to the thought of the advertisement. When the reader is more conscious of the border than of the advertisement, and his atten-

Fig. 39.—Broken borders.

tion is not led to the text which it encloses, the unitary relationship of the individual parts of that particular advertisement has not been attained. A border which is more attractive within itself than the message which it contains is not concentrating attention for that particular advertisement.

The use of a border should be determined in relation to the feeling of unity. Whenever an advertisement's unity would be created or emphasized by its use, then a border should be chosen. The unity of an advertisement, however, is often assisted by omitting a border. For instance Fig. 37 is an example where the idea to be carried out demands a feeling of space. The idea of flying a kite implies freedom and space. The arrangement of the parts, moreover, is such that a unitary effect is retained.

Classification of Borders.—Advertisements permit of the

FIG. 40.—Novelty effects.

following border classification: first, there are those without borders (Fig. 37); second, those with clearly defined border limits (Fig. 38); third, broken borders (Fig. 39); fourth,

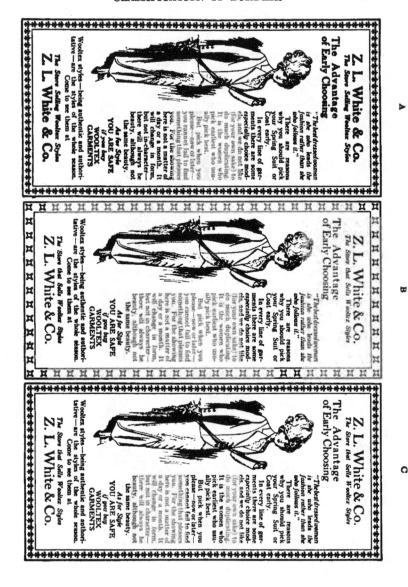

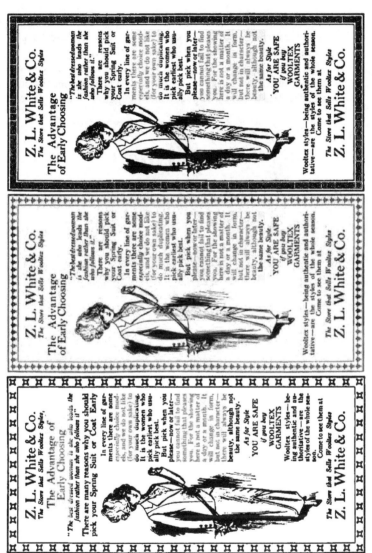

Fig. 42.—Compare the English arrangement with border effects.

there are borders which introduce novelty effects (Fig. 40); fifth, there are those which are broken in a manner to permit an insertion of some idea to be found within the text (Fig. 41).

Whenever the idea of space is desired and a border would tend to destroy this concept, the entire advertisement should be without a border or that part which suggests space. The idea

Fig. 43.—Where an idea within the text is an integral part of the border.

of unity, however, should be held in mind. The special effect should not be such as to lead one away from the thought of the advertisement. Fig. 37 illustrates the effective union of space and thought.

Fig. 39 is an example of the effectiveness to be obtained by breaking the border. It tends to create an atmosphere of freedom and slightly to increase the size of the advertisement.

Fig. 40 introduces a novelty effect which creates atmosphere before we have entered under the shade trees. The dignity of the outside effect is greatly enhanced by the announcement of designs and engravings. The thought is " These people have succeeded in living up to their claims of a beautiful design." The bottom of the advertisement is detailed, yet is quite secondary to the thought of the text.

Fig. 43 illustrates the possibility of weaving the thought of the text into the border. It is appropriate that Cupid should center the attention. It is also true that Cupid tends to force the attention within the advertisement itself. The simple yet artistic line effect of the border is also in keeping with the entire thought of the text, as well as with the beautiful letters which deliver the message.

QUESTIONS

1. Upon what factors should a scientific analysis of an advertisement be based as regarding attention?
2. If attention does not bring with it corresponding financial success, suggest several possible reasons why this is true.
3. What reaction must take place before attention comes into consciousness?
4. If the eye is the specific sense organ of visual sensations, mention some factors of eye experience that the advertiser must heed?
5. Discuss briefly the following forces in attention value: numerical groups, relief spaces, borders, focal point, and geometrical figures.
6. A woman recently entering a street car exclaimed, " My! What an attractive advertising border. I must copy the design." Question the psychology of the advertisement.
7. What is the customary movement of eye exploitation? Suggest how you would psychologically utilize this movement in advertising.

PROBLEMS

1. Locate an advertisement which, though the factors of attention have been violated, still makes an appeal.
2. Advertise the same article in three transitory stages, each succeeding one to further develop attention value.
3. Contrast a simple advertisement with a complex one and point out the advantage and disadvantage of each.
4. How would you answer inquiries as to the best mechanical composition from an attention standpoint for people interested in advertising foodstuffs, schools, and lighting systems?
5. Analyse the six advertisements of the Z. L. White & Company (Figs. 41 and 42) from the standpoint of attention value. Name them in the order of their effectiveness and give your reasons. Discuss from a border point of view.
6. In the two eye illusions (Figs. 44 and 45) note the rapidity of fluctuation in Fig. 45 and the length deception in Fig. 44. Can you explain why? Discuss the relative advantages and disadvantages of such illusions in gaining the attention.

The following six principles relating to attention are suggested:

   1. The power of any object to force itself into our attention depends
   on the absence of counter attractions.

   2. The power of any object to attract our attention depends on the
   intensity of the sensation aroused.

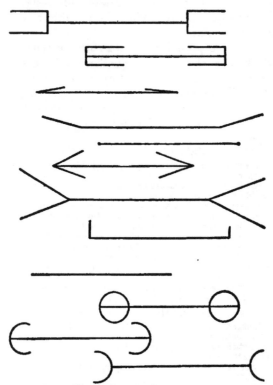

Fig. 44.—A disregard of many of these so-called illustrations in line length often decreases
the possible effectiveness in attention.
(From Witmer's Analytical Psychology)

   3. The attention value of an object depends upon the contrast it forms
   to the object presented with it, preceding or following it.

   4. The power which any object has to attract our attention, or its
   attention value, depends on the ease with which we are able to
   comprehend it.

5. The attention value of an object depends on the number of times it comes before us, or on repetition.
6. The attention value of an object depends on the intensity of the feeling aroused.

Find examples in advertising which illustrate them.

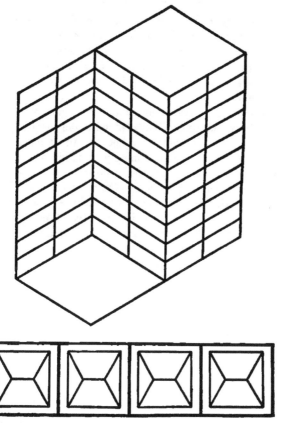

Fig. 45.—Fix the eye steadily upon a single part of the diagram. Describe the effect. (From Witmer's Analytical Psychology)

COLLATERAL READINGS

ANALYTICAL PSYCHOLOGY, LIGHTNER WITMER, Chapter ii.
PRINCIPLES OF ADVERTISING ARRANGEMENT, FRANK A. PARSONS, Chapter v, "Emphasis as Applied in Advertising Construction."
THE ELEMENTARY LAWS OF ADVERTISING, HENRY S. BUNTING, Chapter v.

CHAPTER VII

COLOR, ITS USE AND VALUE IN ADVERTISING

(ANALYZED GENERALLY)

Necessity for Impressive Colors.—The use of color in advertising is rapidly increasing. People have stopped making mere commercial announcements and arguments in black and white, and are now turning towards the more artistic in advertising. With this movement come the increasing use of color and its needed intensive analysis.

But to use color in advertising so that it "gets over" is an art within itself, totally unconnected with the artistic side of any advertisement. My desire is not, for the moment, to tell when to use color and how, but merely to define what color combinations are preferred by different groups of people so that when you, the advertiser, employ colors you can use those whose appeal is to the particular clientele to be reached—colors that, in short, will assist in adding intensive quality. Well applied color is more than attractive; it causes the eyes to linger upon it. There is a certain fascination aroused which makes it *an ideal agent* in the expression of an advertising idea.

To use color properly in advertising, numerous factors must be taken into consideration, for, to be effective, a colored advertisement must appeal especially to those for whom it is intended. It is no more important to use the right kind of language than it is to use the right kind of color and color combinations.

Harmony,—Contrast,—Shades and Tints.—There are a few simple laws of harmony and contrast which need the closest consideration. In all color work it is best to use different colors of the same degree of intensity in order to get an harmonious whole. A deep blue halved on a card with light pink gives a poor impression, while red and blue of the same intensity are a very good combination. While it is bad to divide a surface equally into two or three different color intensities, if there is a predominating degree of intensity, either that, or the other, or both, are accented. This is due to contrast.

103

Contrast has attraction, that is, it has great intensity, but it has very little fascination. It catches the eye but does not hold it. True harmony, on the other hand, has not so much attraction, but it has a great deal more of the power to hold the eye. Thus it depends upon the type of advertisement, as to which process you use. If you wish to attract and impress, use contrast. If you wish the people to study your advertisements, use the principle of harmony.

This, as I have stated it, is a non-technical, general grouping of color principles. Let us now consider more specific instances of how and when color is to be used, by showing color preferences.

Age and Sex Color Preferences.—A general analysis of the color preference of people of different ages in life reveals that every normal individual goes through a well-defined cycle of color preferences. The cycle begins at infancy and ends with old age. It begins with preference for the lightest tints and ends with preference for a fading intensity of color.

Have you ever thought why infants' wear is predominantly white combined with the lightest of light tints? Do the infants prefer pinks and baby blues and whites? Or is it a quality which we merely attribute to them? It seems to be their natural preference, because from psychological investigation we find that children of three and four prefer light, bright colors, and that their preference grows towards darker shades as the years advance until, when at the age of seven or eight, they prefer what is known as the true color. From this time on their color preferances depend a great deal upon their environment, and, too, there is some influence determined by nationality and race.

From the age of the formation of the particular environmental color preferences, which lasts until the individual is between 16 and 24, most people pass through a period of decided preference for black. They would wear black clothing; they would draw and paint in black and white. This period seems to come when the spirit and body have just been through a process of change from girlhood and boyhood to womanhood and manhood. It seems to come directly following the period of adolescence. This period, while it is very strongly marked, is of comparatively short duration, lasting from six months to two years and a half.

From this, people take one of two courses: first, either they gradually drift into using colors thru a process passing from the darker shades to the lighter; or, second, they have a revulsion and turn suddenly to very bright colors. That which they do depends mostly upon environment. Thus the normal person, during the period from 19 to 22, again starts to prefer colors. From this time for the next fifteen or twenty years, they are in what might be termed the prime of their color appreciation. That is, they have reached their standard and are influenced by it.

From this time on they repeat the processes of youth in inverted order. They have a standard and they gradually lose it. That is, they begin again to prefer the brighter colors until as the years go by they prefer fading shades and tints. Thus very old people in second childhood prefer the very bright colors, just as the child of five or six years does. Lavender, a combination of pink and baby blue, is the old folks' color. It ends the color cycle.

The value of this color preference to the advertising man is that, by studying his market with respect to age and color appeal, he introduces positive factors which arouse immediate favorable attention. By connecting age preference with sex, racial, and environmental preferences, the advertiser can be guarded in his use of colors. The difference of natural sex preference for colors seems to vary but little. In modern society, however, the difference of environmental conditions is very great. To this we must attribute what difference there is in sex preference for colors. In uncivilized tribes there seems to be no difference in color taste, which is attributed to the sameness of environment. As the sphere of man and woman separate, so their color preferences tend to grow apart.

In the United States to-day the color preference of the sexes is very different. This is partly due to the standardization of men's clothes, and at the same time to the individuality of the

dress of women. Men are trained by convention to prefer
and buy dark colors and shades, while women are taught that
they must make themselves attractive with bright colors.

Thus it is an interesting thing to note that girls passing
thru the " black period " are, figuratively speaking, between two
fires because they are urged by convention, generally in the
shape of fond match-making mothers, to wear bright " youthful "
colors, while their natural preference is for black. Another
interesting conflict comes when the very old person wishes to
wear the gay " youthful " colors and is discouraged in this by
conventional relatives.

These instances go to show that all thru life there are conflicting factors which influence color taste, and they also show,
generally speaking, that in this conflict environmental factors
are the strongest. The climate one lives in, as well as the type of
the surrounding country's topography, also tend to influence our
appreciation of color. Whether one lives in the city or in the
country, whether his habits relate to a single place, or whether he
travels, are all considered modifying influences. We prefer what
we are accustomed to see, that is, we are nature's creatures, and
wish to harmonize with nature. The inhabitant of the tropics
likes colors that harmonize with tropical vegetation—heavy,
luxuriant colors.

The Italian likes the bright colors that harmonize with his
climate and landscape. He prefers the brightest of bright colors.
Going north in Europe, we find that the French and the Ger-
mans have had their tastes toned by both climate and landscape,
while the English are known for the drab, dull colors which
they wear and use for all purposes.

One general modifying effect, regardless of nationality, is
shown in the influence of the city or town. The color taste
will be more varied and more unsettled in a large city than it is
in the country, or than it is in a smaller city.

Racial and National Color Preferences.—Racial color preferences are those which are predominant in any race of people,
such as the Teuton, Slav, Chinese, Japanese, and the colored

races. National color preferences are not clearly distinguishable from these, but the term may be used in respect to people of different nationalities in America, to whom there must often be made a national appeal. Both national and racial color tastes seem to be the result of years of environment until these color preferences are inherent, and become almost instinctive.

In advertising to a race each has its peculiar color preferences. Taking up the broad divisions, we find that the Teuton likes colors that will harmonize with his flaxen hair and ruddy cheek, and that his favorite color is blue of a tone somewhat lighter than true blue.

The Celts and Iberians, on the other hand, prefer red of a shade darker than the true red. It is merely a question of natural harmony.

The Orientals are much fonder of yellow than we are, and all of their colors seem to be thick, to have a certain yellowish tendency. Their reds are brownish reds rather than rose reds, and their blacks are black blacks to conform with their own colors.

The Indians made pottery colored in red, of almost their own tint, and black to match their raven locks.

The black and brown races like the rich luxuriant colors of the tropics. Purple of a deep, bright tone satisfies them.

So we find that we can especially appeal to different races thru their color instincts and that as nationalities are a blending of certain racial and local characteristics, by study we can directly appeal to the color susceptibilities of the different nationalities. This is especially valuable for the local advertiser in the United States where so often he is advertising to a certain racial or national group, especially where this group has not had time to be changed by its new environment.

Local Color Preference.—Local color tastes are fluctuating, but in certain localities, especially in Europe, they have been fixed for years. For instance, in the highlands of Scotland there has been the local plaid, which shows the unhampered spirit and freedom of the people, and, at the same time, the variety of their outlook. Almost the same colors and combinations are used in the Tyrol of Switzerland and Italy. In time we should expect the mountaineers of our own country to develop this type of color preference too.

Deserts have their colors just as the mountains have, and one will find the same colors predominating in our own western deserts as in the Sahara and other great deserts the world over.

Localities where there is a certain type of vegetation predominant will gradually get to harmonize with it. Even the quarrying of a certain color stone in a locality may greatly influence the color tastes of the people living there.

Seasonal Color Tastes.—In climates where there are well-defined seasons there is a great deal of seasonal color preference. As the animal's fur is changed by nature to harmonize with the background, man finds that he, too, has the same tendency to change his garb with the seasons. He goes in for tints in the summer and shades in the winter. An interesting thing that has come to our attention with respect to this very close following of nature, is the fact that each year, in the early fall, the clothing salesmen for men's clothes predict that brown will be the style in color for the winter. Brown suits are sold for a certain short period, but after that time has passed, the demand has ceased. The season for brown has passed.

Conclusion.—The reader has seen that there are many things which help to form the color tastes of different groups of people. Each is of paramount importance in analysing a given group or class of individuals. By adhering to the principles herein set forth, greater efficiency in advertising should result.

The thing that has not been so far sufficiently emphasized is the fact that there must be harmony within the advertisement as well as between the advertisement and outside influences. An inharmonious advertisement is repellent to us and would tend to make us think unfavorably of the article advertised.

One of the things that poor coloring work does is to make the advertisement appear cheap. This should always be avoided. One of the most valuable factors which comes into use in relation to advertising is the power of association. Color is a most powerful factor in causing mental associations, and has been utilized by mankind throughout each age in establishing various customs of thought. Blue, of a certain shade, and white, mean Holland; plaid brings up Scotland to our minds, etc.

There are two colors which are the natural background colors. These are green and blue. For effective harmonic backgrounds one cannot go far wrong in using them. Combinations of contrasting colors will give intensity, while harmonizing colors will give attraction.

The most important message of this chapter is that the human factor of the market must be studied; that the advertiser must know his clientele before he can do efficient advertising. But after he knows his clientele, one of the greatest factors in a well-rounded advertising campaign is color, properly used.

CHAPTER VIII

COLOR IN ITS RELATION TO ATTENTION

(FROM THE ARTIST'S POINT OF VIEW)

Variety of Effects of Saturated Colors.—In presenting general color appeals the importance of deep or saturated colors upon different groups of people is generally recognized. There are those who respond instinctively to color when presented and who are thus subjugated to its immediate influence because of temperament. In other cases, previous education prevails. In advertising, however, color should be reduced to the simple basis of pure and legitimate pigments, so used and filled with life that they at once force, attract and hold the eye.

Use of Emphatic Color.—The colors which immediately most forcibly strike the eye of the multitude in advertising are red, yellow, blue, green, white and black. These colors, which we shall here designate the emphatic colors, are the foundation upon which artistic results are often attained. On the other hand, the color itself is many times so shrieking in nature as to force unpleasant attention. When we wish to present an advertisement, however, which accurately interprets a subject, we are often forced to use shades and tones of the emphatic colors. In their proper blending or in correct contrast effects, the eye becomes aware of a pleasing softening process or feeling of constant change. When this condition prevails attention at least has been obtained. There are numerous color presentations, however, which do not thus control the eye movement. Hence, their color effect should be analysed and their undesirable impressions changed.

Our general experience forces us to accept the emphatic colors as too startling to be used in great quantities. This develops an appreciation for the so-called secondary colors, orange, green and violet. Tertiary colors, or browns and grays, are in turn the result of blending the primary and secondary, which often seem to satisfy the artistic sense even better than the use of secondary colors. The advertiser's work is to catch and hold the attention of the general public. Hence, the crowds' non-discriminating sense forces the use of these emphatic colors in their pure form. Their proper use at least attracts the attention and introduces a bit of life, full of vigor and often dancing quality, with respect to the sensation of color itself. These emphatic colors then serve as a foundation to work upon, the pigments of which should be laid strong and even so as to create a sentiment suggesting quality.

It is certain that of these emphatic colors some are more impressive than others. Professor Harlow Gale has made some experiments to determine what the attention value of the different colors is. His results are as follows: red has the greatest attention value, green is second and black third. Black on a white background is more effective than white on a black background.

Various Effects of Colors.—Let us analyse the different effects of color from the artist's point of view. Red at once attracts and holds the attention and is so appealing that it is called the advancing color. Suppose, for instance, that we are seated on the observation platform of a swiftly moving train. Let us fix our eyes upon the red eye of a switchlight. Notice how it will apparently keep up with a moving train. So strongly does it advance upon the vision that in competition with other colors it will be the last bright spot on the track line. Green and blue, on the other hand, seem to lack the quality of attracting the same amount of attention and are appropriately termed receding colors. Now take the green light on the reverse side of a switchlight and notice how quickly this color fades from you. It tends to recede quite as rapidly as the red has tended to advance.

The same truth applied to advertising compels us to state that the color used to depict some one sign or design in presenting an article demands attention accordingly as the brilliancy and evenness in tone of color is adapted to the public eye.

A red ground with white or black letters is always one that attracts the eye and tends to cause a halt in movement. Mentally, it often leaves an impression which tantalizes the reader until the advertisement is again read. Color thus forces its message. It must be stated, however, that the forcing of this message does not necessarily imply pleasure. In combination, green and red are unfortunate colors to use unless it be on a large billboard, for they literally dance and become confused, while the eye is wearied by a constant endeavor to separate the colors.

Yellow suggests light and can be aptly used in connection with red. Yellow with green and blue tends to liven these colors considerably and thus to increase their attraction-power. Take, for instance, the sun filtering through trees or bushes. Note how the oftentimes dull green is brightened by the yellow rays of the sunlight. Again, in advertising lighting fixtures, the essential color—the one to attract the eye—is yellow. Yellow typifies light, which should be made strong enough in its tone to suggest illumination. Other parts of the design composing the entire picture can be introduced without in any way detracting from the general color scheme,—yellow.

Street Car Advertisements.—The placing of street car cards has become a very important factor in the advertising world. It is here that the eye of the community, in its partial repose, makes possible an appeal thru color. The space allotted one of these cards in a car is small compared to the signs one sees on stationary objects and should, therefore, be clear and to the point without too much drawing and too many colors to confuse the eye. A simple and direct design is likely to attract more attention than one complex in nature.

Booklets.—Booklets and small hand advertising may be treated in quite a different manner since close eye-range means the ability and supposed patience to fathom out and study the subject in hand. This fact should modify our use of color.

Labels.—The size of the label demands a drawn design in keeping with the proportion, and that again means a study as to the spreading of color over the surface.

Trade-Marks.—Trade-marks with their demanded power to attract and hold the attention, have at the same time, the function of stamping indelibly upon the mind that here is an article that has been esteemed sufficient and worthy of so stamping. The design should be clear-cut and free of any kind of a puzzle effect which tends to confuse the mind of the reader. Clear-cut lettering and design are two essentials, and striking colors with a sense of judgment shown in their use also help greatly in bringing to a focus the mental attitude of the reader. After all, a trade-mark is merely a stamp of approval that a certain firm places on its goods as a reminder to the public that it wishes its good-will, appreciation, and lasting favor.

Bill Boards.—Bill boards, with their expansive surface and long-distance range of vision, should embody all that the artist of color advertising can conjure. Brilliant hues, carefully blended; subdued colors evenly spread, and lettering which emphasizes the illustration, are the essentials of an attractive bill board. The ornate is to be discouraged.

Posters.—Posters, with their artistic, commercial, individual and universal value, require skill of the highest order to justify the great expense which their creation implies. A poster may be of unquestioned technique, but if it does not embody the main factors of the desires of those to whom it would appeal, it is of small commercial value.

Significance of Colors.—Francis William Vreeland has written an article in the " American Printer " in which he expresses quite clearly the subject of color. Its contents is as follows:

" The disc of the sun and the color effect of its light are yellow, deepening into orange. The sun is the source of light, heat and life, and the sunshine of happiness. Hence the colors of yellow and orange are symbols of warmth, light, life, sunshine and happiness.

" The glow of the fire and the life blood of man and beast are red. Red, therefore, signifies heat, vitality, energy and those things which result from an abundance of all these in mankind, *i.e.,* love and passion.

" The sky is blue and the atmospheric effect upon snow is bluish white, deepening into positive blue in the distant landscape—blue and bluish white emblemize cold, sky, air and snow.

8

Hence, also does the artist and colorist make the distinction of warm and cold colors, designating orange, orange-red and yellow, and all colors showing a strong influence of any or all of these, as *warm* colors; and blue and such colors as likewise show its influence, as *cold* colors. We, therefore, have warm and cold greens, purples, browns, greys, etc., according to either their tendency toward orange, red and yellow or toward blue. But to continue our limited list of color symbols: Sprouting herbs, leafing trees, etc., as well as the fully developed foliage of plants and shrubs, in nature are for the most part, green. Green, for these reasons, also symbolizes life—especially budding life—and vitality. It (green) is, in man's mind, also associated with things relative to poisonous substances and metallic decay and corrosion, which makes this color also the symbol of treachery, jealousy and envy—for, do these things not result from the poison and morally corroded and decayed center of thought?

" And for similar reasons sea green is the symbol of water; steel grey, of strength, weight, solidity, hardness, durability and resistance; purple, of caste, royalty, pomp, etc.; white, of purity; grey, of solemnity; black, of ill omen and death; yellow and warm grey, of dawn, opening and commencement or beginning; brown, of bitterness; gold, of wealth and prosperity, and numerous other colors of things or thoughts which through long employment, association and consistency, appeal to the productive mind as properly representative of the thought to be expressed in a design.

" For our purpose, therefore, one who would achieve the most consistent and artistic results will choose for his color scheme such colors as will accomplish the above purpose. In a word, those which through long employment, association and consistency will, along with all of the other details in this composition, tell the story clearly. And this, too, in the purely decorative or ornamental composition as well as that one which is realistically treated.

" Let us, for example, suppose that we are to produce a cover design for a railroad or steamship booklet,—or poster, if you will,—in which the story is to be of trips or voyages to southern climes. To be consistent with the purpose of the book or poster, our choice should be a color scheme with a predomination of warm colors, such as yellows, oranges, reds, warm greens, etc., with, perhaps just a touch of something of an opposite character for artistic contrast. But always the predomination of those colors is to be symbolical of warmth, sunshine and abundant tropical foliage.

"Suppose now, in an entirely different vein, we are to do a design for the cover of a machinery catalog. Here steel greys and those colors suggesting strength, durability, etc., are the more appropriate, for they will not only be directly symbolical of the proposition, but will also produce a design quiet in tone, dignified and lasting in quality of appeal, and forceful in strength.

"Thus in all manner of color design should one use colors as much for their emblematic value as for their effectiveness. This the advertiser must do if he is to be artistically consistent; for only such designs and pictures are truly artistic."

The following list of color combinations will be useful:

Paper	Inks
Light red:	Olive and gold; rich green; blue and white.
Dark red:	White and gold; dark green; orange and dark blue.
Light yellow:	Light blue; red.
Light brown:	Dark brown and silver; green, grey and lilac.
Dark brown:	Black and white; light drab; orange.
Light blue:	Light red; dark blue; light yellow and yellow brown.
Dark blue:	Dark red and gold; light blue and white; green and orange.
Light green:	Yellow and dark brown; gold and orange; dark green.
Dark green:	Black and light green; gold and white.
White:	Crimson red; navy blue; emerald green.
Black:	Dark red; gold and white; light blue and silver.
Light gray:	Dark gray and red; dark blue and gold.

QUESTIONS

1. Which is the most effective style of advertisement—black and white, or colored? Why?
2. What are the different ideas of color combinations in advertisements and their effect upon the reader?
3. What are the general factors that determine color preferences in advertising?
4. (a) What is meant by racial and by national color preferences? Give examples. (b) Why is this an important feature for the advertiser in the United States to observe?
5. How do the color tastes of an individual harmonize with: (a) Locality. (b) Seasonal changes?
6. What would be the basis of your choice of colors for a bill board as compared with a booklet?
7. What do you think would be the probable effect of large red letters on a bill board of white as compared with the same sized letters, white, on a dark blue background?
8. If you have a red bill board with green letters would you have the letters closely or widely spaced? Why?
9. Which would be more effective on a poster, a green background with white letters or the green background with black letters? Why?
10. What color would you outline white letters with on a green background in order to give more character? Does this added color conflict with the background?

COLLATERAL READINGS

ADVERTISING AND SELLING, HARRY L. HOLLINGWORTH, Chapter x.
PRINCIPLES OF ADVERTISING ARRANGEMENT, FRANK ALVA PARSONS, Chapter viii.
ADVERTISING, STARCH, Artistic-Value of Different Colors, page 76.

CHAPTER IX

THE ADVERTISER'S TYPE

Classification of Different Styles of Type.—There are many hundred different styles of letters used in printing, but those most common may be classified in the following groups: Old Style Roman, Modern Roman, Italics, Script, Old English, Antique, and Gothic. Each of these groups has many varieties.

Confusion in the mind of the student of typography may be caused by the fact that similar types have different names when made by different founders. For instance the Post Old Style, Ben Franklin, Plymouth, Blanchard and Buffalo are some of the names given to type of a very similar design. Again, two or more founders will give the same name to type of a very different design. The De Vinne of the American Type Founders Company and the De Vinne of the Linotype Company are not at all alike. The Monotype Company designates all of its type faces by numbers instead of using the standard names.

Modern Roman and Old Style Type.—Most of the text matter of books and magazines is set in Modern Roman and Old Style Type, and practically all newspapers are set in Modern Roman. These types can always be depended on for the body matter of any piece of printing from a book to a label, and in many cases can be used for the head-lines as well. They are standard and are, by far, the most useful of type faces.

Italics and Bold Face Type.—In formal works *Italics* ordinarily indicate emphasis and are frequently so used in advertisements. But the Italics are often not as strong as their corresponding Roman type. In advertising, it is often better to emphasize by using the thicker or what is known as **bold face type,** or by underscoring, or by the use of larger type. Of these, the use of bold face is the best, as well as the most economical. ***Bold face italics,*** however, are especially strong. An excess of italics or other emphasized words is to be avoided, as it not only disfigures the page but defeats its own purpose.*

---

* See Fig. 2, page 43.

Script.—Script is seldom used in advertisements, its attention value being decidedly weaker than certain other equivalent forms, as well as more expensive from the printer's standpoint.

Old English Type.—**𝔒𝔩𝔡 𝔈𝔫𝔤𝔩𝔦𝔰𝔥 𝔗𝔶𝔭𝔢** is used in church or legal printing and in formal or artistic cards and announcements. It is, however, difficult to read and for that reason should be sparingly used in advertisements. Capitals of Old English run together and are illegible, and for these reasons should not be used.

Antique Type.—**Antique type,** which is a heavier face than the Roman, but not heavy enough to be considered a bold face is used in formal books, text books, dictionaries, etc., for the headings or beginnings of paragraphs, and can be so used in advertisements. In fact Antique is a good type for almost any advertising purpose.

Gothic Type.—The type which printers and type founders call **Gothic** is the plainest possible, without shading or serifs. It is made for a great variety of purposes and can be had very light or very heavy, thin, regular or expanded, and is one of the most useful of types. Many advertisers prefer Gothic for bold, strong display. Capitals of Gothic in the smaller sizes are good for the text of advertisements, cards and other forms, but should be used with great discretion. A long paragraph of Gothic capitals is monotonous and difficult to read.

Lower Case Type.—This criticism likewise applies to paragraphs set in all capitals of any style. On account of its great irregularity, *lower case* (commonly called " small letters ") is always easier to read. The best advertisements are those most easily read; and, for this reason, lower case is being used more than ever before in display lines, as well as in the body of the advertisement. Not only is lower case more legible, but more words can be put in a line. It is estimated that three lines of lower case can be read as easily as one line of capitals, whatever the type face.

Type Families.—Many faces of type are now made in " families." This makes possible a more harmonious appearance of printed matter. Thus the Cheltenham family is made up of the

regular width of letter and strength of face, known as Cheltenham, the italics, bold, bold italics, bold extended, bold condensed,
and bold extra condensed. Each of these different faces has the
same distinguishing characteristics.

This line is Cheltenham.

This line is Cheltenham italic.

This line is Cheltenham extended.

This line is Cheltenham Bold.

This line is Cheltenham bold italic.

This line is Cheltenham bold extended.

This line is Cheltenham bold condensed.

This line is Cheltenham bold extra condensed.

Harmony of Type with the Subject Matter.—In selecting
type, the advertiser should try as nearly as possible to choose
that kind which is in harmony with the subject under discussion.
A light delicate type is appropriate for millinery or jewelry
advertising, but a bolder, stronger type is better for coal, lumber
or iron advertising. Type should also be made to harmonize
with the size and shape of the space to be filled. For instance,
a thin, narrow page looks well in a laterally compressed type;
and a page wider than its height is better set in a regular or
expanded letter.

Harmony of Paper and Type.—The harmony between paper
and type also should be considered. A rough finish paper should
be printed in an old style or antique type. These types, however, are not out of place on any kind of paper. Small, weak
letters on a high finish, glossy paper are difficult to read and
should be avoided.

It is not advisable to print shaded or very thin type on rough
finish paper or on blotters by the letter press method of printing.
The difficulty is mechanical, as the fine lines of shading soon fill
with fuzz from the paper and with ink, producing the effect
of a worn type. Good results are obtained, however, by the
lithographic or intaglio processes.

Emphasis Gained by Type in Color.—In preparing an advertisement which is to be printed in two or more colors, it should be noted that black and white make the strongest possible contrast. If color is to be used for emphasis, it is necessary to set the emphasized words in a heavier type. Unless this is done, the intended emphasis will in reality appear weaker than the rest of the matter. If the entire advertisement is to be printed in color, old style antique is decidedly effective.

Definition of a Font.—A font is the unit of type sold by the type founder to the printer. The word also indicates the amount of type a printer has of a certain kind, as a fifty-pound font or a twenty-five-pound font, but it has no useful meaning for the advertiser.

Measurement of Type.—In America type is measured according to a system adopted by the type founders in 1886 and known as the point system. A point is nearly one seventy-second of an inch; so a letter measured by a number of points is known as six point, ten point, etc., according to the height of its body. As the body must be made large enough for the ascending and descending letters, measuring the face of type will not give the size of the body. The only letters which reach from the top to the bottom of the type body are the capital " Q " and the lower case " j ". As the name of the size of type refers to the height only, and not to width, an eighteen-point letter may be actually larger in area than a twenty-four point letter. This should be borne in mind when specifying sizes. If type is set with the lines close to each other,—solid,—it is measured by a special type gauge. Or, it may be measured by counting the lines of type in one inch and dividing into 72 to get the number of points in each line; thus, if there are six lines of type to the inch, divide six into seventy-two and the answer (12) indicates that the type is 12 point; or nine lines to the inch would indicate eight point. However, type is usually set leaded; that is, with thin strips of metal between the lines. Thus, the above method is not practical where there is doubt about the matter being set solid. Six lines to the inch may, and usually do, indicate 10 point type separated with two-point leads.

These lines are set in six point solid. Six point, which was called "Nonpareil" before the days of the point system, is the most used of all the small sizes. It is used more than other type for setting tables of figures, as it is half of the standard, which is twelve point. Printer's spacing materials and brass rules used in printing lines are always cut to even multiples of the six point body.

These lines are set in six point opened with two point leads. Six point is used for foot notes and is a splendid type for compact books of reference. It may be used for technical information in catalogs and booklets, and for inscriptions under engravings. Type smaller than six point is hard to read, and its appearance discourages the attempt. The use of smaller type in advertising should be avoided as a waste of money and effort.

These lines are set in eight point solid, which was formerly called "Brevier," probably on account of its being used in the early days for the printing of breviaries. It is now the most widely used type for newspapers and is used to a considerable extent in the printing of magazines. Many books are printed in eight point.

These lines are set in eight point separated with two point leads. Eight point is nearly twice the size of six point in area and is correspondingly more legible. It is one of the most useful sizes for the body matter of advertisements and for printing catalogs and booklets. Eight point capitals are specified by law as the smallest letters allowed for statement of contents on labels for goods sold by the package.

These lines are set in ten point solid. This is the nearest size, now made, to the "Long Primer" of former days. Ten point is the great text letter for magazines and books, and is the smallest size allowed for lawyers' paper books.

These lines are set in ten point leaded with two point leads. Ten point is easily read and is an excellent size for advertising in periodicals or for making catalogs and booklets. It would be a good rule to use ten point for the body of all advertisements unless there is a special reason for the use of some other size.

These lines are set in twelve point solid. Twelve point, formerly called "Pica," was the standard of type measurement, and still is, to a large extent. The American point system is based on this size and all printers' spacing materials and brass rules, as well as the larger sizes of type, are made in multiples of it.

These lines are set in twelve point with two point leads. This size can be used for the body matter of advertisements, circulars, booklets and catalogs, and is an excellent head letter size for use with smaller body types.

This line is fourteen point.

This line is sixteen point.

This line is eighteen point.

This line is twenty point.

This line is twenty-four point.

This line is thirty point.

This line is thirty-six point.

An " em " in type measurement is the square of the body as an eight point em or a ten point em. It is the basis of compensation for compositors and machine operators.

Type and Space Computations.—The approximate number of words in a square inch of ordinary text matter is as follows:

Words to square inch			Words to square inch		
18 point, solid	....	7	9 point, leaded	....	21
14 " solid	....	11	8 " solid	....	32
12 " solid	....	14	8 " leaded	....	23
12 " leaded	....	11	7 " solid	....	38
11 " solid	....	17	7 " leaded	....	27
11 " leaded	....	14	6 " solid	....	47
10 " solid	....	21	6 " leaded	....	34
10 " leaded	....	16	5 " solid	....	69
9 " solid	....	28	5 " leaded	....	50

It should always be borne in mind that tables of words per square inch are not accurate for two reasons: first, because words vary in size, and second, because different styles of types of the same body vary in width.

Foundry type, hand set, contains more words per square inch than the same size set on the linotype. Type set on the monotype machine may be either close set, as foundry type, or a trifle wider, as linotype matter.

If it is required to find the number of words per square inch in type other than plain Roman, a good method is to mark off 4 × 6 square inches on a page printed in the type desired, and by counting the words, find the average number to the square inch.

The regular sizes of type are six, eight, ten, twelve and fourteen point, and they are the main dependence of the advertiser. The five, seven, nine and eleven point sizes are called irregular and are not made in many of the best advertising faces. These should be avoided. In laying out advertisements the regular sizes only should be specified.

" Agate," or five and one-half point type, measures about fourteen lines to the inch. It is used for setting want advertisements in newspapers and for other places where compactness is required. A line of this size is used largely as the unit in selling advertising space.

To find the amount of space a manuscript will occupy in type, count the words and divide by the number in one square inch as given by the above table. If a manuscript has ten thousand words to be printed in a pamphlet, 6 × 9 inches, with type-pages of ten point leaded 4¼ × 7¼ inches, or 31 square inches, and it is desired to find how many pages it will take, the method is as follows: we find that one page contains 31 × 16, or 496 words. Ten thousand words will require twenty and one-sixth pages or practically, allowing for discrepancies, a twenty-four page pamphlet.

The method of determining the correct size type to be used to fill a certain space is as follows: if a manuscript has one thousand words and it is desired to print in four pages, 3 × 5 inches, we find each page to contain fifteen square inches and four pages have sixty square inches. If we put one thousand words in sixty square inches, each square inch will contain 16 words and, referring to the table, we find ten point leaded type will completely fill the space. Practically, however, it is well to allow five to ten per cent. more room than the exact amount to hold the manuscript.

Number of words required to fill a certain space with certain type is computed as follows: if it is found necessary to fill a space 4 × 5 inches in an advertisement and eight point type is desired, by multiplying the number of square inches (20) by the number of words to the square inch, we find we will need 640 words, if the type is solid, or 430 words if the type is leaded.

Practical Aspects of Type Arrangement.—In the making of an advertisement, as in any other work, a clear plan should be first laid out and everything made to conform to it from the beginning. In this way much time and expense will be saved. The space to be filled, or the size of the page, should be ascertained and the proper margins arranged. In booklet making, about one-half of the page will be in the margins, leaving the other half for the printing. Thus a booklet with pages 4 × 6 inches (24 square inches) should have type pages 2½ × 4½ inches or 11¼ square inches; and a catalog with pages 6 × 9 inches (54 square inches) will have a type page 4¼ × 7¼ inches or about 31 square inches. If proper margins are not provided a good appearance cannot be obtained.

Engravings should be made to fit the space for which they are intended on the plan. They will not only look better, but will save delay and expense in setting type on the balance of the page. All manuscripts should be typewritten on one side of the paper only, and preferably double spaced. Handwriting should be in ink and, if names or technical words are used, each letter should be legibly written.

Each printing plant has its own outfit of type and no two are equipped alike. In specifying type, allowance should be made for this fact. A great deal of advertising is placed on competitive bidding, and it may be that the printer who gets the order does not have the exact type requested. When in doubt it is always best to let the printer choose the type for the work, the advertiser giving only the general style wanted.

Conditions in printing establishments are vastly different now from the more easy-going days of the past. High wages and short working days make it necessary to account for all the time of each workman. Time reports are now required for each operation on every order. These have opened the eyes of the managers to the great waste of carelessly prepared manuscript and printing instructions. But when efficiency has been introduced and the work is done according to a carefully arranged plan, corresponding economy has resulted. Just as it is more expensive to tear down a brick wall than to change an architect's plans, so it is very costly to make alterations in the proof that should have been made in the manuscript.

While the labor cost in printing establishments is constantly rising, the use of improved machines is tending to hold down costs on work adapted to them. In ordering printing, it is well to keep this fact clearly in mind. The largest quantity that can be used economically should be ordered at one time, and the printer should be consulted as to the laying out of the work at the time the plan is started. If the cost is a consideration, as it almost always is, the size of the page should be adapted to the standard sizes of paper and to the machines on which the work is to be printed. The size of the engravings and the fineness of the screen should be determined at the same time.

The style of binding and the material of the cover of a catalog should be chosen before any actual work is done. It should be remembered that books can only be bound in multiples of four pages. Sixteen pages is the most economical number, for it takes three right angle folds and makes a better and cheaper book than one of twelve or twenty pages. Thirty-two small pages can be printed at one time while, if the pages are nine by twelve or larger, eight pages should be put in a form.

In designing the type page it should be kept in mind that the rectangular page is the cheapest, and any running of type around engravings or cut-in heads or notes in the margin add to the expense of the work. The old style and modern Roman types are always to be found on the typesetting machines and should be used for quick economical work.

Copy and lay-out were recently sent to a printer with the type for each line specified. It was set accordingly but, on the return of the proof, it was found that all the display lines were marked to be changed to another face of type. This increased the cost of typesetting more than fifty per cent. without material change in the appearance of the advertisement.

If the lay-out man does not know his own mind, and if he does not know *exactly* how an advertisement will look in the type of his selection, he had far better not specify the type at all.

In specifying type sizes, great care should be taken not to overflow the allotted space, and lines should not be marked for a certain type when there is the least doubt that the space is wide enough to allow the number of letters to be put in the line. Sometimes manuscript has the lines marked for twenty-four point when it is impossible to get them in eighteen point type.

The wiser policy is to permit the printer to change the specifications to a certain extent, for there are conditions which the writer may overlook, or of which he may be ignorant. For instance, the bottom shoulder on some of the larger types is as much as one-eighth inch, a fact which often deceives the lay-out man. He cannot understand why a line of small type should not come close to the large line above.

Sometimes the designer of an advertisement will take a proof of a picture and with his scissors cut it to fit the desired space, forgetting that it is quite another matter to cut down the copper engraving.

In laying out catalogs with vignette half-tones, care should be taken not to crowd them. These engravings have a large margin into which the shading fades away, and a part of the engraving does not show on the proof. Not only for mechanical reasons, but for the sake of appearance, ample space for these illustrations must be allowed, as their beauty is lost, if crowded into the adjoining type.

The following questions and answers regarding lay-out,

selected from the Curtis Publishing Company's booklet of general instructions, are to be heeded by all advertisers:

Q. What is a lay-out?

A. A lay-out is a draft of the general appearance desired for an advertisement. It is intended for the guidance of the compositor in assembling and arranging type-matter and cuts, and also serves as a guide to work done on the material by the engraver.

Q. What should the lay-out show?

A. The lay-out should indicate clearly and beyond question the relative position of each illustration, and of display and body type. It should also give exact instructions as to whether a border is to be used and, if so, what kind.

Q. What are the most common defects in lay-outs?

A. First, showing a cut not the same as the one sent us. Second, failing to tell us whether or not a border is desired. Third, insufficient or confusing instructions about the arrangement of type.

Q. Does it pay to prepare good lay-outs?

A. It pays well. The compositor's ambition is stirred and his best effort is put into a well-laid-out advertisement. No compositor can do his best on a piece of carelessly prepared copy.

As to typesetting in general, a great improvement has been made in the last fifteen or twenty years in the direction of simplicity. The old fancy types which were used in the most incongruous manner are now seldom seen. The curved rule and typographic flowers are out of date. People no longer insist on type set in curved lines. All these things added greatly to the cost of setting type, especially the curved lines which took an indefinite time to set, and caused an equal amount of trouble on the press.

Ornamentation and decoration are now left to the artist and the engraver, and the faces of type used in advertising are of plain design made in such carefully graded sizes that harmony of design in the advertisement is easily secured. Typography is confined to its own work of making the advertisement legible and pleasing.

No ¶	No new paragraph.
Run in	Let there be no break in the reading. ·
¶	Make a new paragraph.
∨ ∨ ∨	Correct uneven spacing of words.
⌀	Strike out the marked type, word, or sentence.
ꝺ	Reverse this type.
#	More space where caret ∧ is marked.
‿	Contract the spacing.
⊃⊂	Take out all spacing.
Γ	Move this to the left.
⌐	Move this to the right.
⌐	Raise this line or letter.
⌐	Depress this line or letter.
‖	Make parallel at the side with other lines.
☐	Indent line an em.
⊥	Push down a space that blackens the proof.
×	Change this bruised type.
w.f.	Change this faulty type of a wrong font.
tr.	Transpose words or letters underlined.
l.c.	Put in lower-case, or small letters.
s.c.	Put in small capitals.
caps.	Put in capitals.
᾿	Insert apostrophe. Superior characters are put over an inverted caret, as ᾿ ᾿ ᾿ ᾿, etc.; for inferior characters the caret is put in its usual position, as in ⌃.
rom.	Change from italic to roman.

FIG. 47a—Proofreader's signs. (Correct Composition, T. L. De Vinne).

ital.	Change from roman to italic.
⊙	Insert period.
,/	Insert comma.
;/	Insert semicolon.
:/	Insert colon.
-/	Insert hyphen.
/—/	One-em dash.
/—²—/	Two-em dash.
℈	Take out cancelled character and close up.
Qu. or *?*	Is this right? See to it.
∧	Insert letter or word marked in margin.
| | | |	Hair-space letters as marked.
Stet	Restore crossed-out word or letter.
....	Dots put below the crossed word mean: Cancel the correction first made, and let the types stand as they were.
⌒	Over two or three letters. Change for the diphthong or for a logotype, as $\widehat{ae}$, $\widehat{ffi}$.
≡	Straighten lines.
////	Diagonal lines crossing the text indicate that the composition is out of square.
Out, see copy.	Here is an omission; see copy.

Corrections or textual improvements suggested to the author should be accompanied by the interrogation-point and be inclosed in parentheses or "ringed," as (*tr.* / *?*) or (℈ / *?*).

Corrections should always be made in the margin, and never in the text; faults in the types or text to be indicated only by light pen marks.

FIG. 47*b.*—Proofreader's signs,—Continued. (Correct Composition, T. L. De Vinne)

We should bear in mind that printing is simply a means for the conveyance of thoughts. While it is best when it is artistic and in good taste, it is more important that it be legible. Good advertising printing will never obtrude its own personality to such an extent that it obscures the purpose of the advertisement.

Printing, like language, might be compared to window glass. It is best when it is clearest. When we can clearly see through it the thoughts of the author, we know that it is good.

An analysis of the practical relation between type and space is illustrated in the following paragraph:

This is ten point type set leaded, and is printed to give advertisers an opportunity to see, and to show their clients, just how a proposed advertisement will look if printed in ten point type. It is intended to be used with the dummy or lay-out sheet. To use it, find the space to be occupied, and cut from this sheet a piece the exact size. Paste this piece on the lay-out sheet in its correct location. Each square inch of this type contains an average of sixteen words, and, by measuring the size of the piece cut out, the number of words which the space contains can be readily found. Be sure to cut this sheet showing type size the exact size of the type matter, allowing proper margins. This type, however, is "leaded"; that is, it has thin strips of metal two points thick between each line. If it is necessary to crowd in more words, these strips of metal (leads) can be taken out and then each square inch will contain twenty-one words. It will be impossible for the printer to crowd more words in the space, if ten point type is used; and great care should be exercised not to put more words in the manuscript than the space will contain. If necessary to have more words, a smaller type will be required. By the use of this sheet a correct idea of the appearance of the advertisement will be obtained, and, if the number of words in the manuscript is confined exactly to the capacity of the space, the printer will have no reason to substitute a different size. Printers' bills for alterations can thus be avoided. In placing engravings in manuscripts, be sure to allow room for the full size of the engraving and not only for the part which shows in print. A margin of an eighth to a quarter of an inch is required on all sides of the engraving for blocking.

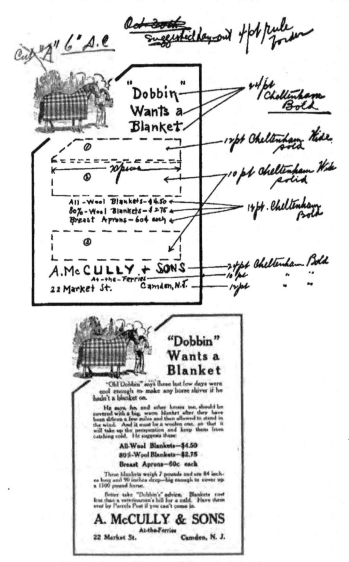

Fig. 46.—Suggested lay-out and the finished advertisement.

The copy, form, suggested type and finished advertisement (Fig. 46) indicate the precision demanded to secure the most excellent results:—

COPY FOR OCT. 30TH

"Dobbin" Wants a Blanket

"Old Dobbin" says these last few days were cool enough to make any horse shiver if he hadn't a blanket on.

He says, he, and other horses, too, should be covered with a big, warm blanket after they have been driven a few miles and then allowed to stand in the wind. And it must be a woollen blanket, so that it will take up the perspiration and keep them from catching cold. He suggests these:

          All-Wool Blankets $4.50
          80%-Wool Blankets $2.75
          Breast Aprons .... 60c. each

These blankets weigh 7 pounds and are 84 inches long and 90 inches deep—big enough to cover up a 1500-pound horse.

Better take "Dobbin's" advice. Blankets cost less than a veterinarian's bill for a cold. Have them sent by Parcels Post if you can't come in.

A. McCULLY & SONS
At-the-Ferries
22 Market St.   Camden, N. J.

QUESTIONS

1. What is meant by the following terms in connection with type: point system; leaded type; em; lay-out; copy.
2. What are three fundamental principles which should be considered in choosing type?
3. What is the danger of judging the effect of an advertisement by cutting out an illustration and inserting it into the desired space to be filled?
4. What should be the relationship between the type and white space of any advertisement?

PROBLEMS

1. How many pages will a manuscript make that contains eight thousand words? The type page to be 2½ x 4 inches and set in 10 point leaded type.
2. Will a pamphlet of 32 pages, no cover, 6 x 9 inches with half-tone engravings go through the mail for one cent? How did you estimate?
3. How can we make a book as thick and pretentious as possible but with a small manuscript? Suggest four factors.

COLLATERAL READINGS

THE TYPOGRAPHY OF ADVERTISEMENTS, TREZISE, Chapter ix, "On Choosing Type."

PRINCIPLES OF ADVERTISING ARRANGEMENT, FRANK A. PARSONS, Chapter ix.

HOW TO ADVERTISE TO MEN, SYSTEM, page 39, "Determining Amount of Space and Amount of Copy."

A THEORY OF PURE DESIGN, DENMAN W. ROSS, page 186, "Composition."

ADS AND SALES, HERBERT N. CASSON, Chapter viii.

ADVERTISING MEDIUMS, DEAN CHAS. O'CONNOR, Chapter xxxv (2nd Edition).

CORRECT COMPOSITION, THEODORE L. DE VINNE.

PLAIN PRINTING TYPES, THEODORE L. DE VINNE.

THOUGH several differing opinions exist as to the individual by whom the art of printing was first discovered; yet all authorities concur in admitting Peter Schoeffer to be the person who invented *cast metal types*, having learned the art of of *cutting* the letters from the Gutenbergs he is also supposed to have been the first whoengraved on copper plates. The following testimony is preseved in the family, by Jo. Fred. Faustus, of Ascheffenburg: 'Peter Schoeffer, of Gernsheim, perceiving his master Fausts design, and being himself desirous ardently to improve the art, found out (by the good providence of God) the method of cutting (*incidendi*) the characters in a *matrix*, that the letters might easily be singly *cast* instead of bieng *cut*. He privately *cut matrices* for the whole alphabet: Faust was so pleased with the contrivance, that he promised Peter to give him his only daughter Christina in marriage, a promise which he soon after performed.

But there were many difficulties at first with these *letters*, as there had been before with wooden ones, the metal being too soft to support the force of the im pression: but this defect was soon remedied, by mixing a substance with the metal which sufficiently hardened it

and when he showed his master the letters cast from these matrices,

FIG. 48.—Example of use of proofreader's marks.

CHAPTER X

THE ILLUSTRATION—MECHANICAL MAKE-UP

Psychology of the Illustration.—When one contemplates getting his message to the world, the illustration arises immediately as one of the best mediums. Where words fail to arouse interest, pictures always succeed. A decidedly attractive illustration will be read and will often sell the goods where only cold type matter may be met with indifference. The cartoons in our daily papers are most important factors in creating sentiment or thrusting a philosophy upon their observers. It would seem that the illustration, with the possibility of picturing or calling up a multitude of sensations at one time, has so aptly adjusted itself to the mind of humanity that even he who " runs " may receive the message. It seems to be natural for the masses to think in terms of things. If you could have lived in London three hundred years ago, you would have found each tradesman with the symbol of his particular goods hung before the door. Business organizations in Brussels of the Old World took the form of guilds and these guilds in turn modified their architectural structures. To see an illustration of these picturesque old guild-houses is to experience a sensation and association of ideas not entirely appreciated in a written description. Thus it is that our thought is constantly expressing itself in a concrete thing. The universal appreciation of moving pictures is indicative only of the mind's tendency easily to grasp the thought expressed in terms of things. When the tiny life within a drop of water, the unfolding of beautiful flowers, the most exacting color detail of a Durbar celebration is brought entertainingly before us, we sit in wonderment or pleasure. But wonderment or pleasure is likely to lead to thinking, and thinking leads to action. Thus, if I can combine in an illustration a series of factors which, united in their effects, make my particular article stand unchallenged in the public mind; or more, if I can so climax my picture that my article becomes an immediate need to the interested one, then the illustration has served its true commercial purpose.

134

Union of Illustration and Text.—In the use of the illustration one danger is to be guarded against. Generally speaking, the illustration should not be such as to take one's thought away from the particular selling proposition involved. There are times when the face of a beautiful girl is not to be desired. Illustrations should be talking points in the sale of an article. Amusement or knowledge are incidental factors to the main commercial idea which the advertiser is attempting to present.

Two Purposes of an Illustration.—The illustration may serve one of two purposes in an advertisement; either it should prove an adjunct in re-emphasizing the text, or it should be supplementary to the text in the sense that the advertisement is only fully comprehended when both have been read. Each should so explain or re-enforce the other as to produce a feeling of unity. The advertiser should be constantly on the watch for good photographs which might be used to give individuality to his work. The fundamental principle of selection is that of universality. When we look upon the Gibson or Fisher pictures, there is something in them that reminds us of many people whom we know. They are never just like one person, but many.

Hamlet has said, " Suit the action to the word, the word to the action, with this special observance, that you o'erstep not the modesty of nature." In advertising we are to suit the illustration to the text and the text to the illustration, else we may drag the reader into confusion.

Having clearly in mind the advantage of illustrations, the need of those possessing originality as well as universal interest, and the union of text and illustration to produce the best impression, let us proceed to an intensive study of the mechanical factors involved in good illustrating.

Co-operation Between Advertiser, Artist and Printer.—There is often too little sympathy between advertiser, artist and printer. The advertiser with a vivid imagination and limited expense account has an idea, the artist is often incapable, and the printer is limited in equipment. In attempting to reproduce the idea of the artist, these human and physical difficulties often result in work disappointing to all parties concerned. But it is here that the advertiser must display great intelligence. He must know when to allow his own judgment of effects to be overruled by either the artist or the printer. Sincerity of purpose in co-operation for the production of excellent work, is the spirit which should associate itself in their combined effort. Mutual respect and sincere criticism are necessary human qualities in order to get the best results. When the association of these three people is not characterized by such qualities, it is better that they separate. A change in printer and artist on the part of the advertiser should not be based primarily on money. Workmanship and results are the most important factors. It is often, however, the executive having control of, and yet lacking sympathy with the advertising man, who overlooks the human factor herein involved. He bases his judgment of the transaction solely on the money consideration. Our art galleries, cameras, moving pictures, highly illustrated books, and individual traveling experiences are educating the masses into an appreciation of good pictures; the advertiser must become an expert in satisfying the æsthetic taste of his particular group of prospective customers. He must also affiliate himself with the best artist and the best printer in order to get maximum results, the utilization of whose efforts, from a monetary point of view, often sacrifices the immediate present for the future.

The blend of colors, design and size for any kind of work should be at the suggestion of the artist. Circulars, pamphlets, and folders increase their attention almost doubly by a correct color presentation, and it is to the artist, who feels these relative values, that we can most profitably and savingly turn.

Size of a Reproduction.—It is often desired to get some conception of the size of a reproduced illustration, especially if it is to be decreased in size. This can be ascertained as follows: A line is drawn from the lower left hand corner (A) to and passing thru the upper right corner of the picture (C). If the picture is to be reduced to a given width (A B^1), and it is desired to find what the height would be, measure off the width along the lower edge from the lower left hand corner (A to B^1); from the point (B^1) a measure is made vertically upward to the diagonal line and the exact height will be obtained ($B^1 C^1$). If the height is given and the width is unknown, measure from the lower left corner to the desired height ($A D^1$) and then across to the diagonal line ($D^1 C^1$). See Fig. 49.

In considering the illustration, an accommodating camera will handle any drawing of reasonable dimension. It is much easier to reduce the size of the drawing than to enlarge it. In the latter instance a new drawing of a larger size is advised. On an enlarged drawing the defects become magnified and the results are often unsatisfactory. In either event, if other

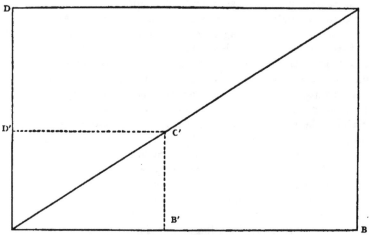

FIG. 49.—Method of finding proportions.

than proportionate changes are desired, illustrations must be redrawn.

Various Processes of Reproduction.—In newspapers and magazines there are three kinds of processes used in developing an illustration; namely, the zinc etching, the half-tone, and the wood engraving. These three are originals of which replicas are needed to meet the demands of economy, and such replicas are known as electrotypes, nickeltypes and stereotypes.

The *zinc etching* is a reproduction of any pen and ink drawing, type matter or tracing, but not blue print. The copy is placed before a camera and a negative obtained. No screen is used. This negative is usually printed upon a zinc plate, though for finer effects copper is used. The zinc between the photographed lines is removed by the use of nitric acid until in this etching bath the proper printing depth has been obtained. Many thousand impressions may be made from this zinc etching, but if the illustration is to be used for a long time an electrotype should be made from it. Fig. 50 is a simple pen drawing con-

Courtesy U. G. I., Phila,

Fig. 50.—Best for cheap paper.

sisting of black and white lines from which a most excellent zinc etching can be made. The use of the line plate is generally restricted to the following: trade-marks, drawn lettering, borders, and artistic pen or pencil sketches.

To make an *electrotype,* an impression of the zinc etching is made in wax and suspended with a plate of copper in an acidulated solution of copper sulphate. An electric current is then turned on and the waxened impression begins to be plated. When of sufficient thickness, the wax is removed from the plate, and after mechanical adjustment the new impression or electrotype is ready for the printing press. This same process is carried out in the reproduction of half-tones and wood engravings.

Nickeltype is made by depositing nickel instead of copper on the face of the mold by means of the electrotype process. A nickeltype is an electrotype whose use is made necessary because of its inherent quality to reproduce certain colors more effectively than the pure copper.

Half-tone engravings are taken from either the object itself, photographs or wash drawings in black. The first step in the half-tone process is the photographing of the object of illustration thru a screen interposed between the copy and a sensitized plate in the camera. The result is a negative the surface of which has been broken up into very small dots. In proportion to their size these dots give all degrees of tone except positive blacks or whites. Hence the name " half-tone." The negative is printed on a copper plate and goes thru the etching process above described. Afterward, all the defects are taken out and the half-tone engraving is prepared for mounting. Figs. 55 will reveal different screen processes, as well as the varied effects to be created by each when printed on different grades of paper.

Nearly all photographs for engraving need retouching. Distinctness of detail and outline is the desirable characteristic. A half-tone made from a half-tone is seldom satisfactory, while anything having colors should always first be photographed. The quality of paper upon which the half-tone is to be printed decides what screen is to be used.

The *wood cut* was the original method of reproducing a drawing. This is obtained either from a drawing or a photograph. Either, however, should be absolutely correct in detail as this process produces an illustration which is clear and distinct above the others. It is this necessity for care and skill on the part of the engraver which makes wood engraving more expensive than the others. Because of the sharpness of outline, this process seems to be the best for mechanical subjects and illustrations which are to be used extensively. The wood cut itself, however, is merely to serve as a pattern for an electrotype.

Combining Different Parts of Different Illustrations.—If it is desired to combine different parts of illustrations so as to carry out some conception of the advertiser, the following suggestion is made by Fowler in his " Building Business ":

" Lay a piece of blue carbon paper, face downward, on some white bristol board; fasten all three in position on a drawing board with thumb tacks. Next, trace with a sharp point all the principal lines of the figure, being careful to follow them exactly, and only tracing such lines as bind the important details of the design or illustration.

" When the clipping and carbon paper are removed, a tracing will be found on the bristol board that will give all the principal lines of the figure. These should be inked over with Higgins's black waterproof drawing ink, care being taken to make the lines as smooth as possible.

" If this tracing is carefully made, any engraver can make a good zinc etching of it. It is always desirable that the engraving be smaller than the drawing, so as to permit considerable reduction in size as such reduction obliterates much of the roughness in the lines and the poor workmanship that is common with the amateur draftsmen, or with people who have little artistic ability.

" No one has the right to use a copyright picture, however, unless he changes its identity."

Stereotypes.—The newspapers have a process for duplicating their forms known as *stereotyping*. If you are an advertiser and wish to insert the same advertisement in several papers, by sending a copy to one newspaper and asking for a number of stereotypes, it is sometimes possible thus to duplicate your advertisement for the other newspapers.

Stereotypes are made by beating a moistened paper pulp substance against the form into which the lay-out for the advertisement has been put until this substance contains an exact reproduction of the surface desired. This pulp with its impression is then heated, dried and placed on a half cylinder, when molten type metal is run into the space between the cylinder and the paper. By a mechanical device, this molten type is hardened

FIG. 51D.—Blue plate.

FIG. 51C.—Showing result of the printing of the red and yellow plates.

FIG. 51B.—Red plate.

is then heated, dried and placed on a half cylinder, when molten
type metal is run into the space between the cylinder and the
paper. By a mechanical device, this molten type is hardened

Fig. 310   Blue plate.

Fig. 311   Showing result of the printing of the red and yellow plates.

Fig. 312   Red plate.

Fig. 51c.—Showing result of the printing of the red and yellow plates.

Fig. 51n.—Red plate.

Fig. 51b - Bed plate.

into the desired impression before the paper has been even scorched.

Kinds of Engraving.—There are three other kinds of engraving with which every advertiser should be familiar: steel and copper engraving; color effects through a combination of half-tones and the Ben Day process; and lithography.

Steel and Copper Engravings.—The difficulty and nicety of detail required in the production of steel and copper engravings make this method quite expensive. The rich and dignified effects are enough to warrant the expense, if one wishes to be characterized as of positively good taste. A calling card upon which the name has been steel engraved suggests the feeling of quality. Engraving is to be recommended for both professional and business cards. The traveling man finds their use an aid in introduction. It advertises the taste of the user.

When the plate for a steel or a copper engraving has been made, its entire smooth surface is inked, the ink being forced into the engraved crevices. The plate's smooth surface is then cleaned with benzine and polished with whiting. Then the card or paper to be printed is placed over the plate, and a powerful press forces the card and plate together until the ink has been transferred from the crevices on to the card.

Three-Color Process.—By the three-color process (that is, the combination of the three primary colors,—yellow, red and blue, Fig. 51) all the colors of an oil painting or water color may be faithfully reproduced if properly handled by a first-class, three-color photo-engraver, which in lithography might require 7 to 11 or more color impressions. These plates are made by making three half-tone negatives, one for each of the three color plates, thru proper color screens placed inside of the camera back of the lens. The negative for the yellow plate is made by photographing all the yellow of the picture and that portion of the yellow which enters into the combination of other colors, by placing a violet screen back of the lens. The negative for the red plate ·is made by photographing thru a green screen, and the negative for the blue plate is made by photographing thru an orange screen. It is absolutely necessary that these three negatives be made of exactly one size to insure a perfect register in printing.

When these colored negatives are correctly made, and the plates properly etched by a skilled artist or re-etcher, and printed by a competent pressman, the result is a counterpart of the original copy; but the work must be handled by the most expert workmen throughout in order to get satisfactory results.

Half-tones and Colors.—Colored printing differs with the

Courtesy U. G. I., Phila.

Fig. 52.—Ben Day screen.

number of colors and kind of illustration to be produced. There are excellent results to be obtained in the printing of three colors where each engraving is a half-tone. Take, for instance: " a " is a half-tone printed in yellow; " b " is a half-tone printed in red; " c " is a combination of these two; " d " is a half-tone blue which, combined with " c," produces " e," the finished picture. Four color half-tone process in addition to the three half-tone plates has a fourth one, black or grey black, which serves as a key plate and brings out greater detail and strength.

The introduction of half-tones to produce a single picture

Fig 54.—Ben Day color process.

4. Name the three kinds of processes used in developing an illustration and characterize each.
5. What numerical screen-lines would you advise for newspapers and magazine work?
6. Give the three kinds of engravings and describe each.

PROBLEMS

1. Solve the problem of mal-adjustment often existing between artist, advertiser, and printer.
2. Find a written advertisement and from it design an illustration concretely expressing the main thought.
3. It is desirable to run this advertisement in to-night's paper at one-half its width. Graphically show how it will look when reduced to this proportion.
4. Clip several half-tone cuts from various sources and designate their approximate screen density.
5. Differentiate between the color process and the " Ben Day " process.
6. Locate two advertisements which you believe illustrate the steel and copper process, and that of lithography.
7. Discuss: (1) advisable sizes of half-tone reproduction;
   (2) advisability of " odd " and " even " color tones;
   (3) expense involved in all processes and engravings.
8. Name the different kinds of plates presented by advertisers for general advertising use.
9. What is the significant difference in the following: " line cut and zinc etching "; " half-tone and electrotype "; " stereotype and electrotype "; " electrotype and zinc etching "?

COLLATERAL READINGS

THE TYPOGRAPHY OF ADVERTISEMENTS, TREZISE, Chapter ix, page 110.
ÆSTHETIC EDUCATION, CHAS. DEGARMO, Chapter ix, page 130.
PRINCIPLES OF ADVERTISING ARRANGEMENT, FRANK A. PARSONS, Chapter ii.
I. C. S. ADVERTISER'S HANDBOOK, pages 169 to 189, " Advertisement Illustration."

CHAPTER XI

THE ILLUSTRATION

THE following pages are self-explanatory, showing how the different screens are adapted to the different qualities of paper:—

65 LINE SCREEN HALF-TONE ON ZINC (FIG. 55)

Made From.—Photographs and wash drawings.

Where Used.—City newspapers that print from stereotype plates.

Why Used.—A screen that is coarse enough to stereotype.

Style.—Portraits, scenes, interiors, exteriors can be made square, oval, or circular finish, preferably with line border. Portraits can also be made outline finish, that is, part of the background being cut away. Avoid the use of this screen with vignette.

Paper.—The very cheapest grades of paper such as used in newspapers.

Caution.—Never use this screen for illustrating any picture showing small fine detail.

Subjects Used.—Portraits, scenes, interiors, exteriors.

85 LINE SCREEN HALF-TONE ON ZINC (FIGS. 55 AND 56).

Made From.—Photographs and wash drawings.

Where Used.—Weekly papers using cylinder press.

Why Used.—This screen is still coarse but permits of details. Will electrotype, but will not stereotype.

Style.—Portraits, scenes, interiors, exteriors can be made square, oval, or circular finish with or without line border. Portraits can also be made outline finish, that is, part of the background being cut away. Never use this screen with vignette or outline finish for any article of merchandise.

Paper.—The better grades of paper such as used in weekly newspaper, machine finish, S. S. & C. book, plate and coated papers.

Caution.—Never use this screen for illustrating articles of

---

*Due courtesy is hereby given Mr. C. F. Teller, of the Onondago Lithographic Company, Syracuse, N. Y., for this intensive analysis.

merchandise. Use zinc etching. Never use this screen for stereotyping.

Subjects Used.—Portraits, scenes, interiors, exteriors.

100 LINE SCREEN HALF-TONE ON ZINC (FIGS. 56 AND 57)

Made From.—Photographs and wash drawings.

Where Used.—Weekly newspapers, certain farm journals, mail order publications, and in some magazines using a cylinder press.

Why Used.—This screen is not so coarse as the 85 line screen and therefore shows more detail. Will electrotype, but will not stereotype.

Style.—Portraits, scenes, interiors, exteriors can be made square, oval, or circular finish with or without line border. Portraits can also be made outline finish, that is, part of the background being cut away. Never use this screen with vignette or outline finish for any article of merchandise.

Paper.—The better grades of paper such as used in weekly newspapers, machine finish, magazine text, S. S. & C. book, plate and coated papers.

Caution.—Never use this screen for illustrating articles of merchandise. Use zinc etching. Never use this screen for stereotyping.

Subjects Used.—Portraits, scenes, interiors, exteriors.

120 LINE SCREEN HALF-TONE ON COPPER (FIGS. 56 AND 57)

Made From.—Photographs and wash drawings.

Where Used.—Trade papers, general magazines, better grades of mail order publications, farm papers, good class of catalogs and circulars, and duograph or duotype half-tone plates.

Why Used.—This screen is finer than the 110 line screen, therefore will show more detail. It is the most suitable screen from which to make copper and nickel electrotypes. Will not stereotype. This screen and the 110 line screen on copper are the best for magazine advertising.

Style.—Portraits, scenes, interiors, exteriors and articles of merchandise can be made square, oval, or circular finish, with or without line border and outline finish. Never use this screen vignette finish (use outline finish) in any magazine or publication. A half-tone vignette finish is the most difficult engraving to print and should never be made on a screen coarser than 133 line.

Style.—A half-tone vignette finish should be printed on the best coated papers, costing not less than 7½ to 8 cents per lb.; best grades of half-tone ink; all make ready necessary to produce perfect printed results.

Paper.—Good grades of S. S. & C. book, plate and coated papers, and for medium grades of printing on dull finish papers.

Caution.—Never use this screen for illustrating articles of merchandise in newspapers, mail order publications, farm papers and magazines using news or machine finish papers. Use zinc etchings. Never use this screen for stereotyping.

Subjects Used.—Portraits, scenes, interiors, exteriors and for the illustration of any article of merchandise on smooth or dull coated papers.

133 LINE SCREEN HALF-TONE ON COPPER (FIGS. 56 AND 57)

Made From.—Photographs and wash drawings.

Where Used.—Good grades of catalog and circular work, and the better duograph or duotype half-tone plates.

Why Used.—This screen is fine enough to show detail well. It is the best screen universally used for good grades of printing. It is the finest screen that will electrotype, but will not stereotype. Never electrotype a half-tone plate 133 line screen made vignette finish.

Style.—Portraits, scenes, interiors, exteriors and articles of merchandise can be made square, oval, circular finish with or without line border and outline or vignette finish. Never use outline or vignette finish for advertising in any publication; use 110 line screen or 120 line screen. A half-tone vignette engraving is the most difficult engraving to print and it should never be made on a screen coarser than 133 line screen. A half-tone vignette finish should be printed on the best coated papers, costing not less than 7½ to 8 cents per lb.; best grades of half-tone ink; all make-ready necessary to produce perfect printed results.

Paper.—Better grades of coated papers, and for the best grades of printing on dull finish papers.

Caution.—Never use this screen for advertising any articles of merchandise in newspapers, mail order publications, farm papers, trade papers, or general magazines. This is due to the fact that the average publication's electrotyped pages are generally run under poor printing conditions. Use 110 line screen or the 120 line screen. Never use this screen for stereotyping.

Subjects Used.—Portraits, scenes, interiors, exteriors and illustrations of any article of merchandise on smooth or dull finish coated papers.

150 LINE SCREEN HALF-TONE ON COPPER (FIG. 57)

Made From.—Photographs and wash drawings.

Where Used.—Fine grade of catalog and circular work, and the best duograph or duotype half-tone plates.

Why Used.—This screen is the finest for practical use, as it shows the most detail. It should never be electrotyped or stereotyped.

Style.—Portraits, scenes, interiors, exteriors and articles of merchandise can be made square, oval, or circular finish, with or without line border and outline or vignette finish. A half-tone vignette finish is the most difficult engraving to print and it should never be made on a screen coarser than 133 line. A half-tone vignette finish should be printed on the best coated papers, costing not less than $7\frac{1}{2}$ to 8 cents per lb.; best grades of half-tone ink; all make-ready necessary to produce perfect printed results. Never use this screen for any style of advertising or in any magazine or publication. Use the 110 line screen or the 120 line screen. Never electrotype half-tone plates 150 line screen any finish.

Paper.—The best coated papers costing not less than 8 cents per lb.

Caution.—This screen should never be used for dull finish papers. Never use this screen for advertising any article of merchandise in newspapers, mail order publications, farm papers, trade papers or general magazines. This is due to the fact that the average publication's electrotyped pages are generally run under poor printing conditions. Use the 110 line screen or the 120 line screen. Never use this screen for electrotyping or stereotyping.

Square finish with line, shown in three different screens.

Vignette finish, shown in three different screens.

Combination of outline and vignette finish, shown in three different screens.

Outline finish, shown in three different screens.

Courtesy Gatchel & Manning, Phila.

FIG. 58.—Four Styles or finishes for half-tone engravings.

Subjects Used.—Portraits, scenes, interiors, exteriors and for the illustration of any article of merchandise on the best grades of coated papers.

The Selection of the Style or Finish for Half-tone Engravings.—A square, oval or circular finish, with or without line, of portrait, scene, interior, or exterior is optional with the buyer; it is simply a matter of taste (Fig. 58a). Care should be used in ordering oval or circular finish half-tones from oblong or square finish photographs. The oval or circular finish will always remove the corners of the photograph, so attention should be paid to see that these finishes do not remove anything essential to the illustration. In numbers of portraits where some are oblong and others oval, the oval finish is advised. It is often difficult to make square finish half-tones from many oval portraits on account of the missing corners, a good artist can, however, paint in a suitable addition to the background which will not be noticable when reproduced.

Half-tone Vignette Finish.—This is a half-tone with the edges on all sides of the subjects fading away in an irregular edge of diminishing color intensity (Fig. 58b). This finish lends itself effectively in a number of subjects but can only be employed where good paper and presswork are demanded. The plates require special work on the part of the engraver and add approximately 50c to 75c per plate of moderate size.

Half-tone Outline and Vignette Finish.—This is a half-tone in which part of the background is cut away and part vignette (Fig. 58c). A half-tone outline and vignette finish costs about 75 cents for the artist's work to prepare the photograph. A half-tone outline and vignette finish is the most suitable for high-grade catalogs and circulars printed under excellent conditions. A half-tone outline and vignette finish is the most difficult engraving to print. It should be printed on the best coated papers costing not less than 7½ to 8 cents per lb.; best grades of half-tone ink; all make ready necessary to produce perfect printed results. A half-tone outline and vignette should never be made on a screen coarser than a 133 line. A half-tone outline and vignette finish should never be used in newspapers, magazines or in any publication of this kind. (Use square, oval, circular, or outline finish.)

Half-tone Outline Finish.—This is a half-tone with the

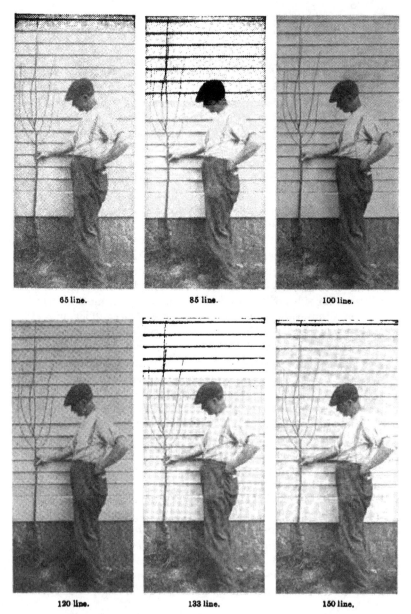

65 line.   85 line.   100 line.

120 line.   133 line.   150 line.

FIG. 55.—Showing different half-tone screen results on machine finish paper.

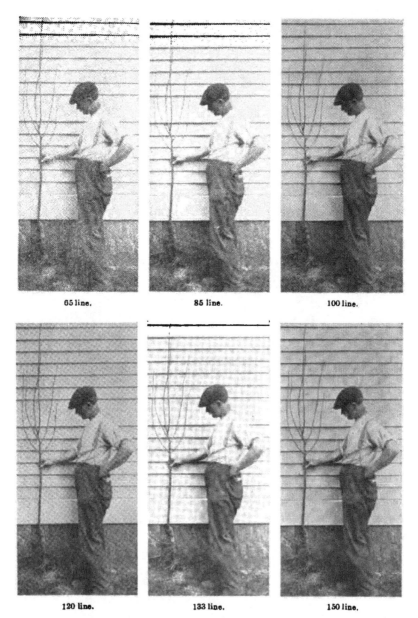

65 line.

85 line.

100 line.

120 line.

133 line.

150 line.

Fig. 56.—Showing different half-tone screen results on super-calendered paper.

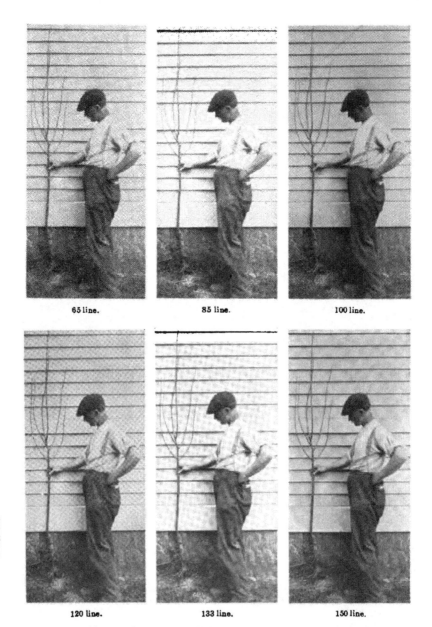

65 line. 85 line. 100 line.

120 line. 133 line. 150 line.

FIG. 57.—Showing different half-tone screen results on coated paper.

background cut entirely away, leaving a definite edge without shading or vignetting (Fig. 58d). A half-tone outline finish is recommended where space is valuable in advertising or to show the object larger in a given space. This can be made from photographs or from any portrait, without artist's work.

Half-tone Square and Vignette Finish.—This is a half-tone in which part of the outside edges are rectangular and parallel, and part vignette. A half-tone square and vignette finish requires from two to five dollars' worth of artist's work, according to the conditions of the photograph and time necessary to secure artistic results. A half-tone square vignette finish is most suitable for high-grade catalogs and circulars printed under excellent conditions. A half-tone vignette finish is the most difficult engraving to print. It should be printed on the best, coated papers, costing not less than $7\frac{1}{2}$ to 8 cents per lb.; best grades of half-tone ink; all make-ready necessary to produce perfect printed results. A half-tone square and vignette finish should never be made on a screen coarser than the 133 line. A half-tone square and vignette finish should never be electrotyped. A half-tone square and vignette finish should never be used in newspapers, magazines, or publications of any kind. (Use square or oval finish.)

Artist's Work.—*Retouching of Photograph by the Artist.*—The retouching of photographs by the artist is the using of a plain photograph as a base and bringing out more clearly the details of construction, the elimination of reflections and the correcting of minor distortions. Good touching demands as little work upon the original photograph as possible, hence the necessity for the best photographs. In poor photographs it is necessary to paint over nearly the entire surface in order to bring the copy to a uniform tone value with necessary high-lights and shadows for contrast. Poor photographs greatly increase the cost of artist's work, and detract from the naturalness of the photograph.

Half-tone Square Finish with Line.—A half-tone square finish should never be used in advertising any article of merchandise, especially machinery or furniture, unless the background is directly related or absolutely necessary to show position of machine in relation to other machines; or unless there is to be particular emphasis on some distinctive feature of the machine. The square finish background tends to detract from the article of merchandise illustrated. The article would be more prominently displayed if made outline finish.

Wash Drawings.—Where photographs are greatly distorted, wash drawings are always used. In the case of an article of merchandise which it has been impossible to photograph or where blue prints or tracings are the only records of detail that can be obtained, a lead pencil sketch of the article is made to give the right perspective and detail. When once this pencil drawing is mechanically and technically correct, it is then washed in by the artist either by hand or by means of an air brush. (The latter is an instrument used in laying colors on the copy by means of compressed air.)

Wash Drawings of Buildings and Plants.—It is impossible to make photographs of many large buildings which give an adequate conception of their size or details of construction. In photographing long or high buildings they are likely to be found somewhat distorted. In either of these cases wash drawings are made by the artist from actual lead pencil sketches of the building or from photographs showing specific details. The large pencil lay-out is made on a card-board 20 × 40 inches and the colors are washed in upon the drawing either by hand or by the air brush.

Price for Artist's Work.—It is impossible to make a schedule of prices which would serve as a basis for the artist's work. In retouching of photographs the cost of artist's work depends upon the quality of the photograph; that is, whether it has many reflections, whether the details are plain and distinct, or whether there are any distortions to correct. The cost for retouching a photograph is often governed by the value of the article of merchandise as well as the value of the illustration to the buyer of the artist's work; for instance, if the artist's work on the photograph is to be used in a fine catalog or a cheap booklet, the expense is varied accordingly.

If good photographs are secured, the cost for retouching is

reduced, and better results are obtained. The engraver should know the value of the article of merchandise and where the illustration is to be used. This enables him to give a much more intelligent quotation.

Sketches.—It is impossible for many concerns to make sketches free, as the artists employed in the art departments receive a stipulated salary. To illustrate: A sketch of a trotting horse on a sulky is desired. No artist can draw this from memory—he must have some information of the detail of construction of the sulky and the position of the horse in trotting. A considerable amount of time must necessarily be consumed in securing this information. The engraver cannot afford to make a ten-dollar sketch on a chance of getting a twenty-dollar contract. When the order is placed for a design or illustration, sketches are prepared for approval of the customer, and should these not prove satisfactory desired changes and, if required, new sketches are made.

In placing orders for drawings, furnish all possible information as to ornamental or conventional designs, style of lettering, and whatsoever other information will prove helpful.

Cover Designs.—Distinctively designed covers for catalogs and small booklets are absolutely necessary in gaining the attention of the buyer. If it is an attractive design, harmonious in color scheme, and printed on the right kind of cover stock, the catalog will be both read and filed away for future use. It is the cover with poor type arrangement and distasteful color scheme that finds its place in the waste basket. At a small cost, color sketches for all cover designs are furnished. Before submitting color sketches for cover design, it is necessary to know the size of the catalog, whether regular or broad fold, and the wording to be used. Does the buyer desire a conventional or an ornamental design, and does he have any preference as to the color of the cover stock, these details must be specified.

Embossed Covers.—There are two kinds of embossing plates, brass die embossing plates and zinc embossing plates. The brass die embossing plate such as used on many covers is hand-cut in

brass. It shows two or three depths in the embossing and
gives a clear, sharp embossing edge. Zinc embossing plates cost
less money than the brass die embossing plate, for instead of it
being hand cut in brass it is a positive etching etched deeper by
nitric acid. The zinc embossing plate will not permit of two or
three depths, nor such sharp lines as are obtained in the brass
embossing plates.

Pen and Ink Drawing.—Pen and ink drawings are made
for cover designs, advertising ideas, trade-marks, and signatures
reproduced by zinc etchings. They should always be made with
India ink on white paper stock, for if made with ordinary
writing ink, which is not absolutely black, it is impossible to
secure a good zinc etching. If the ink is of a decided bluish
tint, it is impossible to produce a zinc etching.

Pen and Ink Drawing Made from Photographs.—To save
the cost of a pencil lay-out in making a pen and ink drawing
of an article of merchandise, a photograph or wash drawing can
be rephotographed and a silver print made from the negative.
This silver print would be the same as a pencil lay-out, and it
saves the time in making tracings or lead pencil sketch to get
the right proportion and perspective. After the photograph is
inked, the print is bleached and a pen and ink drawing is produced at a moderate cost.

Cost of Pen and Ink Drawings.—The actual time spent in
making a pen and ink drawing is not considerable. The greater
part of the time is generally consumed in making a lead pencil
lay-out so as to get a balance of harmony and correct details.
For the artist to get correct details in connection with his work
it is necessary for him to have in hand details of the sketch in
some form or other. The getting of this material often con-
sumes a great deal of time.

Photographs.—The basis of all good half-tone illustrations,
other than those made from wash drawings, is the *photograph*.
The purchasing of the best photographs that money can buy
is advised, for they are free from distortions, and free from
bad reflections. A good photograph will always show more detail.

The best artist's work can be done on the best photographs, where it is possible to retain the photographic value without the necessity of covering it with paint. The trouble with photographs made by amateurs is caused either by cheap lens or lack of experience. The greatest faults in photographs made by amateurs are distortions, bad reflections, and lack of clear details, all of which increase the cost of retouching the photograph.

Reduction Sizes.—For the photographing of articles of merchandise unless the article is large, the 8 × 10 size is best. For a photograph of groups in parts, the 11 × 14 size is advised. On small articles of merchandise, not having much detail, the 5 × 7 size should be used. Smaller sizes are difficult to bring out the details of retouching.

Prints.—Always furnish two prints so that the artist can use one as a guide and reference for bringing out the details in retouching the photograph. All photographs should be mounted or they are liable to be bent, cracked, or torn in shipping or handling.

Paper for Photographs.—In the retouching of photographs the artist should have a black and white velox print with semi-mat surface. Red as a color always represents peculiar difficulties in photographing. If the prints are toned red they give different color values in the half-tone engravings. A black and white photograph on gelatine paper, smoothly burnished with intense shadows and bright high-lights, will make the best half-tone reproduction.

Avoid dead unburnished copies or photographs containing a bluish tone. It is almost impossible to make perfect work from rough paper, matt finish or gray photograph. In selecting photographic prints for copies consider the following: solio papers or any of the print out papers, toned to a black and white are good. Aristo-platino paper does not reproduce well. Velox paper (glossy) is the best in its class of papers, if developed to a greenish tint; carbon velvet is also good. Platinum paper (smooth) with good black color makes a good copy; sepia color makes a poor copy. Negatives and tin-types should never be

offered as copy. It requires extra expense in rephotographing
the half-tone or making refixed photographs of the negative. Un-
fixed photographs or proofs should never be sent to the engraver,
as they turn black when exposed to the light.

ZINC ETCHING WITH GRAINED BACKGROUND (FIG. 59)
(Produces an effect of two colors with one printing)

Made From.—Pen and ink drawing and type matter.

Where Used.—Newspapers, magazines, catalogs and circulars.

Why Used.—For the reproduction of two color effect by one
impression of the printing press. Since a zinc etching with
grained background is produced in the making of the plates it is

Fig. 59.—Zinc etching with grained background.

not necessary to have a grained effect in the pen and ink drawing
or type matter.

Paper.—Any kind of paper.

Ink.—Any kind of ink.

Caution.—Cannot be made from blue prints, brown prints,
wash drawings or photographs. Cannot be made from any copy
printed in blue ink or printed on red or yellow paper.

A zinc etching with grained background should never be
enlarged over twice its original size. Enlargements magnify the
imperfections of the copy and tend to make the lines of the zinc
etching ragged. A zinc etching with a grained background should
not be reduced over four times the size of the copy, unless the
lines of the copy are heavy enough to permit being reduced to
$\frac{1}{4}$ of their width.

Proper Subjects.—Zinc etching with grained background made from pen and ink drawing or type matter is especially suitable where particular prominence is desired or a reproduction of two color effect by one impression of the printing press in newspapers, magazine publications, catalogs and circulars.

ZINC ETCHING WITH BEN DAY BORDER (FIG. 60)

Made From.—Pen and ink drawing and type matter.

Where Used.—Trade papers, general magazines, better grades of mail order publications, farm papers, and the better class of catalogs and circulars.

Why Used.—For the reproduction of two color effect with one impression of the printing press. A zinc etching with a Ben Day

FIG. 60.—Zinc etching with Ben Day border.

border is produced in the making of the plate, and it is not necessary to have the Ben Day effect in the pen and ink drawing or type matter.

Paper.—Magazine text, S. S. & C. book, plate and coated papers.

Caution.—Cannot be made from blue prints, brown prints, wash drawings, or photographs. Cannot be made from any copy printed in blue ink or printed on red or yellow paper.

Zinc etching with Ben Day border should never be enlarged over twice its original size. Enlargements magnify the imperfections of the copy and tend to make the lines of the zinc etching ragged. Zinc etching with Ben Day border should not be reduced over four times the size of the copy, unless the lines of the copy are heavy enough to permit being reduced to $1/4$ of their width.

Subjects Used.—Zinc etching with Ben Day effects from pen and ink drawings and type matter are especially suitable where a two-color effect is desired with one impression of the printing press. These are used in trade papers, magazines, various grades of catalogs and circulars.

ZINC ETCHING WITH BLACK BORDER (FIG. 61)

Made From.—Pen and ink drawings, tracings and type matter.

Where Used.—Any newspaper, magazine publication, catalog or circular.

Why Used.—For the reproduction of pen and ink drawings,

Quality-Service
DESIGNS · PHOTO - ENGRAVINGS
IN ONE OR MORE COLORS
MADE IN
· PHILADELPHIA ·

Fig. 61.—Zinc etching with black border.

tracings or type matter, any size desired. Excellent for stereotyping and electrotyping.

Paper.—Any kind of paper.

Caution.—Cannot be made from blue prints, brown prints, wash drawings, or photographs. Cannot be made from any copy printed in blue ink or printed on red or yellow paper.

A Zinc etching should never be enlarged over twice its original size. Enlargements magnify the imperfections of the copy and tend to make the lines of the zinc etching ragged. A zinc etching should not be reduced over four times the size of the copy, unless the lines of the copy are heavy enough to permit being reduced to $\frac{1}{4}$ of their width.

Subjects Used.—Zinc etchings should always be used in illustrating articles of merchandise in newspapers, certain mail order publications, farm papers and magazines using cheaper grades of paper than magazine text and S. S. & C. book. Cover designs, letter heads, maps, tracings, type matter, and advertising designs printed on smooth or rough stock.

POSITIVE ETCHING OF REVERSED PLATE (FIG. 62)
(Plates where the blacks of the original will print white; and the whites will print black)

Made From.—Pen and ink drawings and type matter which may be straight or reversed.

Where Used.—Any newspaper, magazine publication, catalog or circular.

Why Used.—For the reproduction of a reversed effect from

FIG. 62.—Positive etching or reversed plate.

a pen and ink drawing, tracing, and from type matter where the black lines print white, and the whites print black.

Caution.—Cannot be made from blue prints, brown prints, wash drawings, or photographs. Cannot be made from any copy printed in blue ink or printed on red or yellow paper.

A positive etching should never be enlarged over twice its original size. Enlargements magnify the imperfections of the copy and tend to make the lines of positive etching ragged. A positive etching should never be reduced over four times the size of the copy, unless the lines of the copy are heavy enough to permit being reduced to $\frac{1}{4}$ of their width.

Subjects Used.—Positive etchings made from pen and ink drawings and type matter, each of which may be straight or reversed. It is especially suitable where particular prominence is desired in newspapers, magazine publications, catalogs or circulars.

CHAPTER XII

THE TRADE-MARK

Definition of a Trade-Mark.—Popularly speaking, a trade-mark is the pen and ink personality of the manufacturer. owner of a trade-mark residing in a foreign country, if the latter name affixed in some conspicuous way to an article, which identifies that article as the product of a particular manufacturer, and at the same time distinguishes it from all other articles of the same kind or class.

A valid trade-mark, once adopted and registered, may be used on the labels, packages, cartons, and advertisements of the concern to which it belongs, for there is no limitation set upon the scope of its use; this depends entirely upon the business policy of the firm.

History and Development.—Back in the sixteenth century, the trade-mark was, as the name implies, a mere mark used to designate the origin of manufacture. It was first used in connection with textiles. To-day, however, the trade-mark represents a significant link in the evolution of selling methods. Fifty years ago, the indirect method of marketing goods thru the middleman or jobber was at its zenith. The consumer seldom, if at all, ever came into direct touch with the manufacturer, inasmuch as the latter's sales-campaign, from advertising to the employment of salesmen, was directed almost exclusively by the jobber. The course of evolution brought the realization that a business policy, founded on the direct personal relation between manufacturer and ultimate purchaser, would eliminate the economic waste of the middleman, would tend to create in the public mind a feeling of confidence in the goods, and also promote a greater stability of demand. The trade-mark is the crystallised idea following from the realization. And by means of an ever-expanding network of railroads, combined with nation-wide advertising, the trade-mark came to symbolise, as it were, the standard of workmanship, the quality of goods, and the entire business policy of the commercial house using it.

Principles Governing Creation of a Trade-Mark.—The careful construction of a trade-mark is of fundamental importance to its user. It has been said very truly that " there is no servant more diligent, more faithful, more persistent, or more efficient than a good trade-mark." Conversely, the pernicious influence of a poor trade mark is just as far reaching. Moreover, the heavy expense likely to be incurred in launching a new or revised trade-mark before the public, and the concurrent lapse of time before the same is associated with the particular goods in question, render the altering of a trade-mark, once it has become generally known, an inadvisable step.

A trade-mark, therefore, should contain all the elements conducive to permanency. If it is a symbol, the rules relating to the threshold of sensation, attention, focal point, eye movement, etc., are primarily involved; if a name alone, the principles of typography and color are to be followed; if a portait or picture, the functions of our sense experiences must be heeded. In a word, it should represent all the general laws of advertising psychology summarised and compressed into a device or sign of a distinct individuality. In the selection of the form of a trade-mark, no general rule is applicable for every instance. The trade-mark is always modified by the nature of the product, and the class of people to whom it appeals. But there are certain facts which it is well to keep in mind. Experience has shown that a name, as such, can be fixed in the public's mind within a few weeks, while it requires years to accomplish the same end by the use of a symbol. However, a symbol is easier to remember. Usually, a combination of the name and the symbol proves most effective.

Importance of Trade-Mark Individuality.—To claim the protection of the law, a trade-mark must possess a distinct individuality. Therefore, the field of industry in which a specific trade-mark is expected to flourish ought to be thoroughly investigated so as to avoid any possibility of immediate or remote resemblance to trade-marks that have preceded it. A contemplation of the fact that the trade-marks of some of the national advertisers are valued at five millions of dollars, emphasizes the

11

importance of using painstaking care in the selection of a trade-mark. This amount of wealth may be destroyed in an instant, if it can be proven that the trade-mark sustaining it has no legal right to exist. Before entering into a discussion of the legal rights and liabilities which the owner of a trade-mark is invested with, a distinction ought to be drawn between the remedy accorded a genuine trade-mark and a mere so-called trade symbol or trade sign. A trade-mark is safeguarded by the common and statute law appertaining to trade-marks; while a trade symbol is protected by the principles related to unfair competition. As expressed by one Court, " Unfair competition is distinguishable from the infringement of a trade-mark in this: that it does not involve necessarily the question of the exclusive right of another to the use of the name, symbol, or device. A word may be purely generic or descriptive, and so not capable of becoming an arbitrary trade-mark, and yet there may be an unfair use of such a word or symbol which will constitute unfair competition. The right to the use of an arbitrary name or device as indicia of origin is protected upon the ground of a legal right to its use by the person appropriating it. The doctrine of unfair competition is possibly lodged upon the theory of the protection of the public whose rights are infringed or jeopardised by the confusion of goods produced by unfair methods of trade, as well as upon the right of the complainant to enjoy the good-will of a trade built up by his efforts, and sought to be taken from him by unfair methods."

Registration of a Trade-Mark Versus Adoption and Use.— Once having been decided upon, the trade-mark ought to be registered immediately with the U. S. government, or its adoption and use as a trade-mark be made known; otherwise, it will be afforded no legal protection. Registering a trade-mark is a simple process, conducted in accordance with the regulation of the Patent Office. The protection granted by this process is peculiarly valuable, namely, an injunction issued by reason of an infringement of a registered trade-mark is valid throughout the United States; and, furthermore, being listed in the public records that are open for examination at all times, very often it obviates unintentional infringement. On the other hand, for a trade-mark made such by adoption and use rather than by registration, the protection is a little more difficult of access. Unless the amount involved is $3,000 or more, and the litigants are citizens of different states, the case cannot be docketed in the Federal courts; which means that the scope of the injunction is confined to the territorial limits of the state. Moreover, the owner must prove its notorious adoption and use, and the working of fraud by the infringing symbol not only upon the owner, but also upon the public.

Essentials of a Valid Trade-Mark.—To be valid a trade-mark must fulfil certain requirements, on the one hand, and on the other must satisfy certain restrictions. Specifically a valid trade-mark must be:—

1. Used in lawful trade.

2. Affixed by some means to the article or its cartons. The method of affixation is immaterial, but it must be written, printed, branded, woven or otherwise impressed in a distinctive manner.

3. Arbitrary in its character and selection, and not a mere description of the article with which it is associated. Examples of the trade-mark arbitrarily chosen are numerous. Thus, the word " Kodak " exemplifies an arbitrary combination of letters, held to be a valid trade-mark. Moreover, a trade-mark may be suggestive, as distinguished from descriptive, and yet not violate the above rule; as, for instance, " Uneeda." Nor will misspelling, hyphening, or a peculiar arrangement of letters render valid a trade-mark which otherwise would be invalid; hence, P-I-T-T-S-B-U-R-G P-U-M-P is not a valid trade-mark. Advertisements, directions, and cautions do not amount to a trade-mark, and the same is true of the mere form or appearance of the commodity. Nevertheless, the Federal trade-mark law recognizes one exception to the above restriction relating to descriptiveness, in that a trade-mark though descriptive of the character of the product, may be registered, if it has been used for ten years prior to February 20, 1905.

Coined words indicative of origin and ownership are valid trade-marks ; however the words themselves must not suggest the quality, character, or ingredients of the article. Trade-marks consisting of coined words are myriad; as, " Postum," " Oldsmobile," " Shawknit," " Nabisco," " Pianola." Where a coined word has secured such a wide usage as to practically become idiomatic, such as " kodak," and " celluloid," this interesting question presents itself: whether by its evolution into an idiom, the owner is deprived of his legal rights attached thereto. The rule seems to be: where a trade-mark has become an accepted part of the vernacular, the public may use the word for all purposes, *except* as a trade-mark or in other unfair competition. Thus, the legal rights ensuing from the possession of a trade-mark are reserved to the owner.

Words in common use when given a fanciful meaning constitute valid trade-marks; for example,—" White House " as the name of a coffee, has been so sustained; as has been " Club " for a cocktail. Likewise, advertising " catch " phrases which establish the identity of the manufactory, and so denote the origin of the article will be protected as trade-marks. Furthermore, catch phrases, though not trade-marks, are safeguarded, by the principles governing unfair competition. In this connection, as disclosing the extent to which this protection is carried, there is the incident involving Wilson's Whiskey. May Irwin, the celebrated comedienne, was appearing in a play entitled, " Mrs. Wilson, That's All." On the ground that this title worked an injury to this business, the whiskey concern started legal proceedings that eventually necessitated the alteration of the title to " Mrs. Wilson."

4. Such a complete identification of the article as will distinguish it from all other articles of the same kind or class. A valid trade-mark dare not be the same as another trade-mark already in use for an article of the same kind. Moreover, if one trade-mark is likely to delude or confuse the public on account of a close similitude to another, the former cannot be upheld as valid. Thus, since the three letters " B.V.D." are registered as a valid trade-mark for a particular kind of underwear, it has been held that any other combination of individual letters to advertise the same product would be an infringement of the

"B.V.D." rights, restrainable by injunction and for which damages can be recovered. Of course, there is no objection to the use of a trade-mark previously applied to goods of a different character, though this latter fact must first be established.

What a Trade-Mark Must Not Be.—On the other hand a valid trade-mark.

1. Must not be a mere geographical or a proper name. Unless used in an arbitrary sense, geographical names are not valid trade-marks. The exception is well illustrated by the name "Vienna Bread." In the course of its reasoning in the latter case, the court declared: "As a mark for bread it is purely arbitrary, and is in no manner descriptive either of the ingredients or the quality of the article. . . . By the use of the word 'Vienna' in that connection, no deception is practiced, because the place of its manufacture is given, and it is known that bread cannot be imported from abroad for use here."

2. Must not be the name of a building, or business location. However, the use of such names may be upheld as a valid trade-mark, provided they are arbitrary and not misleading. A brief statement of two cases will illustrate the line of demarcation here. When Edwin Booth founded his theatre in New York City, he called it "Booth's Theatre"; the ownership of which finally passed out of the Booth family, though the name of the institution remained unchanged. In an action by the Booths to enjoin the use of the old name, it was decided that there was little likelihood of the public being led into the mistaken belief that Booth acted there, since the name related to the building. However, where one of the partners in an association carried on in the name of "Caswell, Hazard & Company, Established 1780," assigned his interest to the remaining partners, and later set up, in competition with the old firm, another business whose name included the phrase "Established 1780," the use of the last two words was enjoined on the ground of unfair competition in trade.

3. Must not be the name or portrait of a living person unless the consent of such a person or his legal guardian be first obtained. Moreover, from a psychological point of view, only strong reasons

will warrant the use of a portait alone as a trademark; it ought to characterise with a distinctive tone either the product or the manufacture, for sheer prettiness or a dilated ego are not of themselves sufficient qualifications.

4. Must not be constructed of the flag or of the various other insignia of the United States, a state or municipality. Moreover, Legally, a trade-mark is a distinctive mark, device, symbol or American National Red Cross, unless the person so using the same is a member of that organization and privileged to utilise it. A trade-mark comprising the insignia of any fraternal order is invalid.

5. Must not be obscene or otherwise immoral, nor connected with articles deleterious to the public welfare.

6. Must not be a specious statement of the origin, manufacture, quality or contents of the article to which it is attached; and to associate a valid trade-mark with advertising misrepresentative of the above-mentioned features is also to be condemned. The courts, guided by public opinion, have grown rather strict in their interpretation of this principle. As a result the position of the honest advertiser in the business world is strengthened. Judgment in one case was pronounced in the following words: " The idea seems to be that it is natural for men to exaggerate in advertising their goods, wares and merchandise, and that courts ought to sympathise with this human weakness or natural business tendency, and sanction it as a necessary business expedient. We may be compelled to tolerate, but ought not to sanction such measures. . . . With honest exaggeration or extravagance of statement born of zeal or overestimate of quality, this court finds no fault. But when exaggeration assumes the form of intentional misrepresentation as to the uses, qualities, and composition, etc., of articles of this description, the courts are bound in common honesty to refuse to sanction it in any way." In fact, the courts are more and more inclined to compel the introduction of positive evidence establishing that the article fulfils in every respect its advertised attributes, before admitting evidence showing the infringement. In the Moxie case, the

above rule was applied even though Moxie was manufactured by a secret process.

7. Must not be an obvious description of the nature or quality of the article. Hence, the bare designation of material, such as paper, leather, etc., or the bare delineation of the form, size, color, weight, and method of construction of the package, label, or of the article itself will render a symbol worthless as a trademark. The ensuing is an excellent test in determining whether or not a trade-mark is descriptive: " Will the public as a whole regard the mark as an arbitrary symbol denoting the origin and ownership of the product or commodity, or as an advertisement of some desirable quality ? " " Dessicated Codfish " and " Hygienic Underwear " were declared invalid trade-marks as indicating the nature of the article, while " Veribest " was rejected as a trade mark because it denoted quality. The term " Syrup of Figs," since it discloses ingredients, is not a valid trade-mark.

Creation of a Trade-Mark by Adoption and Use.—Where trade-marks derive their legal existence from adoption and use, as distinguished from registration, some new rules of law apply. For example, the intermittent use of a trade-mark which afterwards is discontinued altogether, secures to the manufacturer no protection against one who has used the same trade-mark permanently. As to what period of time may elapse between the adoption and the use of a trade-mark, depends entirely upon the peculiar circumstances of each case, though it is well settled that during this interval there must be no abandonment or an intention thereof, if the trade-mark is to acquire any vested rights. Moreover, the use of the trade-mark must extend beyond mere advertising, so as to embrace an affixation on the article itself or its packages; otherwise, the consumer would be hampered in tracing the origin and identity of the product.

Steps Incidental to Registration.—Anyone, irrespective of his citizenship, may register a trade-mark in most of the States, though in a minority of jurisdictions registration is confined to citizens thereof. However, the Federal law makes provision for the registration of a trade-mark by any person, natural or artificial, domiciled in this country, provided the trade-mark is used in commerce with foreign nations, among the several States, or with the Indian tribes; and the same right is granted to the owner of a trade-mark residing in a foreign country, if the latter has also extended registration privileges to United States citizens.

After a trade-mark has once been determined registrable, upon the payment of a fee of $10 a certificate will be granted under seal of the Patent Office, stating that the trade-mark is entitled to registration. Ordinarily the legal protection afforded by registration under the Federal Trade-Mark Act continues for a period of twenty years from the date of the certificate. However, should a trade-mark be previously registered in a foreign country, the protection in the United States ceases on the same date as it does in that country, unless the term in that country is for longer than twenty years. Of course trade-mark protection may be renewed for like periods of twenty years by the original registrant, his legal representatives, or assigns, upon the payment of $10 for each renewal; and the law is such that any number of successive registrations may be secured. This practically allows the registrant to secure a perpetual monopoly in a trademark.

All trade-marks registered in the United States Patent Office are published in its Official Gazette, and this contains the name and address of each registrant, a brief description of the trademark, together with a list of the articles to which it is applied. A person having reasonable cause to believe that he would be damaged by the registration of a particular trade-mark may ask the Patent Office to cancel the registration thereof; and, moreover, where there are conflicting applications for registration of a trade-mark, or any other dispute between an applicant and a registrant, the Patent Office will suspend any action it ordinarily would take in order to allow one of the parties to establish priority of use.

Infringements of a Trade-Mark and Remedies Therefor.— Infringements of a trade-mark assume several forms. There may be an imitation of the name, symbol, emblem, color, size, shape, and decoration of the package enclosing the article, or by a combination of such features.   To work an infringement it is not essential that the imitation be identical with the original, the simple fact that the general public has been or is likely to be deceived is sufficient.   Thus, " Appolonis " was held to be an infringement of " Appolinaris," " Cocoine " as an infringement of " Cocaine," and " Gold Drop " as an infringement of " Gold Dust."   And the fact that names are pronounced the same, though different in spelling, will nevertheless constitute an infringement.   The honest intention of the infringer is immaterial; if the mark which he is using is at all likely to delude the public as to the goods which it is buying, this will constitute an infringement.   Furthermore, the liability for infringement reaches beyond the person who originates the infringing trade-mark and includes those persons who in any way participate in it, such as the middle-man, the retailer or the employees concerned in its engraving and printing.   The remedy for an infringement is of a two-fold character: a single suit is brought by which the infringement may be restrained through an injunction and at the same time, damages are awarded.   The measure of damages is the whole profit of the infringer on the sale of the commodity associated with the trade-mark, as well as the loss sustained by the advertiser of the original trade-mark.

The trade-mark is the personal handshake of the manufacturer.   Therefore, it should be forceful; it should be constructed with a summary of the principles of psychology in mind; it should be such as to inspire and retain public confidence, and the legal principles underlying and regulating its composition should be followed.

QUESTIONS

1. Trace the evolution of the trade-mark and describe the underlying economic conditions which brought it to its present status.
2. In what way and to what degree is the trade-mark related to advertising generally?   What kind of a mark is likely to be most effective for permanent use?
3. Distinguish between the legal protection afforded a registered trade-mark and one not registered, and give the underlying theory therefor.
4. Enumerate the requisites and non-requisites of a valid trade-mark.   Does non-registration affect the right to recover for an infringement of a trade-mark?   State the rule for determining whether a trade-mark is suggestive or descriptive.

5. Give examples and discuss in their relations to the law of trade-marks the following terms: " Arbitrary in character and selection; " " coined words; " " catch words and phrases."
6. Discuss the attitude of the courts toward misrepresentative advertising and the trade-mark connected therewith.
7. What additional rules of law apply if trade-mark rights are claimed merely from adoption and use? Describe the forms that infringement of a trade-mark may assume, and give examples. What is the remedy for an infringement?
8. Discuss the probable effectiveness of " Made in America " with the statement " Made in the United States."
9. From a legal point of view, what is the limitation imposed upon an advertiser's use of imagination in the construction of a campaign?

COLLATERAL READINGS

ADVERTISING AS A BUSINESS FORCE, PAUL CHERINGTON, Chapter xi, " Trade-Mark Problems."
THE LAWS OF ADVERTISING AND SELLING, CHAPMAN, volumes i and ii.
I. C. S. ADVERTISER'S HANDBOOK, pages 262–273.

CHAPTER XIII

THE ADVERTISING CAMPAIGN

A Careful Detailed Analysis Essential.—An advertising campaign consists in a recognition of the numerous ways, means, conditions, methods, etc., by which a business house introduces its product or products to the general public. The manner of introduction or the method used for an increased publicity may vary as widely as there are different kinds of businesses. One fundemental principle, however, is followed by every successful advertiser: he analyses carefully and logically his entire proposition with respect to the product itself, the field of activity, and the distribution facilities that he will employ. There is a definite plan formulated and adhered to thruout the specified time during which the campaign operates. The cost of the project is carefully considered. All details of advertisement insertions are planned and executed with the one idea of more sales, and consequently greater profits. The problem before every business man is, " How can I educate the public to a knowledge of my article ? " " How can I prove to the general public that my products are the best on the market ? " He solves this problem partly by a successful advertising campaign, and partly by a successful sales-force coöperation.

Field Covered by Analysis.—In advertising a specific article or proposition, your campaign will contain an analysis of the following factors:

First, a statement of the amount of money to be expended and how the appropriation is to be determined.

Second, a regard for such laws as will create an honest cam- · paign.

Third, the method of distribution of the advertised goods. This means, whether your goods are going to the jobber alone or to both the jobber and the retailer. As an advertiser of a specific article or proposition you must indicate whether you as a manufacturer are to advertise to the consumer, to the jobber, or to the retailer, or to a combination of two or more of them.

171

Fourth, the area of activity. In other words, is your campaign to be local or national in nature? Accordingly as it is either or a combination of both, analyse the possibilities for maximum returns with respect to population, classes of people, distribution facilities, etc.

Fifth, the competition to be met.

Sixth, the kind of sales organization, whether salesmen or mail. Any successful campaign must consider a proper relation between salemanship and advertising.

Methods of Making Appropriations.—Appropriations for advertising campaigns result from either one of two main sources. First, the appropriation may be a definitely determined amount, based upon a certain fixed percentage of the gross sales, or profits of the previous year. These percentages vary from as low as one-half of one per cent. to as high as fifty per cent., according to the type of business under consideration. Second, the appropriation may be a lump sum, provided by vote of the board of directors of a business, or its managers, without regard to its relation to sales or profits, but simply based upon the estimated requirements, as submitted in the budget or report of its own Advertising Department, or by the Agency which conducts its campaigns.

It is undoubtedly becoming more general to find the appropriation determined by the first-mentioned method, and this naturally appeals to one as a more scientific means of arriving at the proper amount of money to spend. There is one important criticism to be made of this method, that in periods of falling sales or profits, the appropriations likewise decrease as a result of the fixed percentage used, whereas it is at such time that the appropriation should be increased. Falling sales, or profits, other things being equal, should be the barometer by which the necessity for increased advertising should be measured in order to restore at least normal conditions.

The second method prevails quite commonly where a firm employs advertising agencies to conduct its campaigns. Here the proposition takes the form of many other business deals in that several agencies may be asked to submit a proposition and estimates, showing the relative costs and results that may be expected

from various forms of advertising. When these propositions
have been received they are carefully considered and close comparisons of the figures submitted are made. Considerable scaling
down may result from this inspection, and finally the successful
bidder is engaged to prosecute his previously outlined campaign.
Thus one may see that while the appropriation, even in this case,
may have a definite relation to sales or profits, nevertheless, the
main reason which determined its amount arose from the desire
or necessity of attaining a certain result; namely, a definite
amount of sales.

Mediums.—Another factor consists in an intensive analysis
of mediums, the relative expenditure of each with respect to the
advertising appropriation and the amount of space to be devoted
to each particular kind of advertising. The amount of expenditure for any size of an advertisement should be determined,
as nearly as possible, by the amount of money necessary to be
paid for space in a particular magazine, and by determining the
amount of business that an advertisement increasingly creates.
In other words, there is a certain size advertisement which brings
maximum return, an increase of which means a loss to the advertiser rather than a gain. Therefore, as nearly as possible, determine what size of insertion will " pull " maximum returns.

Summary.—To be specific, analyse your article with respect to:

1. *Economic Factors*
   Money
   Laws
   Post Office Regula-
     tions
   P a s s i n g economic
     conditions: as, ca-
     lamities, w a r s,
     public policies, etc.

2. *Human Factors*
   Instincts
   Customs
   Habits
   Desires
   Classes of people
   Interests
   Attention
   Will
   Memory ⎰ Repetition
          ⎱ Intensity
          ⎰ Association
          ⎱ Ingenuity
   Curiosity
   Psychic Tendencies
   Morality
   Honesty

3. *Article*
   Utility
   Emotion
   Environment

4. *Means of Getting Attention (Mental)*	*Means of Getting Attention (Physical)*	5. *The Advertiser Himself*
Suggestion	Form	His adaptability to
Reason	Focal point	people
Imagination	Eye movement	Belief in proposition
	Adjustment	Relation to business
Means of Getting Attention (Physical)	Stimulus	concern
	Proportion	An ethical standard
Color	Symmetry	
Illustration	Balance	
Type	Rhythm, etc.	

This five-fold division enables the advertiser to determine the appeal. The following articles, on the advertiser himself, appropriation, campaign plans, sales policy, and method of keying advertisements, will give you concrete examples of the significance of an advertising campaign and illustrate the practical application of the classified factors stated above. The reprinting is a courtesy extended thru *Printer's Ink* and the Business Bourse, both of New York City.

DISCUSSION OF MR. H. TIPPER'S PAPER ON "THE VALUE OF TRAINED MEN FOR WORK IN THE ADVERTISING DEPARTMENT" JUNE 10, 1914.   PHILADELPHIA, PA.

C. R. Sturdevant, Educational Director, American Steel & Wire Co., Worcester, Mass.

" After all that has been written on the subject of advertising in recent years, and after listening to the very able discussion of the subject here to-day, I cannot hope to add much that is new. I wish merely to emphasize some phases of the subject already known.

" Most men are followers, copyists. Few are endowed naturally with the mental powers necessary for original creative thinking, or for making initial investigation. Our powers of imagination must be cultivated and developed by study and by instruction. We are creatures of habit and like the domestic animal, have to be trained to do anything unusual.

" Anyone would be greatly handicapped who begins any difficult undertaking without first acquainting himself thoroughly with the known and published knowledge pertaining to that particular subject. Without such knowledge any advancement or unfoldment that the individual could make might very likely be but duplications of that previously accomplished by others. But if a man begins his task thoroughly acquainted with all the known facts relating to the subject, then and not until then will he be equipped to bring forth the very best that is in him. We must know much about a subject before we can ever hope to add much of value to it.

"Advertising is an art or profession the function of which is generally to describe in writing and illustrations certain com' modities to prospective buyers in such attractive and forceful manner as either to make purchasers of them, or to aid greatly the selling organization. An advertisement is an appeal to the prospect to purchase something, and in these days when our mail is flooded with advertisements and catalogs of all kinds, and when all our papers, magazines and books are filled with them, it requires a man of unusual knowledge and skill to produce advertising matter that will accomplish effective results. And the future advertiser will find his task more difficult than the present one.

"The man who considers writing an advertisement has certain thoughts in his mind regarding a certain thing or proposition, which he wishes to impress upon the minds of many others. He wishes to secure the attention of those others and to interest them to the extent of investing in his scheme. The writer has to accomplish this through the use of written language, and pictures or cuts. In other words, one mind is trying to mould the thoughts of thousands of other minds, through the medium of the printer's art with regard to a certain thing or proposition. Of the four factors involved, the language used—the written story itself—would seem to be the one requiring most attention, and next in importance would be the manner in which the story was garbed or dressed up by the printer. The main problem is first, what to say, then how to present it.

"Of course no man can do justice in the write-up or description of an article or proposition about which he himself is unfamiliar. It takes a long time to explain what is not known. A story cannot possibly be any clearer or more complete than the writer's own mental conception of it. In this respect the management can offer much assistance to its advertising help, by presenting opportunities for them to become thoroughly familiar with

the finished product, its uses, advantages, and in most cases also
its construction.   On the other hand, the advertising writer
should solicit such opportunities and not wait for them to be
offered.

" No argument is required to show that the successful
advertising man should know much about the printer's art.
He must *know it*.   He should know regarding the styles of type,
about typographical arrangement, about forceful illustrations or
cuts and their best arrangement with respect to the type, about
mediums, the rules for writing copy, and the general technique
of making forceful copy.   If not possible to obtain this experience
in the printing office of the concern itself, then it should be
obtained by service in any one of several technical schools for
printers.

" In determining just what to write for an advertisement,
and the most effective manner of expressing it, the writer must
in general carefully consider many factors, such as the mental
caliber of the people whom he wishes to interest, the proposed
extent of the advertising campaign, what his competitors are
making and what they are advertising, the opportunities and
possibilities of the times, and the district to be covered.   After
determining the resultant of all these considerations and others
of similar character, the writer will then know whether to make
an artistic and elaborate presentation of his subject-matter or
whether to make it very forceful and intellectual, or suggestive,
or perhaps humorous.

" The man who is fully capable of summing up a situation
of this kind and who can then write an advertisement that is
100 per cent. effective, must be a man of unusual knowledge
and ability.   The advertiser, like the actor, has to present his
story from the standpoint of those who are to receive it; if he
wants to put it over the footlights, he must look well to style and
expression.   He must be an artist, as well as a student.

" The old methods and policies will neither do for the present
nor for the future.   The successful advertising man of the future
will of necessity have a very wide general knowledge of business
matters, of human nature, of his own industry, and of those well-
established rules and principles governing the writing and pre-

sentation of advertisements. Language is said to be the index of a man's intellectual attainment. Stylish, elegant, forceful English is required for best expression of thought. No article can be correctly or effectively described by the use of incorrect or inapt words. Of all classes of men in business, the writer of advertisements should have a good command of the English language, and a wide fund of information. Most men have to start early in life to acquire these accomplishments and they are acquired only through continued personal study and by mixing with people. Unless he learned the habit of speaking correctly in his growing years, he will have difficulty later in life to correct his language, to unlearn his vices of speech, and to acquire an extended working vocabulary. The man who is deficient in these respects could with profit make a close analytical study of those advertisements and articles which are attractive and to the point, which are conspicuous successes.

" The value of training men for the advertising department would depend largely on the nature of the training. If of the right kind, it would be indispensable. I should think a man's usefulness in this department would increase in direct proportion with his preparation, or training. To what extent the management could assist in such training would depend on the men to be trained, the extent of the desired training, and the available facilities for training. But in the last analysis the training would depend upon the men themselves and the amount of work they would be willing to do—the pleasures they would be willing to sacrifice for the good of the cause."

CALCULATING THE ADVERTISING APPROPRIATION

ON WHAT SHALL IT BE BASED ?—WHAT SOME ADVERTISERS ARE SPENDING—ANALYSIS OF CONDITIONS IN EACH PARTICULAR CASE MUST PRECEDE AN INTELLIGENT DETERMINATION OF HOW MUCH TO SPEND—PORTION OF AN ADDRESS BEFORE THE TECHNICAL PUBLICITY ASSOCIATION

By L. F. Low, Advertising Manager. H. W. Johns-Manville Co., New York

" Many things must be considered in arriving at the amount to spend for advertising. We must keep in mind whether the concern is already established or just starting in business, the

12

bank balance, the nature of the products, the present consumption, the possible consumption, the capacity of plant, number of competitors, number of dealers who handle the goods (if sold through dealers), the amounts that other concerns in similar lines have found it profitable to spend, and a hundred and one other things.

" We know, for instance, that from one to two per cent. of the gross income can be considered to be the standard advertising appropriation for mechanical and electrical manufacturers, for public service corporations, etc. The advertising appropriations of automobile manufacturers usually range from one and a half to as high as thirty-three and a third per cent. of the gross sales, but will average around four per cent. Department stores are spending an average of from two to four per cent. in local newspapers, while some departments spend as high as eight per cent.; and I have heard of one department store which spent twenty-one per cent. the first year in business. A clothing manufacturer is spending three and a half per cent. One piano manufacturer is spending eight per cent. A stove manufacturer is spending twelve per cent. Many toilet goods manufacturers are said to be spending from twenty-five to sixty-six per cent. of their gross profits. Some of the well-known food manufacturers are spending from one to two per cent. of their gross sales, while it is claimed that one manufacturer in this line is regularly spending fifty per cent. of his profits, which are said to be between two hundred and three hundred per cent. A book manufacturer has recently found it very profitable to spend twenty-five per cent. of his gross sales for advertising. A mail order house is spending twelve and a half per cent. The Union Pacific and the Southern Pacific railroads are spending about six-tenths of one per cent.

" In making up an appropriation for a concern just starting in business, of course we have no gross sales to guide us, and it is then necessary to figure our appropriation on a percentage of the estimated first year's sales. In order to get a quick start, new concerns often make a much larger appropriation for advertising for the first year than they expect to spend after their goods have been introduced.

" After the total annual expenditure has been determined

upon and the fixed advertising expenses, such as salaries of employees of the advertising department and rent, deducted, we must decide on how much of the balance should be spent for catalogs, booklets, art work, engraving, postage, exhibits, periodical space, circular letters, etc. When this has been settled, a margin must be allowed for emergencies, and it is seldom that any advertising plan—no matter how skilfully worked up—can be readily adhered to. Conditions nearly always arise which make it necessary to make some changes in the original plan.

"Now we have decided how much we consider that our firm could profitably spend and how it should be apportioned, but we have yet to get the approval of the board of directors.

"Fortunately, most business men of to-day realize what a tremendous selling force judicious advertising is, and when your board of directors is composed of this modern type of business man it does not require any persuasion to get a reasonable advertising appropriation. But there are still some doubting Thomases, especially among those who have never done any advertising and know nothing about it, and if you have any of this type of man to deal with, it is your duty to point out the advantages of advertising.

"Before attempting to convince these skeptics that advertising is really a wonderful selling force, it is often well to first point out about how much business they should be getting, for I know of at least one instance (and there must be many others) where the manufacturer, when asked to spend some money for advertising, said: 'I don't need to advertise. I am now getting about half the business in my line and my four competitors are dividing the balance between them,' while investigation showed that he was only selling about one-eighth of the total quantity that was being consumed.

"Here is one way to get this information. Of course, nearly every line would have to be handled differently, but this one example will help to illustrate the idea.

"Suppose, for instance, we are trying to influence a manufacturer of spark plugs to advertise. Unless he had analysed the possibilities, he might be selling, say 100,000 plugs and think that he was getting about all the business. He would change his mind, however, if you pointed out that, according to reliable authorities, there were in 1912 in the United States over 900,000 automobiles and 430,000 motor boats, and that about 400,000 automobiles and 70,000 motor boats will be built during 1913, making a total of 1,800,000 automobiles and motor boats that will require an average of four spark plugs each, or a total of at least 7,200,000 plugs.   And as you further pointed out that as there were only nineteen competitors and that as his product was better than that of any of his competitors, he should surely be able, provided he properly advertised and pushed the sale of his goods along modern lines, to sell at least one-twentieth of the total number of plugs sold, or 360,000, which would give him a profit of $54,000, even on a very small selling price, this should at least open his eyes as to the great possibility.

" Some advertisers are of the impression that it is not necessary to advertise continuously. They do not realize that about seventeen out of every 1,000 persons they tell about their goods every year die, and that the birth-rate is thirty-two per thousand, so that there are that many new persons each year to educate to use their goods. They do not stop to consider that thousands of men go into new lines of business every year; that the readers of the publications they use are constantly changing, so that from twenty-five to eighty-five per cent. new readers have to be told about their goods every year, etc.

" And now as to just a few of the advantages of advertising. Advertising largely enhances in value the good will of a business. It is really as much of an investment as machinery, buildings, etc.   That it is so considered by many large concerns is shown by the following table, which gives the price that these concerns place on their good will:

THE RELATION OF THE CAPITAL, ASSETS AND GOOD WILL OF SOME LEADING INDUSTRIAL CORPORATIONS.   AS REPORTED BY BOSTON NEWS BUREAU

Name	Capital	Assets	Good Will	Per Cent. Assets
Goodrich	$90,000,000	$100,877,604	$57,000,000	56.5
Woolworth	65,000,000	65,157,155	50,075,000	76.8
Sears, Roebuck	48,500,000	60,768,949	30,000,000	49.3
Studebaker	43,500,000	56,467,143	19,807,277	35.0
May Dept.	20,000,000	21,377,229	14,343,957	67.0
Underwood	13,500,000	15,476,785	7,995,720	52.2
Loose-Wiles	13,000,000	15,247,152	7,970,543	51.6

" If, for instance, the factories, the goods, and everything else that could be called tangible property of the above concerns or of such concerns as the H. W. Johns-Manville Company, or the General Electric Company, were swept away, the privilege of manufacturing goods and marketing them under the name of ' J. M.' or ' G. E.' would be worth a lot of money.   For this reason, any money that has been spent for advertising is invested as much as if put into machinery, buildings, etc.

" Advertising and trade-marking goods enables a manufacturer to own his business and goods instead of letting the dealer own them.

" Mr. Tipper, advertising manager of the Texas Oil Company, made an investigation some years ago which showed that his salesmen sold from sixty to seventy per cent. of the people they called on before the goods were advertised and that after four months advertising, the same salesmen sold from eighty to ninety per cent. of the persons called on.

" As an example of what judicious advertising will do, look at the record of the following mail order houses:

" For instance, Sears, Roebuck & Company, of Chicago, did a gross business in 1912 of $64,112,194, which is an increase of about sixty-five per cent. in six years.   Their common stock was selling a couple of days ago at $217 a share.   There are very few concerns in this country that are doing such a remarkably profitable business.

" The Baltimore Bargain House did a business in 1911 of $13,345,789.55, or an increase of $551,879.72 over 1910.   It costs them about two and one-fourth per cent. to sell goods by mail, against a selling cost of seven to ten per cent. through salesmen.

" One of the hardest things in the world to sell is life insurance.   Yet the Postal Life of New York, which sells life insurance entirely by advertising, is said to have nearly doubled its business in 1911 on an advertising appropriation of between $23,000 and $24,000.   By advertising, this company is getting business at a cost of about ten dollars per $1,000 against an average cost of securing business through agents of from twelve to twenty-five dollars per $1,000 for the first year and then a yearly commission of about seven and a half per cent. for seven and a half years, or a total cost for the whole period of from twenty-two to thirty-five dollars per $1,000.

" The National Cloak and Suit Company of this city is said to have started business in one small room about twenty-two years ago, and to-day they occupy a large eleven-story building.

" Gordon Van Tine & Company sold building material in the regular way through salesmen for about twenty years and then went into the mail order business and sold by advertising alone. The third year after they started advertising they are said to have done a business of more than $1,500,000, or triple the business they did before employing that modern selling force—advertising.

" The Kalamazoo Stove Company started in business about the middle of 1902. It spent $18,000 for advertising the first year and did a business of $40,000. Four years later it did a business of $500,000.

" Butler Brothers, whom it is said started in business about thirty-five years ago with a stock valued at $500, now send out over 2,000,000 catalogs a year describing more than 30,000 items, and occupy large buildings in four of the big cities.

" All of the above concerns are strictly mail order houses and sell their goods entirely by advertising. I have mentioned these concerns for the reason that they employ no salesmen, so no one can say that anything except advertising is responsible for their wonderful success.

" But advertising has done just as well for concerns employing both advertising and salesmen to market their product. Take just one illustration in the National Biscuit Company. It grew from a $4,000,000 corporation to one of $55,000,000 in eight years after it started to advertise, and even in the year of the panic it made a profit of $4,101,415."

An interesting Business Bourse report contains the following:

Analysis of Methods of Determining Advertising Appropriations.—There are still a large number of advertisers who either make no fixed appropriations, or who have formulated no policy for guidance in deciding what sum shall be spent for advertising. Investigation has proved that the advantage in economy and maximum support of the trade is with those who have set policies. Nevertheless, there are comparatively few advertisers who adhere strictly to their appropriation. If there is unusual prosperity there will be spasmodic spurts of generous advertising, but at the sign of decreased sales, there is an abrupt cut.

In arranging an advertising appropriation, these factors are to be considered: (1) whether the campaign is for general publicity; (2) for educational work; or (3) for direct returns.

Methods in Use of Basing Appropriation.—1. Apportioning a percentage of the gross business of the previous year.

2. Apportioning a percentage of the net profits of the previous year.

3. A progressive advertising appropriation, in proportion to the current increase over sales during the same period in the previous year; monthly or quarterly.

4. Grading the appropriation according to the plans for the ensuing year, based on constructive analysis.

Methods of Charging Advertising Appropriations.—As expense, when done to (1) maintain a normal distribution; (2) call attention to temporary terms or prices, or convey special necessary information. As investment, when done to (1) exploit a new article or branch of the business; (2) add to the good-will of the business.

Efficient Methods of Influencing the Making of Appropriations.—1. Presentation of proposed expenditure on the concrete basis of figures showing: (a) possible business in units of material; (b) present consumption and competition; (c) detailed expenditure proposed; (d) logical reasons for expected returns; (e) exact amount of expected profit and returns; and (f) time in which such results are expected to materialize.

2. Securing trade analysis or dealer investigation to study conditions on which to base a policy or strategic angle to be put into effect thru advertising. Such information makes the views and judgment of sales and advertising executives concrete and therefore compelling.

WINNING THE CAMPAIGN BEFORE FIRING A GUN

WHEN ADVERTISEMENTS ARE MERELY SERIAL INSTALMENTS IN
THE WORKING OUT OF PRE-ARRANGED " PLOT "—HOW THE
NATIONAL CANDY COMPANY ELIMINATED GUESSWORK AND
ASSIGNED ADVERTISING TO DO CERTAIN PREDETERMINED
TASKS—THE INTERLOCKING SALES AND ADVERTISING WORK
THAT FOLLOWED

By V. L. Price, Vice-President and Chairman of the Executive Committee of
the National Candy Company (Skylark Chocolate), St. Louis, Missouri

" I sincerely believe that the preparation for the advertising
—the laying out of the ' sales plot,' as it were—is as important, if
not more important, than the actual advertising itself.

" In looking at our own campaign for Skylark Chocolates,
it would be easy to assume that all that would be necessary for
another advertiser to duplicate our success would be to present a
candy of like attractiveness, and use the same mediums. That
assumption would be false, for there was a great deal of work
done in connection with the Skylark campaign, as a preliminary
to the advertising, which does not appear on the surface at all.

" When we decided to put a brand of chocolates on the market
which should be sold by advertising to the consumer, we drew
up a list of things which we should have to consider. First,
the cost; second, how and when that cost is coming back; third,
the product; fourth, our facilities for manufacturing it; fifth,
distribution; sixth, dealer co-operation. All of those were questions which, in our opinion, must be settled before we could
expect success for the new brand.

" We asked our advertising agent to submit an estimate of
what it would cost to advertise the goods properly in the localities we wished to cover. The amount suggested was within that
which we felt willing to spend to prove the practicability of our
plans. Therefore, it was set aside from the surplus on hand,
which is the best place from which to get advertising appropriations.

" We knew that, like every other expenditure, the amount
spent in advertising must be accounted for. It must come back
from somewhere. We didn't want to take it out of the consumer,

the retailer or the wholesaler.   The only other place it could come from was the lower cost of production and lower fixed-cost percentage resulting from increased sales.   The advertising —and the preliminary work—must be productive of a sufficient increase in the number of sales to more than offset the appropriation, else we should come out losers in the end.   That is a fact which it is well to realize beforehand.   When that fact is clearly in mind, it tends to increase the care with which the campaign is conducted.   It is not simply more sales that are wanted but enough more sales to save, in reduced cost of doing business, the cost of the advertising."

CHOOSING THE PRODUCT TO BE ADVERTISED

" In selecting the particular product which we were to advertise we spent a great deal of time.   We went carefully over our already large line of chocolates, selecting the flavors and shapes which were most in demand.   We made careful comparisons with all other lines of chocolates with which we should compete, and wherever our brands seemed to show the slightest disadvantage, we strove to remedy it.   We felt that if Skylark Chocolates could not stand the test with our own men, they never would make good with the consumer.   We knew that the test of comparison was the strongest quality argument we could possibly have.

" Our facilities came next.   Suppose we created the demand which was hoped for, could we take care of it ?   Could we supply dealers promptly enough to keep our lines of distribution unbroken, after they had been once established ?   The analysis of the product determined quality, and we had now to assure ourselves of quantity.   Slow and late shipments are a drawback to many a good advertising campaign, and we resolved to care for the demand before we created it.   Fortunately, our facilities were ample, but we analysed the situation pretty thoroughly before we made up our minds.

" The real, active work began with the process of getting distribution.   We had determined to advertise a brand of chocolates, in the first place, as an entering wedge to territory in which our goods were not well known.   Consequently distribution for the new brand must be built up from the beginning. We started with Chicago, where the whole proposition was new, name and all.

" We selected a corps of fifteen men, and put them to school in our factory. Some of them had sold goods, some had not. The requirements were simply that they be clean, active and honest; willing to learn and willing to work.

" We spent several weeks teaching those men facts about our goods, our advertising, our facilities, our officers. The advertising agency, the street car, bill-board and newspaper representatives all took a hand in the educating process. Every one asked questions, made suggestions, criticised, fought and joked, but all with a sincere desire to get information that would be helpful. There was no secrecy, no ' bull,' no big noise.

" The men were taught to answer the following questions from the retailer: ' What are you going to do for me?' ' Are you going to reach my customers?' ' How long will you keep on helping me?'

" We knew we should have to answer those questions satisfactorily before we should get even the smell of an order, so the men were taught to answer them.

" We divided the city of Chicago into twelve districts. Each district was placed in charge of one of our own new men, whom we called Privates.

" We called in several of our experienced salesmen, and put them on the reserve list as Lieutenants.

" The Captain was the general sales manager, and the General the manager of the factory. A Board of Strategy was organized, consisting of representatives of the advertising agency, the executive officers of the company, and of the factory.

" At the close of each day's work the Privates reported to the Lieutenants their orders and also the customers they had failed to sell, and why. Next day the Lieutenants called upon all those the Privates had failed to sell, and reported to the Captain. The Captain followed the Lieutenants, calling upon all dealers who had refused to stock the goods, and reported failures to the Board of Strategy, as the court of last resort. Any dealer who ' got past ' the Board of Strategy was a hard nut to crack, indeed.

" I may be wrong about it, of course, but if I should be asked to express my opinion as to just how much of the success of the Skylark campaign was due to advertising itself,—the actual filling the space with copy,—I should say certainly not more than twenty-five per cent. of it.

" Advertising, in that restricted sense, is such an intangible thing when it comes to figuring out what the matter with it is, that the answer to the question is often a matter of opinion.   The mail-order man, selling direct to the consumer by means of advertising alone, can easily figure out just what is due to advertising, but the man selling through dealers often has difficulty.   The only way to figure out whether advertising is good or bad is to check its cost against its accomplishments, and when you do that there are a lot of factors to be considered which are not usually included in the term ' advertising.'

" I really believe that the great majority of advertising failures are due, not to fool ' copy,' or wrong choice of mediums, but to poor products, poor salesmanship, or poor service.

NECESSARY TO ELIMINATE MYSTERY FROM ADVERTISING

" In numberless cases, the advertiser does not stop to figure out exactly how the money he spends is going to come back to him.   He has a vague notion that it *is* coming back, with interest, but as to how, when and where from, he hasn't a notion.   Advertising is no mysterious power which materializes profits from the atmosphere.   There are only three ways in which the money can come back: from debasing the quality of the product so that it costs less to make, from increasing the price so as to leave a greater margin of profit, or from increasing the sales so as to lower the cost of production and the overhead expense, yet leaving quality the same.

" Now, when a man thoroughly realizes that fact, and understands that the only rational method of making his advertising a success is to increase his sales to a point where the economies of production will more than offset the additional expense, he is in a fair way to go further and analyse the problem as it should be analysed.

" But, here again, sometimes he falls down. He confuses *increased demand* with *increased sales*. They are not the same thing, by any means. Has he the facilities to make the supply equal the demand? In other words, it is necessary to finish what has been started. The amount of increased business which it is necessary to secure to ' break even ' can be reduced to figures which are approximately accurate, and the question must be answered as to whether or not that increased business can be handled.

" Our own campaign is interesting chiefly as showing how the problem was worked out in one specific instance. Every problem of like nature can be similarly analysed, and in my opinion, when that happens more frequently there will be fewer failures chalked up to the score of advertising."

HOW TO LOOK BEFORE YOU LEAP

SUCCESSFUL CAMPAIGNS ARE WON BEFORE A SHOT IS FIRED—
MAKING CERTAIN ON THREE GREAT ESSENTIALS—KNOWLEDGE
OF YOUR PRODUCT THE FIRST OF THESE—QUESTIONS TO ASK
YOUR BRAND BEFORE YOU CAN HOPE TO WIN A MARKET

By R. E. Fowler, Advertising Manager of the Printz-Bieferman Company, Cleveland, Ohio

" If we are to take the trade reports of business failures as a barometer of business conditions, we must admit that there are many firms, striving to win a market, which miserably fail— firms, which in the first flush of business endeavor, seem successful, but which eventually become business derelicts and in many instances a menace to the fundamental principles of business.

" There must be some good and sufficient reason for these failures. There must be something left undone in their business propaganda that put a bar to successful effort.

" If we can uncover some of the weaknesses of their policy, we may be able to place over these shoals of business a beacon light that will act as a warning to other navigators.

" Many manufacturers seem to think that winning a market consists of the manufacturing of a product, the engaging of a sales force and the setting aside of an advertising appropriation. And when you mention an advertising appropriation it brings to mind the appalling ease with which hard-headed business men are led into the spending of vast sums of money—men who could not be cajoled into the investment of $10,000 in new equipment, no matter how great the need; men who would not think of erecting a business block costing $50,000 without engaging the services of the best architect obtainable and having definite blue-prints of every floor as well as a general reproduction of the exterior shown them, will cheerfully invest, on the advice of a plausible stranger, three times $50,000 in an advertising cam-paign for the promotion of a new product without a clear con-ception of how the money is to be expended, or whether there is a logical market for his product or not.

" Isn't it time to stop to think; to analyse; to dig a little deeper into the garden of facts?   Isn't it time to take the truths that we have at our command, and from them draft a consistent plan of action by which we can work intelligently and with reasonable chance of success?

" What I say will be directed more to the men who are just launching their crafts than to the men of the other ships, but even the complacent man who feels that he has won his market can well afford to listen.

" The fundamentals required for winning a market are: First, a clear, concise and logical analysis of your *product;* second, a clear, concise and logical analysis of the *field* in which your product can be profitably sold; third, a complete analysis of the scheme of *distribution* you intend to employ and of the media through which you intend to tell the story of your product to the retailer and to the purchasing public.

UPON THESE ROCKS YOU MAY BUILD

" The analysis of these three factors is your foundation. Running through them and flowing out of them are many other factors that have a bearing on the success of your business.   Some of these are service, co-operation and efficiency.

" I will treat these factors in their logical order, beginning first with the analysis of your product. (See chart on page 196.)

" To the man just starting; to the man who has bucked the game for years without winning, and to the man who has won a measure of success, I say: *Analyse your product!* I wish that I could burn this into the top of the desk of every man who is now or who will be engaged in a business venture, for on the proper assimilation of its import, and upon the proper application of this analysis rests the entire structure that he would rear.

" Be sparing of the questions you ask your product and you invite failure. Be searching in your analysis and you are reasonably sure of success.

IF A DEMAND EXISTS

" The first question that naturally arises is, ' Is there a demand for this article ? ' and leading out of the question, if there is a demand, we immediately find a number of others. The first: ' Is it developed or undeveloped ? ' and upon the answer to this question may stand or fall the success of your venture. If the answer should be ' Developed,' you immediately know that the heavy expense of an educational campaign is eliminated from your calculations and that your plan will be to convince the jobbers, dealers and consumers that your product is desirable. On the other hand, this answer to this question immediately brings into the arena the element of competition with established concerns which will be taken up later.

" You will also want to know if this developed demand was caused by necessity or whether it was the result of an educational campaign.

" If, however, the answer should be ' Undeveloped,' you are face to face with a condition, which, if you desire national distribution, will call for great sums of money for educational purposes; not for a season or a year but for a period of years, and you must realize in the beginning that your venture, saddled with these tremendous expenditures, cannot be profitable to you for some time to come.

" In fact, given a product of undeveloped demand and a limited amount of capital for educational purposes, it would be foolhardy to attempt to acquire national distribution. It is being attempted, however, every day, and in many cases the firms who attempt it are numbered among the missing within a few years. The only logical thing to do would be to use your capital in local educational work and in creating local demand and then using this local demand as a nucleus to reach out for a territorial or sectional demand. In this way you would be safe. You would not only be working along the lines of least resistance, but you would also be concentrating your entire educational force on a given community and, consequently, could look forward with reasonable hope to accomplishing your purpose.

" The next two divisions: Is it a forced demand, buoyed up by the heavy advertising campaigns and skilful salesmanship? or is it a natural demand because of supplying an existing want? are answered by the above so we can pass on to the next division.

" Is it a permanent, all-year-round demand, or is it a seasonable demand? The answer to this question is going to decide to a great extent the manufacturing conditions with which you must contend. It's going to have a bearing on the wages you will have to pay your employees. It is going to have a bearing on your moral, social and religious life.

" If the answer be ' Permanent Demand,' it means the steady whirring of wheels from January to January with just enough machinery to keep a step ahead of the demand. It means contented workmen because their positions are permanent year in and year out and their working hours regular. It means that you can enjoy life, become acquainted with your family and sleep like a boy at night.

" If the answer be ' Seasonable,' it means thousands of dollars in machinery that for months out of each year will stand idle and that at other times will race madly to gather as much as possible of the fleeting demand. It means high pressure, overtime, crowding of your employees, alternating with periods of absolute idleness. This causes poor workmanship under the hurried conditions, dissatisfaction, labor troubles and expense.

" To you it means long hours on high gear, night work, Sunday planning, estrangement from your family and friends and a speculative business that you are never sure of.

" Let us proceed to the next sub-division, serviceability. Running out of serviceability we will find five very pertinent questions that we must ask your product and the first is, ' Is it a necessity ? '   Is it something that the buying public need and have use for every day ? If it is we know that you are assured of a widespread demand, but if the answer should be, ' No, it is a luxury,' we immediately find our selling field narrowed to those people who are able to afford the gratification of their luxurious tastes.

" The next question, ' Is it a convenience ? '   ' Does it make some operation easier ? '   ' Does it in some way shorten the time necessary to complete a task ? '   ' Does it add something to the sum total of human happiness by making the way smoother for its purchaser ? '

" Vacuum cleaners are a convenience. Vacuum cleaners make sweeping easier ; they shorten the time necessary to thoroughly sweep a room, and they do add something to the total of woman's happiness by robbing of its drudgery the very necessary task of sweeping. Around this one point the campaigns of the vacuum cleaner companies were built. They adopted the previous efforts of the carpet sweeper people and improved on them.

" ' Is it durable ? '   ' Is it economical in use ? '   Both of these questions are vital ; for an article may be a necessity ; may be a convenience ; may have a permanent, natural, developed demand, but if the article is not durable and is not economical in use it cannot be profitably marketed.

" No one cares to buy an article, no matter how much one needs it, unless one is convinced that the article will perform its functions economically and at the same time render an efficient and lasting service because of its durability. Be careful with these questions, and if your product cannot answer both of them affirmatively, postpone your quest for a market and experiment with your product until you absolutely can answer them as they deserve to be answered.

"The next sub-division, quality, has a direct bearing on the previous division and in many cases, if properly analysed, will answer affirmatively the questions which I have just said must be given the most careful consideration. 'What is the quality of your raw materials?' 'Are you using only the best, and carefully examining and testing them?'

HOW DOES IT LOOK?

"What is the quality of your design? Is it suitable to the article and to the use the article must be put? Closely allied with this question is the quality of appearance. Don't pass these two sub-divisions carelessly. You are going out to bid for the approval of a vast audience. Things that will sway one portion will leave the other untouched, but you want your article to be as near psychologically perfect as it is possible to be, so that you can appeal to and influence the majority of all men and women; the first impression that your buying public will receive of your product will be through the medium of the eyes, so see that not only the quality of the design is right but also that the quality of appearance is 100 per cent. pleasing.

"Quality of workmanship. Examine this carefully; for be the quality of raw materials of the highest rank, the quality of design and appearance all that you could ask for, but the quality of workmanship mediocre, you will find that the good qualities are outweighed by this one bad quality and your articles of negligible selling value. The quality of workmanship will seriously affect our next step, quality of finish, which is deserving of as painstaking care as any of the others. One may think that I am dwelling unnecessarily long on the subject of quality, but you will discover, if you have not already, that the buying public *is looking for quality and regardless of the price they pay;* also that your article will be weighed in the scale of their minds by its comparison with competing articles already on the market or that are daily being added.

13

" See to it that the scales of division balance true to your product when the comparison is made.

THE FIELD OF PROFITABLE SALE

" Price to the jobber, the broker, the retailer and the consumer will, to a great extent, determine the field of profitable sales for your product. If you are fortunate enough to have an article of medium or low price it opens up for you the widespread buying power of the masses, but if your price must be high your strongest demand will be derived from the people of easy fortune, and statistics say that but five per cent. of the men of this country have an income of $3,000 per year or over; so that you can easily see the very limited demand for a high-priced article.

" Remember, also, that your product will be weighed and compared with competing articles on the question of price as well as on the question of quality.

" Our next step is profit to the manufacturer, meaning yourself; to the jobber; to the broker and to the retailer. You have now arrived at the ' reason why ' of all business endeavor. You have uncovered the mainspring of business life; the great motor that turns the wheels of our commercial activities. See that all parties that are engaged in the distribution of your product are handsomely rewarded in profits gained, and each one of them will be a consistent booster of your sales; but if profits be cut below that of competing articles and the demand be undeveloped, your sales will languish in spite of your most strenuous promotion efforts.

" See that your profit be of sufficient size to enable you to bear the burden of manufacture. See that the jobber, the broker and the retailer are also well taken care of; for you and your product will be weighed again in the scales of decision and compared with all other competing articles on the basis of profit.

THE NATURE OF YOUR COMPETITION

" The last step in the analysis of the product is your competition. This sub-division not only will affect your product but will also influence your field of distribution.

"You must know your competition. You must know its officers; whether young or old; working on the supposition that if officered by young men that their methods will be sharp and aggressive and that every onslaught you direct at the market will be pursued by plans as clever as your own.

"The length of time that your competition has been established should be considered; whether they have a strong box filled with the profits of past efforts or whether each day's sales must contribute its share toward the merchandising program of the future.

"You must know their sales plan; their advertising campaign; their sales manager and their sales force—not with the intention of undermining them, but with the expressed understanding that your promotion efforts may be devoted to lines of attack that will gain your goal in spite of the competition.

"You must familiarize yourself with their policy toward customers and credits so that you may profit by their successful efforts and learn from their mistakes.

"Modern business is warfare, and you as a modern business man are one of the fighting generals. Your department heads and foremen are your colonels and captains; your employees, your privates, your army corps of fighters; and your ability to plan and direct, your ability to analyse, your ability to educate your employees to see the same as you do are your siege-guns with which to batter down the walls of opposition.

"Ask of your product the questions that the other subdivisions of the analysis have touched on; for from these questions and answers will come, not only the knowledge of whether your product is practical or not, but also the ammunition necessary for your salesmen in their selling campaign. Insist on answers that fit in as part of the structure you wish to rear and then and not until then will you be able to say, ' My product is deserving of a market and I am going to discover the *natural field* for it.' "

CHART

Demand	Developed .... Undeveloped Forced or Natural Permanent or Seasonable	By education By necessity	

Serviceability
- Is it a necessity?
- Is it a luxury?
- Is it a convenience?
- Is it durable?
- Is it economical in use?

Quality .....
- Of raw materials
- Of design
- Of workmanship
- Of appearance
- Of finish

How does it compare with competing articles on these items?

Price to.....
- Jobber
- Broker
- Retailer
- Consumer

High
Medium
Low

How does it compare with competing articles?

Profit to ....
- Manufacturer
- Jobber
- Broker
- Retailer

Larger than on competing lines
Same as on competing lines
Smaller than on competing lines

Competition .
- Officered by old men
- Officered by young men
- Aggressive
- Lax
- Long established
- Newly established
- Wealthy
- Limited means
- Their sales plans
- The advertising campaign
- Their policy toward consumers
- Their sales manager
- Their sales force
- Their credit department's attitude toward customers

SALES POLICY ANALYSIS BEHIND ADVERTISING CAMPAIGNS
(Business Bourse Report)

" An advertising campaign is simply a big kit of tools with which to do whatever needs to be done upon a job of selling. Just exactly what tools to use and what general method idea to base the campaign upon, depends wholly upon the strategic selling situation.

" Consequently, the manufacturer who is a careful analyst,

and the advertising agent who analyses for him, are obliged, in order to be efficient, to be skilled strategists and conduct an advertising campaign from the strategic angle which will meet the situation most exactly.

" In order to know what kind of analysis may be arrived at in planning an advertising campaign, it is interesting to outline the various strategic foundation bases for an advertising campaign. Any one, or a group, of these basic reasons for an advertising campaign are used; all methods, the copy, and even the illustration and the mediums used may be spent and shaped to meet the desired strategic end.   It is in the efficient watching and careful adjusting of the sales policy along the lines of strategy as laid out below, that has really produced the biggest and best successes. To say that advertising is simply done ' to sell goods ' is far too superficial.   Advertising must be done for purposes of policy to meet the current and individual situation.

" The following are among the policies of trade strategy which may be behind an advertising campaign:

"(1) To ' file a caveat ' with the public for a new proposition, in order to be recognized as first in field, no matter how complicated the situation with patents or trade-marks.

"(2) To dispel a popular impression about a concern, such as that it makes only one line of goods.

"(3) To bring an entire group of products into the shelter and help of the prestige of a single trade-mark.

"(4) To dominate a field, or to insure against, or to forestall domination by others.

"(5) To widen the uses and application of an article.

"(6) To build fortifications against substitution and combat it.

"(7) To bring the consumer closer to the maker, for acquaintance, confidence, and human interest.

"(8) To fill out ' valleys ' in production or seasons.

"(9) To bring about a more automatic demand.

"(10) To detract attention from a new competitive development.

"(11) To affect the psychology of dealers.

"(12) To take steps toward greater control of distribution.

"(13) To get your story told to consumers as you want it told.

"(14) To annihilate time in establishing a new or wider market.

"(15) To meet declining sales, depressions, special conditions, indifference, price considerations, etc."

FIGURING AN ADVERTISING CAMPAIGN DOWN TO A DEFINITE EFFICIENCY BASIS

" There are many concerns who spend too much or too little money in advertising, because there has not been sufficient investigation of the market, and, consequently, there is lacking the basis for building a correctly proportioned campaign. The size of the appropriation is very frequently influenced by the personal impressions of the salesmen or sales manager of the volume of business that ought to be produced, instead of what *can* be produced. A careful and unbiased investigation for specific data has time and again unearthed facts which contradicted such surface impressions, and formed a substantial basis for a strong selling plan. Some of the information demanded by the alert advertising or sales manager before making advertising plans are given herewith, also the result of an advertising campaign that followed such an analysis. These figures are prepared so that the concrete results can be quickly grasped by interested executives.

CONSUMPTION OF PRODUCT

1. Present consumption.
2. Total possible consumption.
3. Increase in consumption during a period of years.
4. Consumption by states and zones, showing up strong and weak territories.
5. Consumption per capita; consumption per square mile.

DISTRIBUTION

1. Number of competitors in field.
2. Number of dealers who handle the article.
3. Number of dealers who could handle.
4. Dealers per square mile and per thousand population.

PRODUCTION AND EXPENSE

1. Capacity of the plant.
2. Market price of the product and competitive articles.
3. Total amount of money involved in the business.
4. Total profit involved in the business.
5. Approximate possible profit considering consumption and production costs.
6. Possible amount of advertising and selling expense available.

STATEMENT OF RETURNS FOR SIX MONTHS

Character of Return		Character of Industries	
Coupons	300	City and Civil Engineers	500
Letters	250	State Engineers	30
Post Cards	400	Contractors	300
Return Post Cards	75	Road and Street Commissioners	150
Through Offices	100	Students	70
		Miscellaneous	175

STATEMENT OF EFFICIENCY

Total Circulation	48,000 per issue
Circulation of interest	18,000 per issue
Number of issues	26 cost $8,000
Cost per issue	$308.00
Cost per person of interest	.016
Total number of inquiries received	1,225
Total number of inquiries per issue	47
Per cent. inquiries to circulation	$\frac{1}{8}$ of 1 per cent.
Cost per inquiry	$6.53
Amount of material asked for	3,500 tons
Amount per inquiry	$2.85
Cost per unit of material	2.34
Percentage cost per unit	12 per cent.
Net efficiency per unit of material	.0234 per cent.

METHOD OF KEYING ADVERTISEMENTS
(Business Bourse Report)

" The average method of keying is very inadequate and make-shift. It does not provide for the thorough comparison which should be the object of any inquiry.

" The most common is a variation of street address, or a letter of the alphabet representing a ' department.' The trouble with these is they do not give wide enough scope for the various mediums, etc. The trouble with ' Box No.' is that it sounds too artificial and is an extra incumbrance to the address. Varying the street number discloses itself to readers of more than one publication.

" The most efficient plan for average purposes is to vary the number of a booklet or catalog or department and make a combination with a letter of the alphabet so that the cumulative replies months after appearance may be traced. In fact, accounts may be opened charging up to each key not only (1) number of inquiries, but (2) amount spent on that particular key, (3) money received, (4) character of inquiry, (5) cost and frequency of follow-up, etc. These accounts should be known by their key number, which is never repeated.

" A large advertiser has worked out his keying system with especial thoroughness, assigning a particular circular or enclosure for inquiries from each particular medium. This brings circular matter into the field of analysable returns. This advertiser also asks his agents to keep records of mail inquiries.

" The following is a sample of the key number list:

19 { December—McClure's / Xmas Bookcase Circular

20 { February—McClure's / Filing Cabinet Catalog

21 { March—McClure's / " Filing and Finding Papers " / Bookcase Catalog

22 { April—McClure's / " Filing and Finding Papers "

23 { May—McClure's / Filing Cabinet, Unifile or Cabinet Safe Catalog

24 { October—Metropolitan / Circular for individual librarian

25 { November—Metropolitan / Bookcase Catalog

26 { September—Metropolitan / Bookcase Catalog

27 { December—Metropolitan / Xmas Bookcase Circular and Catalog

28 { November—Munsey's / Bookcase Catalog

29 { December—Munsey's / Xmas Bookcase Circular and Filing Cabinet Catalog

30 { January—Munsey's / " Filing and Finding Papers " and Filing Cabinet Catalog

DETAILS OF INQUIRY ANALYSIS

" The most approved method of analysing inquiry returns is not widely known, nor when known, faithfully followed. A large New York house has perhaps one of the most definite and searching layouts of inquiry and order analysis.

" The following are the headings showing these details:

Claimed circulation	Proceeds per inquiry
Cost of advertising	Orders
Cash returns	Cost per order
Returns per dollar spent	Proceeds per order
Inquiries	Ratio of orders to inquiries
Cost per inquiry	Ratio of inquiries to circulation."

The Advertising Campaign.—The completed advertising campaign will consist of two parts: first, a prospectus suggesting the reasons why you choose a certain article, the present status of that particular business with respect to competitors, etc., the reasons for your choice in advertising media, an analysis of all costs, and what results can be expected, etc.; second, the campaign itself, which should contain the following:

1. A trade-mark.
2. A letter head.
3. A bill head.

4. The article. The capitalization of a firm. The name of a firm.

5. The amount of advertising appropriation. How do you base or apportion this amount?

6. What different kinds of advertising are you to employ— why? (1) Mail order; (2) electric signs; (3) bill boards; (4) street car; (5) newspaper; (6) house organ; (7) magazines, (weekly, monthly, quarterly); (8) hand-bills; (9) letters; (10) calendars; (11) premiums; (12) contests; (13) samples; (14) demonstration; (15) literature; (16) posters; (17) novelties; (18) unique forms.

7. What specific magazines, papers, etc., are to be employed? What are the costs, positions, time or seasons of issue, size, position on page, etc. Likewise, estimate the kinds of cuts to be used and their individual mechanical costs.

8. What is the analysis of your article with respect to habits, customs, traditions, seasons, and desires of prospective groups of consumers or buyers?

9. In creating advertisements, consider borders, focal point, attention, habit, will, etc.

10. If follow-up letters are necessary, create a series.

11. Work out a scheme for the keying of your advertisements.

12. What is the motif or key note of *your* campaign?

13. The specific advertisements.

COLLATERAL READINGS

ADVERTISING AS A BUSINESS FORCE, PAUL CHERINGTON, Chapter iv, page 68, " The Problems of Medium Selection."
ADVERTISING & SELLING, HOLLINGWORTH, Chapter iii.
THE PSYCHOLOGY OF ADVERTISING, WALTER DILL SCOTT, Chapter xvi.
MODERN ADVERTISING, CALKINS AND HOLDEN, Chapter iv.
ADVERTISING MEDIUMS, CHAS. O'CONNOR, Chapter xxxiii.
THE ELEMENTARY LAWS OF ADVERTISING, HENRY S. BUNTING, Chapter iv, " Media and Circulation," page 20.
COLOR DISPLAY IN THE DEALER'S WINDOW AND HOW IT PAYS, CHAS. W. HURD, " Printers' Ink," page 23, May 28, 1914.
AN EXPERT OPINION OF WINDOW DISPLAYS, " Printers' Ink," page 70, April 23, 1914.
POSTERS AS WANT ADS IN ST. LOUIS, " Printers' Ink," vol. 83, No. 7, p. 65, May 15, 1913.
SPACE SELLERS' ESTIMATE WORTH OF THEIR OWN MEDIUMS, " Printers' Ink," vol. 82, No. 7, p. 28, February 13, 1913.
ADVERTISING, STARCH, Chapters x and xi.

CHAPTER XIV

AN ANALYSIS OF ADVERTISING MEDIA

THE relative importance of advertising media estimated by the expenditure of money is suggested in " Printers' Ink " as follows: ·

Newspaper advertising	$250,000,000
Direct mail advertising	100,000,000
Farm and mail order	75,000,000
Magazine advertising	60,000,000
Novelty	30,000,000
Billposting	30,000,000
Outdoor-Electric signs	25,000.000
Demonstration and sampling	18,000,000
Street car advertising	10,000,000
House organs	7,000,000
Distributing	6,000,000
Theatre programs	5,000,000
	$616,000,000

GENERAL CONSIDERATIONS FOR ALL WRITTEN ADVERTISING

1. Is the English clear?

2. Is the English forceful? Does it possess " pulling " power?

3. Is the advertisement universal, for men, for children, or for women?

4. Does it possess interest for the specific class intended?

5. Are the principles of reason, suggestion, emotion or imagination adhered to?

6. Is the general effectiveness more constructive than destructive?

7. Does the advertisement do what you expect from a selling point of view: (a) educate, (b) compete with others, (c) destroy negative ideas?

8. Is it possible to key the advertisement?

COMPOSITION OF INDIVIDUAL ADVERTISEMENTS WHENEVER USED

1. Does it attract attention?

2. Is it interesting?

3. Is self-interest aroused?

202

4. Would an illustration pay?
5. Is it concise?
6. Does it balance?
7. Is it individualistic?
8. Is its fusion effect good?
9. Is its focal point decisive?
10. Is its eye movement gripping?
11. Is its type garb appropriate?
12. Are the headlines striking?
13. Is the shape pleasing?
14. Are the mental pictures aroused illuminating?
15. Is the border appropriate?
16. Is there an appropriate regard for white space?
17. Does it possess intensity?
18. If color, is there harmony, contrast or emphasis?

GENERAL FEATURES OF MAGAZINE ADVERTISING

1. Reaches particular groups of people in all sections of the country.

2. People read magazines more leisurely, as a result, more attention is likely to be paid to the advertisements.

3. Magazine goes into home, is placed on library table, where it remains to be read over a long period of time.

4. A single copy is often read by several persons.

5. Is often suitable for fine cuts and the use of colors.

6. A yearly subscription guarantees the effectiveness of repetition in advertising your product.

7. Types of magazines regarding issues: (a) Weekly, (b) bi-monthly, (c) monthly, (d) quarterly, etc.

8. Types of magazines regarding class appeal: (a) general magazines, (b) trade journals, (c) women's publications, (d) religious papers, (e) agricultural publications, (f) law, (g) science, (h) society, art, music, etc., (i) educational, (j) political, (k) technical, (l) financial, (m) travel, etc.

SPECIFIC QUESTIONS TO ASK IN MAGAZINE ANALYSIS

1. The total amount of advertising which a particular magazine carries.

2. The amount of *your* class of advertising carried by the magazine.

3. The recognized standing of the magazine.

4. The price, size, shape and paper of the specific magazine.

5. The editorial policy of the paper.

6. Is the paper distributed by subscription or thru news-stands?

7. Is the circulation of the paper obtained by club methods, free distribution, or straight subscription?

8. The total circulation of the magazine density.

9. The purchasing power of specific magazine readers.

10. An analysis of subscribers by occupations, financial standing, culture, etc.

11. The size of the advertisement and frequency of circulation most advantageous for you in each magazine.

12. Are you advertising your article at the right season and in the right proportion in order that you may get the best results?

13. An analysis of circulation should include facts related to states, buying centers, groups of cities, and occupations.

14. Occupation analyses as given by "Collier's National Weekly" includes:

Financial Classes: bankers and brokers; bank officials and cashiers; real estate and insurance brokers; insurance and trust officials; treasurers; safe deposit companies.

Professional Classes: physicians, surgeons, and oculists; lawyers; dentists; scientists; professors; teachers; students; secretaries; architects; clergymen; artists and sculptors; mining engineers; miscellaneous.

Building and Allied Trades: including builders, contractors, dealers in lumber, decorators, dealers in building materials.

Government Officials and the Public Service: federal and municipal officials; public service; consulates.

Manufacturing Pursuits: including officials and owners, foremen, expert mechanics, etc.

Retail Dealers: for example, grocers, butchers, druggists and chemists.

Office workers of all classes.

Salesmen and buyers.

Hotels, clubs, restaurants, reading rooms, and public institutions.

Transportation: steamships and Pullman cars; officials; locomotive engineers, despatchers, agents, conductors, etc.

Householders, housekeepers, etc.

Advertisers and advertising agencies.

Newspapers and magazines.

Miscellaneous.

15. Kind of plates, closing dates, regulations, etc., of each magazine.

ESTIMATED VALUE OF PAGE DIVISIONS

1. The following estimate of page values has been made, disregarding unusual modifying circumstances:

(2) Least Value	(1) Most Value

(3)
(1) Most Value
(2)
(4) Least Value

(2)	(1) Most Value
(4) Least Value	(3)

2. It has been estimated that the vertical half pages are a fourth more valuable than the horizontal half pages.

3. The preferred pages are: (a) inside and outside covers; (b) pages next to reading matter; (c) page next to index; (d) the first page after the reading.

GENERAL FEATURES OF NEWSPAPER ADVERTISING

1. Reaches all classes intensively.

2. Permits local emphasis.

3. If attention is gained, will reach a larger percentage of population in a given time than any other medium.

FACTORS TO BE CONSIDERED IN SPECIFIC NEWSPAPER ADVERTISING

1. Reputation of the paper.

2. An examination of the general make-up and tone of the paper.

3. Class or quality of subscribers or the various classes.

4. Attitude of paper may be: (*a*) religious; (*b*) political; (*c*) sporting; (*d*) financial, etc.

5. Discover the facts of its circulation.

6. Number of editions (city circulation) :—

Morning papers:		Evening papers:	
(*a*) Bull dog	10.00 P.M.	(*a*) Noon	10.30 A.M.
(*b*) State	1.00 A.M.	(*b*) Postscript	12.00 M
(*c*) Home	4.00 A.M.	(*c*) Home	2.00 P.M.
(*d*) City	6.00 A.M.	(*d*) Night extra	3.30 P.M.
(*e*) Street	6.30 A.M.	(*e*) Final	6.00 P.M.

7. General analysis of advertisements with respect to: (*a*) class of advertisers in paper; (*b*) advertisements next to yours; (*c*) best position and appropriate size of advertisement.

8. Checking: (*a*) that the advertisement appears in all editions; (*b*) that the cost of the advertisement is proportionate to the circulation; (*c*) that you have full value in space purchase.

OUTDOOR ADVERTISING

1. Outdoor advertising consists of: (*a*) painted bulletins—the advertisement painted on boards; (*b*) dead walls—advertisements painted on sides of building; (*c*) poster advertising—where the lithographic poster is used.

2. National advertisers tend to favor poster advertising.

3. The poster is prepared in sheets, the popular sizes being 8, 16, and 24 sheets.

4. The average life of sheet posters is at least a month.

5. Poster space costs from 7 cents to 20 cents a sheet a month according to the service rendered. Service rendered consists in and is modified by: *A*. (1) Locations, (2) construction, (3) size of town. *B*. The price is subject to a long term discount. *C*. The price of lithographic posters is from 3 cents to 5 cents a sheet according to the art work and number of colors.

6. Each town and city is classified and given a rate which includes the construction of the advertisement as well as the service given to the advertisers.

GENERAL FEATURES

1. Outdoor advertising is valuable because of its flexibility; that is, the advertiser can restrict his advertising to a city block

in order to reach the people of that block, or he can bill a city or a state.

2. Outdoor advertising claims that there is no waste in its circulation.

3. The advertisement is " alive " all the time.

4. There can be co-operation between the selling force and the simultaneous appearance of posters.

5. A poster presents the possibility of reproducing the package in actual color and shape.   The public is thus quickly familiarized.

6. Poster advertising thru color makes possible an immediate appeal to the emotions.

7. Bill board companies tend to insist upon clean advertising.

8. The message should preferably contain one idea.

9. Used by local advertisers of all classes.

10. Used by national advertisers desiring to localize their trade.

11. Size of advertisement often tends to impress article on mind of reader.

12. Its message can reach thousands every day if placed properly.

13. It reinforces other advertising efforts.

14. A local advertisement reaches the same class each day.

PRINCIPLES INVOLVED IN CONSTRUCTION

1. Simplicity: (a) very little copy; (b) symmetry—fusion; (c) ease of comprehension; (d) intensive message—preferably one idea.

2. Attention value—often permits of life-size figures.

3. Universality of message.

4. Intensive regard for color.

5. Should be kept fresh in its message.

FACTORS TO BE CAREFULLY REGARDED

1. The representatives of the Poster Advertising Association place the advertisements.

2. Advertisement should be properly placed in relation to your particular trade.

3. The bill board should be kept in good condition.

4. The checking system should show that the conditions of your contract have been met.

5. Surrounding conditions should be analysed.

6. A railroad bill board should be constructed with regard to distance, repetition and motion.

7. All bill boards should be constructed with regard to angle of vision.

8. Cut-out bill boards are often effective..

9. The color of a given advertisement should be considered in relation to its environment.

GENERAL FEATURES OF ELECTRIC SIGN ADVERTISING

1. Appeals to the people at time when they are out for pleasure, hence in a spending mood.

2. Certain articles appeal at night which do not appeal in the day time: as cigarettes, theatres, cafés.

3. People often see electric sign advertisements because of their uniqueness. The same advertisement loses its effectiveness in day time.

4. Can be used advantageously by either national or local advertisers.

CONSTRUCTION OF SIGN

1. Size of type and figures: (a) Depends upon distance from crowd and its place among other electric advertisements.

2. Color: (a) Excellent opportunity to create attention value.

3. Motion: (a) Encourages greater attention value and is more realistic and fascinating.

DISADVANTAGES

1. Cost is great, due to fact that consumption of power is at peak load.

2. If placed among other electric signs it tends to lose its effectiveness unless very unique.

3. Cost of space is great, unless advertisement is placed on own property.

4. Unless motion flash-light effects are properly timed for attention effectiveness is lost.

STREET CAR ADVERTISING

The advantages for street car advertising claimed by those selling space are as follows:—

Circulation: The following statistics are claimed:—.

1. Passengers a car a day, 600 to 800, exclusive of free transfers.

2. Number of cars in the United States, approximately 50,000.

3. Total number of passengers a day, 30 to 40 millions.

4. Total number of passengers a year, 10 to 12 billions.

5. Average daily passengers of street cars approximate population where run. To illustrate—Philadelphia's population is approximately 1,800,000; average daily passengers are 1,600,-000, exclusive of free transfers.

6. Growth of cities from 1900 to 1910, 34.8 per cent.; growth of rural communities from 1900 to 1910; 11.2 per cent. It is estimated that one-half the people of the United States live in cities. This means that street car advertising covers one-half the total population of the United States.

7. Can be used to advantage either by national or strictly local advertisers.

8. Psychology of street car advertising: While at leisure the minds of the passengers are in a receptive mood and any advertising which attracts and holds their attention tends to impress itself on the mind.

9. Time exposure: The average time each passenger spends on the street car is from 15 to 30 minutes. This means if the passenger is at all interested in the advertising, there is plenty of time to force the copy on his mind, making a much deeper impression than that caused by the fleeting impression obtained from bill boards, painted walls and posters.

10. Repetition: Street cars are usually used by the same people each day, by others once, twice, three or four times a week. This means that the advertising is repeated daily in the majority of cases, and this repeated daily impression causes probably as strong a repetition effect as any other advertising medium.

14

11. Color possibilities: Street car cards allow the same latitude in color effects as can be obtained on magazine covers, bulletins or painted walls. They enable reproduction of product, also contrast of colors. The color possibilities of street car cards are limited only by the ingenuity of the artist, and the cost limit placed by the advertiser on the cards.

12. Flexibility: Street car advertising can be localized to a single town, and can even be limited to certain lines, especially in large cities. To illustrate: in Philadelphia it is possible to buy space in the elevated and subway lines, or to buy space in the 15th Street lines, using only such lines.

In New York you can buy Fifth Avenue space, Broadway space, or subway space.

In Chicago you can buy space in the elevated line or in any particular line. This is also true of all other large cities, which enables the advertiser to select a particular district which he desires to cover.

It is also possible to buy $\frac{1}{4}$, $\frac{1}{2}$, or full run. This means you can buy space in every fourth car, in every other car, or in all the cars. You can also buy space in any one single city.

This flexibility enables the advertiser to make a comparative test between different kinds of advertising. To illustrate: in Philadelphia if he had a new product he could use street cars, and in Chicago, posting, then note difference in results obtained. You could test out different products also. If you wanted to decide which style of color would be the most popular, advertise one style in one city and another style in another city. This flexibility can be used on other products.

13. Card protected: Street car cards are always protected against weather changes, climate and destruction. They are beyond the reach of the ordinary passenger so that they cannot be easily mutilated or destroyed. Neither can they be affected by the rain or weather. This always gives them a neat, attractive, inviting appearance, which naturally makes a better impression upon the passenger.

14. Good Company: As street cars are a public utility, and in many places under the control of public service commissions,

or city authorities, the use of obscene or questionable copy is not permitted. The general public would not permit this, nor would the public service commissions or the city authorities. Further, the revenue derived from the advertising is such a minor part of their total income that the street car companies themselves would not tolerate any copy but that which is neat, clean and above criticism. This position is confirmed by examination of the cards in the cars, and also by the high class of firms using street car space.

15. Cost—How to Buy: The total number of street cars in the United States is approximately 50,000. Advertising privileges of 95 per cent. of these cars are controlled by five companies. One company alone controls 36,000 cars; another company controls the cars in Philadelphia; another company controls practically all the New England cars; another company controls surface and suburban street cars of New York City, while a fifth company controls New York and Brooklyn subway and Brooklyn surface lines. Recently we have been advised that the Brooklyn Rapid Transit Company, controlling Brooklyn cars, will handle, direct with the advertiser, their own advertising space, not selling this privilege to any company.

When street car advertising was originally used, the price was about 20 cents to 30 cents per car. As the value of street car advertising became better known and the method of sale more standardized, with a corresponding efficiency in service, the price has gradually advanced to an average price of 50 cents a month a car. Actual prices range from 30 cents to $2.00 a car a month, the highest price being the surface cars of the Broadway line, New York City. The price of street car advertising is probably as standardized as that of any other medium, although it is possible, in consideration of large contracts, or special seasons, to obtain concessions, if not in price, at least in the way of extra service. Parties buying should investigate this on their own account with each individual company.

16. What Class of People the Cars Carry: There is, perhaps, no more cosmopolitan medium than the street car, for the circulation differs in each city and on different lines. Some lines carry

a larger percentage of well-to-do people, others carry more servants and laborers, while other lines carry farmers, while still others are patronized almost entirely by pleasure seekers. Some lines carry more women than men. All of these factors should be considered by the advertiser.

17. Places Where the Cars Run: There are three kinds of street car service; rural, interurban and congested districts. Naturally each one has a different class of circulation.

18. No Domination: Another point to consider is that there is no domination in street car advertising possible. You cannot buy a whole page compared with your rivals' three inch space.

19. Season: This effects the sale of many products, and street car companies permit making contracts for a period covering the seasons. If you have straw hats, you can make a street car contract for the three summer months. The same is true of the fall, winter, and spring months.

20. Arrangement: The particular seating and lighting arrangement modifies the attention value.

21. Territory: This will also have a bearing on the advisability of using street cars.

22. Street car advertising is often supplementary.

23. The season often affects the number of people riding.

24. The angle of car card needs consideration.

25. The placing of street car cards should regard psychologically:—(1) law of association; (2) intensity; (3) relativity.

Objections to Advertising in Street Cars: Representatives of other mediums often point out the disadvantages of street car advertising, among which are the following: (1) monotony of cards, being same size; (2)being above the eye level it is unnatural for the passenger to look up, requiring a special effort; (3) possibility of many cars standing in the car-barn being used very little or not at all; (4) small size of cards in comparison to painted bulletins, bill boards, etc.; (5) inability to give " reason why " copy or to fully explain product.

By comparisons and tests you can readily realize how necessary it is that the fact of whether or not you should use street car advertising depends altogether upon your product. The safe way is to start small and test out the proposition. If it proves successful, increase. At any rate, you can better afford to make a test than to make a mistake.

MAIL ORDER ADVERTISING

1. Nature of Business:

A. General mail order advertising is made up of all kinds of business, as in the case of Sears, Roebuck & Co. controlling the factory output of (*a*) groceries, (*b*) hardware, (*c*) jewelry, (*d*) farm implements, etc.

B. Special mail order advertising, which consists in selling a single article, as (*a*) hosiery, or (*b*) hats, etc.

2. The field of the mail order business: (*a*) Places remote from purchasing possibilities—as rural districts, (*b*) small towns, (*c*) cities, (*d*) selling to groups.

3. The advantages of the mail order business to the consumer: (*a*) eliminates the middle man, (*b*) sells cheaper than the "home store."

4. One primal advantage to the mail order business is its cash basis.

5. The method of distribution is (*a*) parcels post, (*b*) express, (*c*) freight.

6. A well-conducted advertising campaign considers: (*a*) timely mailing of literature, (*b*) record-keeping and follow-up system, (*c*) the sales correspondent—(1) an able critic, (2) diplomatic, (*d*) knowledge of competitors, (*e*) accurate keying of advertisements.

7. The media: (*a*) farm journals, (*b*) newspapers (Sunday and weekly editions), (*c*) "new feature" catalogs, (*d*) magazines, (*e*) personal letters, (*f*) form letters.

WINDOW DISPLAY ADVERTISING

1. One of the chief means of publicity for the retail merchant.

2. The window display is the magnet above all others which draws people in the store.

3. The window itself and the mechanical fixtures for decorating should be the best obtainable.

4. The decorator should be a man intelligent in the analysis of human nature—keen as a salesman and artistic in the presentation of goods.

5. An itemized account should be kept to show the effect of the windows on business.

6. Should be a relationship between general excellency of the windows and the various departments of the store.

7. Display should not be too unique, else people will look at display and forget all about entering the store.

8. The display window should be as effective in getting results as the written advertisement.

9. A good system is an all-important factor in obtaining a good display in the shortest time.

10. Window display should (a) attract, (b) be pleasing, artistic, etc., (c) appeal, (d) be in season, (e) educate or arouse self-interest.

PROGRAMS

1. People in a receptive mood for such articles as candy, wines, cigars, restaurants, etc.

2. Large percentage of theatre audiences is made up of women. Thus fine millinery, dress goods, hats, and advertisements of similar character are well received.

3. People mostly in a pleasure mood, hence those advertisements are suggested which enter into the spirit of the play or the class of people attending a particular theatre.

NOVELTY AND UNIQUE ADVERTISING—(CALENDARS, BLOTTERS, ETC.)

1. An excellent way of keeping your goods in the mind of the owner.

2. Calendars and blotters should be of good quality, otherwise they will be thrown out.

3. Calendars and blotters should not have too much reading matter as people do not like to have their walls decorated with advertisements.

4. The method of giving a thing, or unique advertising, is often as important as the novelty which is given.

CIRCULARS, BOOKLETS, AND LETTERS

1. The reading matter should be interesting as well as instructive.

2. The lay-out should be severely criticised in relation to type, cuts and general attractiveness.

3. A booklet, catalog or letter which has been sent to a person who has signified that he is interested in the article might profitably differ from that sent to one who has not so signified.

4. The size of envelope as well as grades and weight of paper should be studied with regard to postage, shape, color, and the cuts to be used.

5. The " dummy " sent to the printer should contain all the ideas of its composer.

CATALOGS

Two classes: (a) Manufacturer's catalog—harness, wallpaper, etc.; (b) strictly retail—groceries, dry goods, etc.

1. Should have a hanger so that people will hang it up and refer to it from time to time.

2. Cover should be of good substantial material and a good solid color, not easily soiled.

3. Interior treatment of your catalog and trade conditions in relation to same. Your own manufactured goods should be printed on better paper than jobbers use.

4. Selection of best brands should be emphasized in catalog rather than a large number.

5. Cuts and color should not overly emphasize values. Should, however, portray article to best advantage.

6. In strictly retail catalogs a few pages of general interest should be added—a calendar, as well as a few pages for telephone numbers, addresses, etc.

SAMPLING

1. New things are generally looked at with skepticism, and it is only by sampling that interest can be turned into action.

2. Should consider amount of money you intend to spend

sampling, and then see what advertising space you could purchase for same amount.

3. Should be a true representation of the goods.

4. Goods should be obtainable in that district thru which samples have been distributed.

5. For firms of limited capital sampling by mail, thru demonstrations, or dealers, is an excellent way to get a good footing.

6. As such firms succeed, however, the next step is to make this sampling more effective by the support of magazine, newspaper or street car advertising.

TRADE JOURNALS

1. Used mostly by firms who have articles, or goods, which they wish to sell to firms in a respective trade, and of such a character that they cannot be sold to the public.

2. The advertising here is often trite and monotonous in effect. Much improvement is possible in this field.

3. The previous interest of the trade is often depended upon to obtain results.

4. Many advertisements consist of mere announcements. This is a desire to impress the trade name.

5. Stricter attention should be given in the creation of " human interest " copy.

PREMIUM ADVERTISING

1. It cuts down advertising costs as conducted by individuals by introducing coöperative methods.

2. It gives your goods the added attraction of premium value.

3. It appeals to the " something for nothing " instinct.

4. Definite results from this form of advertising can be calculated.

5. You have your own sales force as well as others pushing your particular product.

6. In many coöperative movements only the most reliable goods are in the enterprise. Your own are thus emphasized most favorably.

CHAPTER XV

THE ADVERTISING AGENCY

The Place of the Agency in Advertising.—Practically every line of advertising which appears in the national publications is prepared by, and placed through, an agency. The same is true of most of the newspaper advertising, except in the case of that of retail and department stores, whose publicity is usually more or less an announcement of bargains or special sales, and for this reason can be more conveniently handled by the advertiser himself.

The great national advertisers, however, whose annual appropriations run into the hundreds of thousands of dollars, employ agents. The National Biscuit Company, the several large tobacco companies, the automobile manufacturers, Victor Talking Machine—all are so-called " agency accounts."

Services of an Agency: Planning Campaign.—The service an agency renders its clients may be enumerated somewhat as follows:

The laying out of a plan of campaign, the buying of space in the publications, preparation of " copy," checking the insertions of the advertising, bookkeeping and trade help.

When an agency takes on a new " account," particularly in case it is that of a firm which has never advertised before, the planning of the campaign naturally plays a most important part in its future success. In the first place, the men of its staff, whom the agency details to handle the " account," must become thoroughly familiar with the product to be advertised. Then comes the question of *how* shall it be advertised? The case must be diagnosed as carefully as a case in medicine, the facts as thoroughly gone into as the evidence in a law suit.

Distribution of Product.—Distribution is of first consideration in the mapping out of an advertising campaign. Many an expensive campaign has failed to give satisfactory results because of lack of harmony between publicity and distribution. Suppose the product to be advertised is a soap or a tobacco,

217

an article of small price and frequent demand. Manifestly, if the advertising is to show results, the article must be easily obtainable by the prospective purchaser. The retail distribution must be good.

However, the agent in the course of his examination into this factor learns from the conference with the sales department that the soap to be advertised has an excellent distribution in the East, a fair one in the South, and is practically unknown in the West. The reason for this condition must be ascertained. It may be known to the advertiser's sales department or, on the other hand, the agent may find it necessary to make his own investigation by sending men to interview the retail dealers and to find out from them, first hand, what the trade conditions are.

Selection of Territory.—Once the factor of distribution has been analyzed, the attention is centered on the methods of advertising the goods.

First, after the advertiser has indicated approximately the limits of the advertising budget, the problem arises as to where the advertising shall be placed. Shall the advertising be concentrated in the East, where the distribution is good, where the prospective purchaser may obtain the goods with the least effort, and where the immediate returns will be proportionately greater? Or shall the appropriation be scattered to cover the South and West as well, with a view toward building up a demand in those sections that will make dealers eager to carry the line. The adoption of the latter plan necessitates the adjustment between distribution and demand. Forcing distribution by first building demand is an expensive process, as much of the advertising must be sacrificed in creating a demand for an article which is not to be had at local stores. It is much more satisfactory first to obtain distribution and then to advertise. So it is that the agent may recommend that an effort be made to " line up " the dealers in the South and West by a promise to move the goods quickly by aggressive national advertising, backed up by newspaper publicity in the dealers' local papers.

Choice of Advertising Media.—Second, having reached a decision as to what territory is to be covered, the means of ac-

complishing this end has to be determined. The division of the
budget among the various advertising media such as magazines,
newspapers, circulars and booklets and bill-boards must be decided upon, and as incidental thereto, a selection has to be
made of the most effective mediums of any particular class.
Every agency has " rate men " or " space buyers " whose function it is to solve these questions. These men are interviewed
constantly by the representatives of various publications from
whom they gather the specific and detailed data requisite for
their work. By means of index cards they have at their finger-
ends, the circulation, the rates, and the class of readers reached
by each publication. This classification is carried, in many
cases, down to such a fine point that the " rate man " can tell,
not only the size of a given publication's subscription list, but
its character as well; as for example, the number of lawyers,
physicians, business men, automobile owners or what not, who
may be reached through the columns of some stated publication.

On the basis of the information supplied by the " rate man "
the list of media to be used is compiled. If the product under
consideration is hosiery, for example, an article which appeals to
men and women alike, general magazines such as *The Saturday
Evening Post, Cosmopolitan, McClure's,* etc., are selected.
Articles such as corsets are best marketed through women's publications like *The Ladies' Home Journal, Vogue, Vanity Fair,*
etc. (the latter two especially, if the article be an expensive one
likely to appeal to a moneyed class of buyers). Articles of
food are most generally advertised in *Good Housekeeping, The
Ladies' Home Journal,* etc.

Circulation aside, the value of a given newspaper may be
determined, according as to whether it is a " home paper,"
" sporting paper " or " class paper." As a typical instance in
Philadelphia the dailies may be roughly classified as follows:

The Evening Bulletin.—The largest circulation. An evening paper that is carried into the home. A good medium for
reaching men and women alike. A paper which justifies its
slogan of " In Philadelphia nearly everybody reads the Bul-

letin." An advertiser who contemplates the use of a single paper would invariably choose *The Bulletin.*

The Public Ledger.—A " class paper." A good medium for any high-priced articles, such as fine jewelry, expensive automobiles, etc.

The Inquirer, Record and North American are given in the order of their respective circulations. A morning paper is a good department and retail store medium, and articles advertised in these papers get the attention of shoppers before they begin their shopping. Articles of food and " women's goods " are profitably exploited in morning papers, but men, as a rule, glance through a morning paper hurriedly.

The late *Evening Times* was reputed to have the best sporting page in the city, and was therefore a good medium for a purely masculine appeal.

The foregoing are given as examples of the data on which the " rate-man " bases his selection of media. It may be said, however, that it is not always an easy matter to draw a sharp distinction as to which articles appeal strictly to men and which to women. Quite frequently, the purchaser and consumer are two distinct persons. It is said that considerably more than 50 per cent. of the men's underwear is purchased by women ; and contrariwise, men are the largest buyers, but not consumers, of expensive candies. Women have the most influence in the purchase of expensive automobiles, while men buy the cheaper grades of cars.

Intensive versus Extensive Campaign.—Third, then, the query is raised as to whether the campaign shall be intensive or extensive. That is, whether the advertising shall be placed in, say, half a dozen national mediums and one paper in each important city, or whether the space per insertion and the number of insertions per medium shall be reduced and a larger number of publications be employed. And in answering this the " rate-man " is confronted with getting the maximum number of possible customers with the minimum of " duplicate circulation."

Campaign Plan Approved by Advertiser.—With these problems threshed out, the agency is prepared to submit its plan to the advertiser. This plan contains a schedule of the publications, the number and dates of insertions and their cost. It may also give the result of the agency's investigations and the conclusions to be drawn therefrom, together with a complete outline of the proposed plan of procedure as regards copy appeal and follow-up work. The plan may be an elaborate affair of 500 pages or it may be a few typewritten sheets. Its length is no indication of its value.

The plan is the blue print of the edifice of publicity which the advertiser and the agency, working together, will erect. Whether the building will be a credit to its creators depends on the soundness of the plan and the faithful adherence thereto. A campaign undertaken without a carefully laid plan and without a very definite goal in sight, can hardly be expected to produce satisfactory results any more than a house begun without a plan can be expected to be either an ornamental or a comfortable residence when completed.

Together, the agent and the advertiser go carefully over the plan, searching for flaws and opportunities for improvement, correcting and revising, until the plan is finally approved by the advertiser.

Essentials Considered in Preparation of Copy.—The agent's next step is the actual preparation of the copy. This work is in the hands of "copy men" or "idea men." While copy is the most important part of agency service, the methods and principles involved in its production having been elaborated elsewhere in this volume, it needs no lengthy discussion here. But there are certain fundamentals which must be born in mind. The man who is to have charge of the preparation of the copy must go into the manufacturer's plant and thoroughly familiarize himself with not only the product, but with all the conditions surrounding its manufacture and sale. If the copy is to be " newsy " and interesting, the "idea man" must be in constant touch and in a confidential relationship with the advertiser's sales department. Copy and selling methods must parallel each other; and if the agency is giving the production sort of service, its " idea men " will be constantly evolving plans to assist the sales department in

its work. Lastly, all copy is submitted to the advertiser for his
approval and is then sent out to the various publications, in
which it is to appear.

Modes of Contracting for Space.—The agency has in most
cases already sent out its orders for space to the publications,
together with a schedule of the insertions to be made. We may
say here that, as a general rule, all space contracted for is cancellable at will at any time before the publication's forms close,
the only exception being in the case of cover pages and other
" preferred positions " which are sold at a higher rate than
ordinary space, and must be bought outright. However, " preferred space " being in great demand, can usually be disposed of
to other advertisers. There are cases also, where an advertiser,
who cancels part of his contract for ordinary space before its
expiration, is called upon to pay a higher rate for the space he
has already used. This is known technically as " paying short
rates," and it is the agent's duty to call the advertiser's attention
to any space contracts carrying a " short rate " clause.

Cost of Agency Services.—Upon the appearance of the publication, the business department of the agency checks up the insertions, settles with the publisher and renders a bill to the advertiser for the total cost of advertising done during the month,
including space-cost and the sundry expenses incidental to the
production of copy, such as drawings, cuts, etc. For all the
service an agency renders, the advertiser pays nothing. His advertising would cost him the same if he prepared his own copy
and placed his own advertising direct with the publication.
The advertiser hires the agent but the publication pays his fee.
This fee is in the form of a commission—usually 15 per cent. on
the gross expense—which the agent deducts when settling with
the publications. Some newspapers, however, allow no agent's
commission on the business of strictly local advertisers, and there
are a great many trade publications also which pay no commissions. In such cases the agent charges the client a service-fee.

Value of Agency to Publisher.—The agent renders the publisher a very real service. For instance, the agent is directly
responsible for his client's advertising bills and, to preserve his

standing as an agent, he must make prompt monthly settlements with the publisher. Moreover, the publisher, by dealing with an agent rather than with a score of advertisers, vastly simplifies his bookkeeping and detail work. Also, it would be impossible for each publisher to solicit business directly from the thousands of individual advertisers, but he *can* solicit their business through their respective agents. A progressive agent, constantly on the lookout for new business, must create that new business: he must induce non-advertisers to become advertisers. Now, a publication which could only hope to get a part of the advertiser's business could not afford to pay high priced solicitors to spend valuable time in the creation of new " acounts." The agent who will handle the entire business *can* afford this expense.

Good service rendered by an agent to an advertiser makes a small advertising appropriation grow into a large one, to the benefit of advertiser, agent and publisher alike.

For the reasons listed above, publishers prefer to do business with agents rather than with advertisers direct. Consequently, where a new advertiser offers his business to a publisher he is almost invariably recommended to place it through an agency. In the days before agencies were as numerous and efficient as they are at present, many publications maintained service departments which prepared copy free of charge for their advertisers, and some of these service departments are still extant. But the most efficient service department cannot hope to compete with a good agency in the matter of service rendered, because it cannot afford either the salaries an agency pays, or the time and attention an agency gives to its accounts. Furthermore, the copy prepared by the service department of one publication would differ entirely from that prepared by the service department of another. A campaign made up of the efforts of half a dozen such organizations would be a patch-work affair totally lacking in continuity and definiteness of appeal. And, on account of these last-named qualities, which every successful campaign must possess to some degree, practically every national account is handled through an agency.

The Individual Advertising Department.—Large advertisers often have a high salaried advertising manager to shape their advertising policies. Sometimes they maintain a large advertising department for the preparation and distribution of their booklets and circulars, and in some few cases this department prepares even the newspaper and magazine publicity, though the actual details of placing is done through an agency. On the other hand, it is safe to say that the greater proportion of the big advertisers usually prefer agency "copy," because of the broader outlook of the agent made possible by his intimate knowledge of advertising and merchandising in so many and varied phases. Of course, the small advertiser who cannot afford to maintain an expensive advertising department, gladly avails himself of the service of his agent in preparing not only his advertising copy but his booklets and follow-up material as well.

Importance of Selecting Responsible Agents.—The selection of an agent is a matter that should have the advertiser's most careful attention. As the question of price does not enter, the selection must be based on a consideration of service alone, although agents differ as to what legitimately may be considered to fall within the scope of agency service. Some regard their duty as ending with the preparation and placing of the magazine and newspaper copy; others consider that an agent should become as nearly as possible the client's advertising department and assume responsibility for the work that properly belongs to such a department, except as concerns actual clerical work, such as the keeping of a follow-up system, attending to the sending out of advertising mail matter and the like.

While each agency has its own individual method of handling its accounts, every agency may be said to departmentize its work somewhat as follows:—the promotion or soliciting department, having charge of the creation of business for the agency; the planning and copy department, the duties of which have already been stated; the art department, whose sole function is the securing of art work; and the business department, which attends to the clerical detail, accounting and checking entailed in the handling of the agency's business.

Value of Agency Experience.—For a man who contemplates advertising as a career there is no better field for harvesting varied and useful experience than in an agency.   And whether he expects to continue in the agency field or qualify for the position of advertising manager of some manufacturing company he will get a better, broader training in an agency than he could in any other way.   Agency work, like advertising work of any kind, is not a sinecure of short hours, easy work and large salaries.   No business and few professions call for more exacting and careful thought, more sincere and painstaking effort.   Naturally, in advertising there are big men and little, successes and failures, but in its very newness, advertising has the one supreme advantage over the older professions.   Hoyle, has, so far, failed to codify the rules.   Few authoritative works have been written on the subject.   In the advertising agency, advertising history is daily in the making and there are opportunities for men who are big enough to make it.   There is plenty of opportunity still for research and exploration.

In the every day surroundings of hundreds of agency "copy" rooms, men are toiling to put " human interest " into the ordinary affairs of every day life, to write " The Romance of Baked Beans " or " The Epic of a Toilet Soap."

To them some advertiser is intrusting perhaps $5000, the cost of one back cover with a circulation of nearly two million a week.   The same piece of copy will appear in perhaps a score of other publications, so that we may raise the figure to $50,000 to be expended on putting before the public a single piece of copy.

The advertiser has set the copy men this task to perform. Bring before your mind's eye that vast audience who comprise the readers of this magazine.   Some are men and women of the highest education and culture.   Most of them are of that intelligent, comfortable, safe and sane multitude we call the " common people."   Throw on the screen a picture and tell that audience in, say, a hundred words, or even less, the story of a specific product.   Weave a romance, set down a history, conjure up a vision of delight, give a heart-to-heart common sense talk.   Do what you will, but bear in mind you are expected to get results.

15

QUESTIONS

1. What economic service does an advertising agency perform for (a) the advertiser; (b) the publisher?
2. Into what departments may agency work be divided? What is the function of each department?
3. Describe the work preliminary to the appearance of an advertising campaign.
4. Give briefly the points to be considered in the selection of advertising "media."
5. What sort of advertising space is usually (a) "cancellable"; (b) "non-cancellable"? (c) What is a "short rate"?
6. How is an advertising agency paid for its services?
7. What class of advertising media is best adapted to the advertising of different articles or propositions, such as: (a) men's underwear; (b) articles of food; (c) department store advertisements; (d) sporting goods?
8. Define intensive and extensive advertising.

COLLATERAL READINGS

ADVERTISING AS A BUSINESS FORCE, PAUL CHERINGTON, Chapter xv.

CHAPTER XVI

CREATING A VOGUE BY MEANS OF ADVERTISING

(A REVIEW OF ALL THE PHYSICAL FACTORS INVOLVED IN ADVERTISING)

Definition of the Term Vogue.—While the immediate functioning factors of advertising are essentially educational in nature, the desired culmination of their operative processes is for the purpose of creating what we might term *a vogue* for a particular article or proposition. By vogue we mean a favorable attitude of mind on the part of a desirable group or groups toward a particular article or proposition. To put the processes of the creation of a vogue in another way, advertising, first thrust out into the realm of human sensitiveness, attempts: first, to attract attention; and second, to establish a feeling on the part of individuals that this particular article has a place in life. When a sufficiently large group of individuals has acquiesced to the appeal of the advertiser in a feeling that the article's or proposition's *raison d'être* is worthy, and the seller likewise feels that enough of the salable has a recognized value, then the vogue has been established. Thus, with respect to the history of any proposition, there seem to be two distinctly developing movements: one, which involves the creation of a vogue; the other, the maintenance of a vogue. A recognition of this division of an article in its career from an unrecognized existence to that of popular continued acceptance involves three specific appeals: first, to become known; second, to be recognized as a vogue; and third, to maintain itself in a progressive realm.

Steps Necessary to Its Creation and Maintenance.—The creation of a vogue for a new article or a proposition involves two steps: first, to gain the attention of the public and simultaneously to arouse the feeling that a worthy new thing has appeared; second, to make a sufficiently large number of people feel that

227

this new thing is worth possessing. After the creation of the vogue for a particular article or a proposition, we again find advertising compelled to regard certain stages which have developed: first, the necessity of keeping the vogue prevalent; and second, to keep your particular article salable in competition with others.

In giving a definition of creative advertising, the idea of competition was apparently excluded, for the subject was then being considered from the progressive standpoint. But progress oftentimes involves the breaking up of the old. It may be said, then, that in so far as the new, thru advertising, becomes a vogue at the expense of some older article or proposition, competitive advertising, and even salesmanship, is involved. Thus we are compelled to say that it is the advertising of the new which involves the creation of a vogue. A vogue usually implies that which is recognized as serviceable to mankind in a progressive sense, and, as such, is pure advertising; but, insofar as this advertising involves the displacement of another article or proposition, competition has entered.

Gaining Attention.—Let us analyse the four steps to be considered in the creation and maintenance of a vogue thru the force of advertising. It is human nature not to accept a new proposition immediately. That which is absolutely new first impresses one curiously and even suspiciously; with a tendency to reject, rather than to accept. Therefore that article or proposition which is thrust upon the market, new in its experience for mankind, is likely to be looked upon somewhat apart from the every day happenings of people. However, as the article persists in its hold upon the attention of people, and the appeal is such as to relate itself intimately with the lives of large groups, curiosity will tend to wane and all other factors being equalized, desire and use will be encouraged.

The question of attention thus becomes the very first step in the consideration of the thrusting of a new article or proposition into the market. The advertiser of the past, in his attempt to gain attention, has developed the bill board, electric light, magazine, newspaper, etc. He has considered the question of attention as the first important factor. Now when attention in advertising is analysed, it reveals two factors: first, form; second, thought. Accordingly as advertising is dependent upon sight for recognition, attention tends to relate itself to form. Attention, thru sight, has thus developed that kind of form which adheres to the laws governing eye movement; or that which tends to shock or to encourage the eye's sensitiveness for pleasurable motion. Thus the mere form of an object becomes of importance. That which is pleasing is rather to be encouraged, and we find the advertiser constantly arranging and re-adjusting that which is to greet the sight, in shapes, which will force the mechanical movements of the eye. Lines, groups, proportion, color, harmony, balance, and contrast blend with each other for complete attention, which attention may be either conscious or unconscious,—the kind of experience which separates the casual reader from all the rest of the world in his contemplation of a specific thing in its unitary presentation. Bearing in mind that the creation of a vogue is the main object of advertising, it necessarily follows that the mechanical make-up of any advertisement should preferably become a secondary experience in the consciousness of the reader, if at all, but, as such, should lead inevitably into thought regarding the article or proposition. Thus, such forms of advertising as detract from the possibility of favorable thought processes in a vogue creation imply a waste of energy or, at least, misdirected energy. Insofar, however, as form which is new, conforms to universal law, and form is thus recognized because of its newness rather than its shock to human sensitiveness, then it is to be encouraged, for with the passing of time and constant repetition, this newer pleasing form is destined to convey its advertising thought in the creation of the vogue. Taking all other things into consideration, we might say, then, that those advertisers who adhere uniquely to the laws which govern pleasing eye movement, are destined in the long run to a more favorable recognition.

Arousing Interest.—But gaining mechanical attention is only the first step. The second factor involved is that of arousing interest on the part of the reader or observer. The pleasurable feeling of mechanical arrangement should pass into conscious attention regarding the article or proposition. But if the feeling either of pleasure or of truth is suggested, the advertisement is most efficiently functioning in the creation of desire. If aroused in a large enough group, desire passes into a vogue. To create a vogue for an article is not always easy, for there are often involved a great many negative ideas on the part of the class about to be reached. And how to overcome these notions and at the same time to construct a new idea, such that the double functioning results in a desire to change the method of living, is one of the serious problems of advertising. Often there seems a state of consciousness on the part of a given group of people where acceptance of the usefulness or the beauty of a thing is recognized, but with apparent stagnation as far as human effort to realize the benefit is concerned. It.is at this point that mental effort in the form of exposition, argumentation or persuasion is likely to prove most effective. We might thus liken the advent of a new article on the market to a play consisting of scenery, action and climax. In the creation of a vogue, the prospective consumer must not be too seriously considering the scenery, nor must he too seriously become infatuated with any one of the acting factors; but he must be led on from scenery into action to the climax, which is the serious consideration of the article or proposition as a vogue in his life's experience.

The Illustration.—One of the most important factors in the creation of advertisements, at the present time, involving the sight, is that of the illustration. While the illustration in part serves to please our desire for mechanical eye adjustment, the climax of such movement is mental in nature. An advertisement, without an illustration, where the typography has adhered to all the laws of unique, mechanical construction, undoubtedly pleases many groups of people and is effective. But there are many other groups whose sensitiveness is caught in the appreciation of an illustration in connection with the text rather than thru print alone. An advertisement containing both illustration and text, then, has the combination of elements, which create a complex situation and the question becomes:—What should be the relationship between the text and the illustration? The ideal advertisement employs a focal point for attention and eye movement, such that the entire advertisement is comprehended; for example, an electric light sign similar to the one in New York City, involving the Ben Hur Chariot Race, should be so constructed in its focal point and light flashing movement as to insist upon an almost simultaneous comprehension of the text to be read above. Mere wonderment, however, is not the state of consciousness desired, unless an extended campaign contemplates wonderment as one of the stages of progressive thinking. And it seems that the ideal advertising campaign might consider mere wonderment at a specific time as all that was necessary, for this same wonderment could be seized upon at a later time and might then be converted into attention toward the article or proposition in the creation of a vogue.

Suggestion and Association of Ideas.—As suggested, one of the important considerations of advertising is that of the thought process involved. The form of an advertisement having forced us from the focal point thru eye movement into thought, the question for every advertiser becomes: What kind of thoughts tinued suggestion. If the associations aroused by an illustration as suggested above, contains innumerable opportunities for continued suggestion. If the associations aroused by an illustration are such as to perpetuate favorable thought in connection with the article or proposition on the part of a continually larger group of individuals, the advertisement might be said to be in the vogue-creating period. If, on the other hand, negative ideas are being aroused and continue to persist in the mind of a continually larger group, the possibility of that article or proposition as a vogue is being diminished. An examination of several hundred advertisements containing both illustration and text reveals the production of three specific types of advertisements from a mechanical arrangement standpoint, each of which has an immediate control upon the thought of the advertisement. For instance, those advertisements which have an eye movement so arranged that some distinct object is made the center of attraction, or whose perspective is so arranged that the mind is taken into a contemplation of ideas apart from the article, these are often such as to make the individual forget that he is reading an advertisement and cause him to contemplate life imaginatively. On the other hand, those advertisements whose eye movement is such as immediately to fall upon that which seems to come out of the advertisement and toward the reader, likewise induce an im-mediate play of the imagination but in a manner which seems to insist upon contemplation of the goods displayed.   The third type of advertisement seems to be purely descriptive in nature, or a reproduction which impresses one with the mere appearance of a thing in connection with other things, such that the idea of commonplaceness is suggested.   In this latter class of advertise-ments we have a feeling of familiarity with respect to what is presented and are inclined merely to go into detail regarding a further knowledge of the specific object.   Imagination does not seem to be aroused.   Exposition seems to be the attitude of mind toward this descriptive presentation of an article or proposition. For lack of a better name we might classify these three ideas as: first, the illustration perspective; second, the illustration pro-jective; and third, the illustration descriptive.   While adver-tisements show these three distinct classifications, there are in-numerable advertisements which show a combination of these three types working enough for us to say, that certain adver-tisements seem to be a cross between any of the two designated.

Various Methods of Making an Appeal.—Psychology de-fines the perception of an object as involving two factors: first, stimulus, and second, apperception.   So, in advertising we might say that when a large group of individuals has perceived ad-vertising such that the stimulus has tended to associate itself with their past experience, that is, apperception, recognition has at least been obtained.   If this recognition is of such a nature that the past is associated in a manner which tends to prove useful to a large group, then vogue for that article or proposition is being established.   If, on the other hand, the stimulus arouses the past of an individual such that it tends to reject the proposition or article, then the possibility of creating a vogue has been dimin-ished.   Relegating the idea of form to the stimulus field, let us contemplate the mental factors involved in creating mind states which, either favorably or unfavorably, affect the minds or the prospective group or groups. A discussion of mental attention, as contrasted with mechanical attention, relates itself to one of three phases of thought in connection with the advertising of an article or proposition, the appeal of which is either in the form of text or an illustration. The advertiser in analyzing possible phases of appeal must ask three questions: Shall I appeal to the environment of my article or proposition? Shall I appeal to the mere usefulness or serviceableness of my article or proposition? Shall I appeal to the emotional elements of my proposition or article?

Appeal Varies with the Class Being Reached.—The advertiser can determine, from his study of human nature, the tendency of a given class to appreciate one phase more than the other, and from this knowledge his appeal should be modified accordingly. For instance, automobile advertising in the past has illustrated completely these three phases. We have seen the automobile sweeping at high speed about some climbing mountain path overlooking beautiful valleys and tumbling waterfalls. The environment into which an autoist could thrust himself thus to conquer time and space—this was the appeal. The desire for the possession of a machine was aroused. Emphasis is placed on the objective in life. Secondly, we have read appeals which dwelt upon the serviceableness of a machine. We have been told that it was a time-saver and an expense reducer. Emphasis is placed on utility. The third appeal is merely the emotional idea, where the pleasures that result are suggested. Emphasis is placed on human feelings. Continued advertising, however, would insist that the entire story of an article or proposition result in a coinciding of emotion, utility and environment. Therefore, that advertising which seizes upon the human mind enough to feel out the thoughts for progress is destined to recognition as a vogue. Having once determined the particular phase of an article's development from any one of these standpoints, or all three, the advertiser, apart from thoroughly understanding the mechanical factors that enter into an exposition of his article or proposition, must regard the human factors in order " to get his article or proposition over," as it is termed in advertising phraseology. The advertiser must connect his article or proposition with the vast mass or group, and when he properly understands the mind of this mass in its adherence to universal principles of mind, action, custom, tradition, precedent, and habit, he is paving the way for the creation of his vogue. With some people an appeal to the senses is necessary; to others an instinctive appeal proves effective; to others an adherence to habit, custom, precedent and tradition becomes overpowering; to certain other groups, imagination, suggestion, persuasion and reason appeal; and whatever the class, there will be found a certain combination of complex circumstances which makes that article or proposition different in its appeal from all other articles or propositions.

Interrelation of Illustration and Text.—Again, the illustration and, likewise, imagination aroused thru text, play a most important part in creating a vogue. That illustration which appeals to our various instincts is likely to meet with immediate response. Instinct implies a complex mental reaction in the presence of stimulus. Whatever advertisement suggests instinct favorably has an attention value more complex and hence more effective—especially if the article is immediately associated— than that advertisement which contains a mere announcement regardless of the individual's personality. Instincts, which under their broadest classifications involve the spiritual, material and social tendencies of life, have their principles of action and reactions, to which the advertiser must conform. The spiritual tendencies of people must be analyzed with respect to that kind of a stimulus which will get a response in terms of creeds and moral inclinations. An advertising campaign which tends to trespass upon the inherited and acquired expressions of this nature is destined to such expressions on the part of people as will discourage the vogue of a particular proposition or article. For instance, the one who attempts to advertise so simple and necessary a product as bread in terms of ill health in a Christian Science paper will meet with peculiar opposition. On the other hand, the advertiser of a new article or proposition who places his advertisement in certain church papers, is destined to a favorable recognition of superiority simply due to the fact that it is in a religious paper. To offend the moral ideas or beliefs of different groups of people is to invite failure in the creation of a vogue.

Discrimination Between Tastes of Different Groups.— Again, in an appeal to the social inclination of people, in so far as they wish companionship and self-esteem in the eyes of their fellow-beings, it becomes necessary to discriminate carefully the likes and dislikes of particular groups. And the advertising realm, in connection with the articles or propositions which are estimated most highly, seems to relate itself to the idea of social prestige. Advertising seems to recognize different groups of people, each acting under prescribed standards. Moreover the creation of desire on the part of innumerable individuals who are not in those groups, but who might become of them, thru imitation, is often suggested.

Utilization of Social Sense.—The advertiser has been quick to recognize the social sense in its various appeals. He moreover tends almost unconsciously to analyze the various groups with respect to the social appeal. For instance, an examination of a large number of advertisements shows two fundamental ideas prevailing in the display of various kinds of goods, where people are involved in their presentation. The idea of serviceableness is differentiated from an idea of the social expression of one's self. In advertising a floor mop which is being manipulated by a girl, the tendency is not to give to this individual extreme beauty above her position, but rather to suggest the type of woman with long features and angular appearance, which suggests the efficiency idea. On the other hand, when an automobile most elaborate in equipment is to be presented, the opposite type is employed to carry out the social concept or type of individual most appropriate for the setting. Many of these advertisements indicate the round-faced, plump individual to hold the observer's gaze. The same might be said in connection with the advertising done by the International Correspondence School.

Efficiency is the motif of their present advertising and the various creations that are presented in their illustrations always suggest the type of man which has the possibility of overcoming obstacles and surmounting difficulties, if only the right attitude of mind is assumed. He is never the type of man whom we would associate with a purely social environment.

The Value of Suggesting Moods.—It is interesting to note at this particular stage of advertising development, the tendency of the so-called Cubist movement and Post-Impressionism to enter the field. The mood of particular classes of people in their appreciation of goods is hinted at, along with the form in which the thought is presented. Thus a suggestion of moods, in connection with our ideal self, becomes quite as important as an appeal to the illustration of realism which is given. Interpretation of those articles or propositions which involve the social tendency of mankind seems to be by far the most important where the idea of style is involved. Style means a constant change. Thus clothing becomes valueless accordingly as it remains upon the seller's shelves from season to season. While there is a tendency for all things to become standardized, yet humanity seems to have an instinctive tendency to want that which has a variation or that which is individual in nature and which differentiates one thing from another. Things born into experience thru the element of style often create a vogue quite transitory in effectiveness. When the statement " they say " in connection with a new article or proposition has made itself felt that particular article or proposition has acquired the vogue experience. Word of mouth statements based on the tendency of human nature to insist upon authority, in connection with what is proper and not proper, are involved in making or undoing a vogue.

The Use of the Material-Self Instincts.—The instincts which are classified under the material self suggest oftener the possibility to construct at the expense of other things. For instance, the lowest instincts, as fear, hoarding, and self-preservation, are involved. Dishonesty, competition, and chance as acquired characteristics suggest themselves as operative mind tendencies in the presence of a new stimulus. We now wish the material to become a part of our life's processes.   It is our desire to make " things " subservient to our human experience, and whatever is forced into our environment which tends to compel a severing of the past and a going to that which is uncertain, or which seems impracticable, or which involves uncertainty in the process of action,—these tend to inhibit rather than to encourage the creation of a vogue.   Although material progress is to be obtained by the regulation of movement in connection with manufacturing processes, yet rechanging and causing the creation of new habits tend to suggest rejection on the part of whole groups of people.   In the same way, the introduction of the washing machine, when presented for the first time, suggests uncertainty on the part of people readily to adjust themselves to a newer material experience and a negative idea with respect to the creation of it as a vogue.   It takes powerful argumentation and persuasion to rearrange the material relations of life involving readjustment of things, where we pass from one kind of habit experience into a new one or where entirely different factors are involved.   Many people today often hesitate to use the telephone; others dislike very much the introduction of a bath-room into their home.   Thus, simply because a thing seems useful, it is no reason why it must win out.   Other forces must assist in the creation of this particular thing as a vogue.   The individual or group must be brought to realize the significance of the saving of energy in the utilization of these greater articles or propositions in connection with their material welfare.

Relation of the Business Man to a Vogue.—In the creation of a vogue the business man is often prone to look suspiciously upon the efforts of the advertiser.   To the former, each advertisement means specific returns.   If an advertisement does not bring immediate results, it is counted as a failure.   If a given concern, whose advertising has extended over seven years, estimates the advertisement of the present month as the one which brings letters in answer, apart from all the previous campaign, it has judged wrongly.   Creating a vogue, implying an educational process, is the setting loose of forces over a long period of time, the result of which cannot be estimated in a single advertisement. It is the cumulative effect of all advertisements. It has often been said that Sunny Jim was a failure as a food advertisement. On the other hand, it is maintained that of all characters thrust into the economic realm to proclaim the qualities of breakfast food, Sunny Jim did best of all; but it is interesting to note that Sunny Jim breakfast food advertising was the first extensive campaign ever conducted in favor of this newer breakfast food. Knowing that that which is new is not accepted immediately, no matter what the merit, Sunny Jim could not expect in a national way, in so short a time, to reap the harvest for his economic friends. But, with his smiling countenance and heart of good cheer, he smiled into the lives of thousands of people a desire for the taste of a new breakfast food, and it is rather difficult to prove that all other breakfast foods do not owe a part of their popularity to the fact that Sunny Jim first introduced them into the possibility of a newer food. I believe Sunny Jim to have advertised all breakfast foods. His universality of character could not do otherwise and, although he did not develop the Force Company as they had wished within the time designated, yet his influence still lives on.

The Vision of the Advertiser.—The above analysis has considered the spirit of advertising, apart from economic laws which tend to modify action. Limitations of money, human prejudices and ignorance, selfishness and fear combined with an inefficient, stubborn humanity constantly modify the vision of an optimistic advertiser. Upon paper within his narrow office, the results seem certain; but, with a multitude of forces operating unforeseen, and even impossible of vision, the results are always different. But, if progress is made at all, the advertiser must have a scientific hope beyond the immediate present conditions; and, in attempting to create a vogue, he must constantly suggest confidence in himself and in the principles which he is observing. Undoubtedly, waste of effort in the creation of wrong cuts; too much advertising space; too little attention to detail; a non-recognition of the right advertising media in connection with expense; a failure to engage the right kind of individual in carrying out ideas; a failure to recognize the competitive force; a rejection of completest knowledge possible;—all these enter into the life of the average advertising man, such that a needless expenditure of money is made. For this we are to be condemned. In so far, however, as we are studying the minimum amount of effort to be put forth with a given expenditure of money, scientifically analysed to procure the maximum return, we are encouraged. And the advertiser, because of the faith element in his work, surrounded by the practical executive, ever feels a force compelling him to keep within the bounds of reason and to bring himself under constant subjection to economic laws.

Salesmanship is the Basis of the Maintenance of a Vogue.— But, after the vogue has been created which involves the idea of advertising, salesmanship combines with advertising to create another specific field in the carrying out of a selling problem in connection with the growth of any establishment. The advertiser is then compelled to modify his form of appeal. He must not only attempt to win the non-vogue class into the user class, but he must be able to compete with those firms selling the same article. The struggle now becomes one where the personal element enters, and where each competitor attempts to proclaim the superior advantages of his article or proposition over others. Advertisements at this stage of development then begin to take a form which involves the principles of both advertising and salesmanship. To continue the vogue means sustaining the business; to increase the vogue is likely to mean growth and profit. And the latter factor is what determines the ultimate success of an advertiser.

QUESTIONS

1. What is the main object of advertising?
2. Thru what two processes must advertising pass in successfully creating a vogue?
3. Name the three specific appeals every unrecognized article, or proposition, must make before it is popularly countenanced.
4. After a vogue has been created what are the necessary stages to be regarded by the efficient advertiser?
5. Can a vogue be created and still fail to impress people with the worth of the new article?
6. What are the four steps to be considered in the creation and maintenance of a vogue thru the force of advertising?
7. Can advertising the old create a vogue?

8. When does pure advertising equal a vogue? Contrast this with the new becoming a vogue at the expense of the old?
9. What should be the relationship between pleasing mechanical attention and consciousness regarding the article, or proposition, itself?
10. When does desire pass into a vogue?
11. Can the stage of mere wonderment ever be justified in an ideal advertising campaign?
12. When may we consider an advertisement to be in a vogue-creating period?
13. Discuss what is meant by the illustration perspective, the illustration projective and the illustration descriptive.
14. Perception involves what two factors? Relate these to advertising.
15. What three questions must the advertiser ask himself in analysing possible phases of appeal? Mention a specific instance wherein these three phases have been illustrated.
16. Mention several universal principles that the advertiser must adhere to in creating a vogue.
17. What new movements are entering the advertising field thru a suggestion to moods?
18. Does style mean a constant change? Discuss.
19. Mention several economic limitations that tend to modify action in advertising.
20. Briefly discuss all possible advertising wastes you recall.
21. Although Sunny Jim was considered a financial failure by the Force Company can you see wherein this character aided advertising in a certain field?

PROBLEMS

1. Compare creative advertising, from the progressive standpoint, with competitive advertising and salesmanship. How do you associate the following quotation with the above: " The new becomes a vogue at the expense of the old, sometimes " ?
2. Justify the standpoint of those advertisers who adhere to the form of an advertisement, sometimes to the point of sacrificing the thought content.
3. You are advertising a certain article to a class of people who consciously accept the usefulness and beauty of your commodity. Still, there is no effort to derive personal benefit manifested thru purchase. How would you proceed to stimulate their desire for possession?
4. After seven years of extensive advertising a certain mail order house discontinued business. Their advertising report showed a profit of $30,000 credited to the last month's business. Analyse this method of presenting advertising gains and justify or discredit this system.
5. Although we distinguish between pure advertising and salesmanship, discuss their relationship after the vogue has been created.

CHAPTER XVII

DISPLAY IN ADVERTISING

(A REVIEW OF THE PRINCIPLES INVOLVED IN ALL FORMS OF ADVERTISING)

Elements of Effective Display.—While the end of advertising from the producer's point of view is that of creating a vogue, from the advertiser's viewpoint, the means by which this vogue is created, becomes equally important. In the consideration of any proposition the advertiser finds himself involved in a double process:—one, where his attention is concentrated on the means by which his message is to be "gotten over," the other, upon the exact thought he wishes the public to get. The word most suitable to express the means of gaining attention in the creation of a vogue is that known as "display." Anything which is done to catch the attention outside of the regular or conventional manner, such that the form of the thing itself tends to emphasize the thought presented, is to be classified as display of advertising. An effective display represents a certain quality or combination of objective factors which need to be analysed in relation to attention. To gain attention as an initial step in the process of advertising involves an understanding of all that goes to make up quality of thought or sensation. It must also contain those elements which continue either conscious or unconscious attention until the display, psychologically speaking, has not been perceived as merely display, but as a thought in connection with the purpose of creating a vogue.

Display and Sense Experiences.—Display in advertising, applied concretely, relates to whatever is perceived thru a single one or any combination of the senses, such that the process by nature leads to an effective perception of the thought intended to be conveyed. The newspaper advertisement which assumes any form other than that of mere news, recognizable upon analysis as an advertisement, is as truly display in its purpose as the most elaborately decorated show window. Likewise the toy balloon, which carries sample soap to the finder, is a form to

16   241

be characterized as display. It therefore follows that such factors as lead into a state of attention become of great importance. In fact, many advertisements are so constructed as to command attention such that the process by which this has been obtained becomes of more interest than the message itself. In this consists the great danger when display is concentrated upon itself, rather than upon the thought which it wishes to convey.

The Problem of Balance.—The first real problem in connection with display, then, becomes one of balance. How much shall I emphasize in order to get the perception of my proposition in spite of the alluring power of the means of display? If the fact of the balloon becomes more important than the message of the soap, display is destroying its *raison d'être*. So in the instance of an elaborate calendar, the spirit of the giver sometimes becomes of more significance than the firm or individual represented. In other words, if a calendar attracts attention in a manner which draws an expression of admiration, and such that the observer is merely told of it as a gift instead of it being the gift from a given concern, the display has not been effective. In this instance the spirit of giving and the idea of quality have not been so united in effort as to suggest a word of emphasis for the giver.

Kinds of Display.—Now display, functioning in our world of experience, exists in one of four relations to mind: first, the display may be of such a nature as to force itself into the consciousness of multitudes of people in a unitary sense without regard for its parts; second, the display is of such a nature as to force itself into the consciousness of people where its parts become as much a matter of interest as the unitary effect obtained: third, the display may be of such a nature as to make the observer conscious of the various parts of itself rather than the unitary comprehension; fourth, the display has the possibility of recognition because of the preperceptive elements which exist on the part of the public mind.

Display Should Be a Simple Unit.—Let us consider the facts in connection with each of the above laws. That display which readily and easily adjusts itself to the state of con-

sciousness where the idea meant to be conveyed harmonizes itself
immediately with the mind—this is to be desired. The difficulty
with the acceptance of this kind of a theory, in connection with
all kinds of display, consists in the fact that humanity does not
tend to adjust itself to the simple until after a long experience
with complexity. When an establishment similar to that of Tiffany reaches a place in public esteem where desire has already
been created, quality of goods recognized, and fairness of price
suggested, with a recognition of the fact that a vogue has been
created determined by this concern's popularity and success, we
have a combination of factors working where advertising can be
reduced to the simplest, individualized form and at the same time
obtain satisfactory returns from the display offered. Having
once won the public mind into an appreciation of the merits and
necessity of a given proposition or article, the form of display
naturally modifies itself until unitary effects alone are desirable.
But even in this instance it becomes a question with respect to
the rising generation, the increasing numbers of wealthy, and the
fixed habits of people, whether other kinds of display would not
prove exceedingly profitable. This would seem to be especially
true where another firm giving equally good value advertises by
other than simple announcement display and obtains a constantly new patronage. The factor of competition, involved in
any form of progress, would imply adopting at least in part
some of the competitor's methods. This necessarily involves a
greater consideration of display.

Unitary display advertising, which considers an harmonious
interpretation of an idea such that it is readily appreciated, with
comparatively small stress on display features, implies that a
vogue has been created and that an announcement is a welcome
reminder of the article or proposition offered. In a competitive
realm, however, simplicity is always brought into contrast with
forms containing greater display value by one who sees the possibilities of suggestion and imagination in the creation of
other than simple display in connection with the article or proposition. And this has its basis in the fact that humanity in general has a tendency to appreciate even the old in a new form.

Intensive and Disseminated Attention Value.—Again, display is often of such a nature as to force itself into the public mind where its parts secure as much conscious attention as the unitary effect afterwards obtained. In this interpretation of the public mind, relative to display, lurk certain dangers. When the unitary effect of the entire display is such as to make one conscious more of the display than the thought which was intended, the real purpose of display in selling goods has partly failed. Undoubtedly, continuous repetition would in time disassociate the minds of people from the display and suggest the real significance of the thought intended. On the other hand, the power of display in attempting to promote an idea in many instances actually serves to re-enforce or punctuate, as it were, the idea. For instance, we are all conscious of the action which is expressed in the Dutch Cleanser advertisements where the Dutch girl continuously suggests the cleansing process. Nearly every advertisement gotten out by this company introduces in its display the so-called " Dutch Kid " in such a relation to the other parts of the advertisement that we are constantly reminded of the process of cleansing, and when these advertisements are talked of afterwards, the factors of display are mentioned in connection with the thought of the article itself.

Maximum Value of Perception.—So we might mention the Campbell's Soup " Kids " which have become rather famous in the advertising realm. The particular display form in which this so-called "Kid" is featured is of such a nature as to make us constantly aware of its uniqueness and at the same time be aware of the idea—Campbell's Soup. On the other hand, innumerable advertisements gotten out by the Ivory soap people, which contain simple illustrations showing the various uses of Ivory soap, while we are conscious of the unique arrangement of each of the advertisements, yet there is not that uniformity of display such that the latest advertisement readily relates itself to the display form of all the past advertisements. Thus the law to be evolved from a realization that display is often effectuated by an unconscious process in its unitary perception is as follows: *In so far as an intensive advertising campaign consists of a unitary display-form which continuously emphasizes, thru repetition, the idea to be conveyed and which is effective in its appeal, that display has reached a maximum regard for perception.* When this law is violated, display is of such a nature as to make the observer conscious of the various parts of itself, rather than a unitary comprehension. When the public mind assumes this latter attitude toward a specific display, the effectiveness of the idea desired to be impressed is lost. If the parts of the display have a certain uniqueness, constant repetition would tend in time to create the idea; but, generally speaking, it would seem better to impress the idea intended from the very first.

Effect of Preperception on Display.—That the public is often deceived by an over emphasized regard of display itself, apart from the idea to be conveyed, is typified in an experiment where advertisements relating to the Karo Syrup people had been asked for. In this experiment several students handed in copy of the Kingsford Corn Starch Company. The class test afterwards confirmed the idea that each kind of copy tended to call up the other, that the display itself had a tendency to become of greater importance than the perception of the advertisement; and that the mind tended immediately to associate itself with its own experiences. Thus if the student were more familiar with the Kingsford Corn Starch display in his search, there would be a tendency to select without serious consideration forms of display gotten out by the Karo Syrup Company. In another instance a foreign poster, presented to a large class, where the rulers of various European countries are represented as wearing a certain brand of suspenders, is often comprehended as advertising some kind of barber preparation. Many of the foreign rulers are represented with beards, a custom not typical of the average American. The kind of display in this instance, again, tends to allow the individual to interpret in terms of his own experience the particular display presented. The construction of this foreign display apart from copy did not consider the preperceptive

factors of Americans, however much it met the demands of the
French people.

Display, once having been thrust into our economic realm,
such that its form has become a habit, in connection with our
process of thinking, tends to create states of mind which modify
our tendencies toward action when different competing display
is presented.   It is a fact that, during any period of time, there
are groups of people deliberately looking for advertisements.   It
is also true that certain people have become accustomed to search
for specific advertisements as typified in the form of department
store display.   The more regularly the same groups are likely to
search in this manner, the less necessary becomes the need for
extraordinary methods of seizing the attention by means of display.   This condition is excellently illustrated in the use of
classified advertising matter.   But even here expediency often
demands an immediate response, so that various sized type,
added punctuation, extra spacing, contrast of color, and an ingenious phrasing, are employed in order to secure attention.   To
the one who inserts the advertisement the idea of emphasis, in
reality, becomes a factor of display.

Basic Principles of Diminution of Display Features.—Now
the classified want advertisements are most personal in nature.
They contain a message which is related to the immediate self-
preservation, need or self-interest of the individual.   That there
are continuous groups of individuals in need is evidenced in the
continuously changing want advertisements to be found in various forms,—be it on the printed page or the bulletin board of
an employment bureau.   *Thus it might be declared a general
law that the nearer an article or proposition becomes a factor for
the preservation, self-interest or need of the individual, with a
realization on the part of the advertiser of such states of mind
constantly growing in various groups, the greater the tendency
to diminish the display feature of an advertisement.*

The reasons why an advertiser has a right to expect the simpler form to get results are: first, that he can depend upon
a continuously changing and large enough group, the individuals
of which are conscious of specific needs.   There must have been

established, however, in the minds of all people ever likely to feel this need, self-interest, or desire, a place and form to which they can go when occasion demands. That the want columns of papers are constantly advertised is evidence of the fact that continuous general education is needed in order to obtain new advertising matter as well as a constant number of readers. Thus it has come to pass that classified advertisements in various forms have a dependable drawing power. Negative ideas as to the profitableness of these forms exist in the minds of many. Nevertheless, with a continuous advertising of their merits, negative ideas become a negligible quantity, and human need itself is drawn to that which is likely, in some manner, to prove a possible source of satisfaction. A second law which follows the law stated above would state: *The greater the need and the fewer the competitive factors, with a form of expression having once become generally recognized, the less is the need for display features. But the greater the need and the greater the competitive elements, the more insistent does advertising display assert itself and the more individual each advertisement tends to become.*

Display Invokes Use of Variety of Senses.—Display as a factor in gaining the attention of a desired group, in order to serve as a stimulus in the perception of an idea, should be based primarily upon those laws which govern our appreciation of sense life. To be conscious of display, in any form whatsoever, is to be conscious of the fact that an idea is attempting to force itself into consciousness. This may be as a result of any one or any combination of the senses. The greater amount of display presented to us, however, relates itself to the sense of sight, and although other senses, as sound, or touch, or smell, do have forms of display which exert a large influence in impressing themselves upon our mind, nevertheless the sense of sight is oftenest employed, in order to give the best interpretation possible to a particular display. For instance, when the perfume shop keeper in Antwerp takes advantage of a national holiday to fill the large urns in front of his store with sweet incense, the odors of which carry for blocks and the smoke of which encircles the entire building, odor is undoubtedly an encroachment upon our sense of smell the complete significance of which, from a display standpoint, is not fully comprehended until the urns themselves, gushing forth their odoriferous smoke, are perceived. So in the case of the calliope of a circus heard at a great distance. The hearer recognizes that sensuous impression is holding his attention and he craves for a greater realization of its significance, the curiosity of which is not at all satisfied until the particular place of location is witnessed. Moreover, psychological tests regarding the tastes of foods, apart from the value of sight, reveal the inability of entire groups of people fully to appreciate what they are eating unless the sense of sight is employed in the process. At any rate, the various senses must be appealed to if we are to meet the demands of display. The senses, in order to be aroused into an appreciation of a stimulus, observe the psychological law which states that any stimulus, in order to arouse the senses, must have within it a certain degree of force. Many street car cards are entirely disregarded by the public simply because they do not recognize the operation of this law related to display. The injection of a deeper color, or the introduction of stronger contrast elements, or an added punctuation mark—any one of these, by actual experimentation, often assists in causing an advertisement clearly to stand forth in good display form in the eye of the public. Or take the instance of a window display. The particular combination of goods might be ever so effective in display form, yet be unseasonable. Hence the public would not desire that particular thing at the time. Or, as in the instance of many displays in windows, the right color contrasts do not abound; the right ideas of proportion are not suggested; the sentiment to be interpreted is not effective. Any one of these might be such as to inhibit a tendency of response. On the other hand, an intensive study of the effect of the display upon the mind of the public would soon suggest that there needed to be introduced such factors as would tend to bring the display from non-consciousness into a state of attention.

Display Stimuli Modify Each Other.—Another psychological tendency of the mind when a stimulus has been presented is to feel the force of surrounding stimuli. Thus, if two advertisements side by side in a street car are of equal display quality, or two show windows side by side are of equal value, and the observer is placed in such a position that both come within range of the sense aroused, there is an immediate tendency to feel the drawing power of both at the same time. However, those ideas which are aroused by way of association with both stimuli acting, will likely determine the effectiveness of one display over the other. For instance, if I am especially interested in a motor cycle and the display of this article in a window seizes my attention quite as much as the grocery display window of Campbell's Soup, the chances are that the motor cycle will receive the greater attention. However, a display with respect to its placing should contain a recognition of those factors which are likely to vie with others for attention value. Thus the pages of many magazines, where the individual advertisements have been powerful each within itself, are oftentimes weakened in their pulling force, because there is not a general recognition that the placing of advertisements tends either to re-enforce or diminish the original effectiveness.

Competitive Elements of Display.—The competitive elements then, of any display, although decidedly effective within itself, consist of external competing stimuli. At this point the introduction of ideas, in connection with a consciousness of the display itself, tends often to re-enforce the thought to be impressed. A strong enough initial factor; recognition that this factor, howsoever strong, is likely to be in competition with other initial factors or display forms; and a recognition of the fact that the thought, which is immediately associated because of the elements of display, is likely to encourage or discourage attention, once secured;—these factors need serious consideration in the writing, forming, and placing of all display.

Display Should Have a Focal Point.—Display, the comprehension of which involves the sense of sight alone, should especially regard the laws of eye movement as related to attention. A focal point is essential in all display. There should be that combination of physical elements such that the eye can easily adjust itself to a given stimulating factor. If this focal point

is so large that the eye cannot readily adjust itself, there is a
feeling which tends to inhibit attention. In other words, the
feeling associated with the process of mechanical adjustment
itself becomes of more importance than the object of attention.
This kind of experience tends to discourage the observer from a
complete comprehension of that which has had a tendency to
take hold upon his attention.   However, the mind is so constructed with respect to its selective tendency in comprehension
that the very opposite condition, as where there are a multitude
of possible focal points, tends to have an attention effect on the
human mind. For instance, innumerable shop windows in London contain, it would seem, almost the entire stock of the storekeeper.   If it happens to be a jewelry window, every conceivable
piece of jewelry and silver ware seems to be placed in the window.
The result is that people who notice the window at all are inclined most carefully to pass from one article to the other.   The
mind is here governed by curiosity, and initiates its own movement. The feeling of value and perhaps desire, with respect to
selective tendencies, all combine to continue interest in this kind
of display. However, for display in general, there is a greater
tendency to appreciate the fact that the eye needs to be focalized
in its contemplation of a given display, and thru this focal point
there should be evolved such possible eye movement that the observer readily comprehends the entire display intended. The focal
point and eye movement become, then, the first general physical
laws to be observed with respect to the creation of an objective
display.   It is by reason of this law of eye movement that a
competitor's advertisement often gains in power.   If the eye
movement of a specific display is of such a nature as to carry
itself naturally into the line movements of another, there is likely
to be a fusion of interest and the display loses its effectiveness. So, in the case of a focal point, if the focal point of another advertisement is such as to be in contrast to the one which
has first stimulated attention, that advertisement which has the
easier appreciation of eye movement in regard to the entire
comprehension of the display, is likely, from the physiological
viewpoint, to win out. However, the thoughts related to the phys-

ical stimulation first received might themselves, thru self-interest, curiosity and other human mind qualities, overcome the mere physical force of a competing focal point and eye movement. When the focal point and eye movement of any display have seized upon the attention thru movement, they should still be related as to produce a feeling of unity of comprehension.

Field of Attention Should Be Well Defined.—Clearly defining the limits of attention in comprehension is obviously the first step in the creation of effective display. Borders, background and contrast assist largely in producing this unitary effect. Ordinary electric light advertisements, where attention is directed thru flashing a message, are based primarily upon this law. Many electric lights are poor from the standpoint of focal point and eye movement. They fail to lead the observer on into an entire comprehension of the thought desired to be impressed. Many lights flashing their message fail to do more than stimulate the sense of sight. The effect of the entire advertisement may be described as one in which the eye has been concentrated on an advertisement, but in the hurry of the passerby, the real force of the message has been lost. Here the display consists of focal point where the intended ideas have been crowded out. Oftentimes color, as far as attention is concerned, · becomes the focal point of attention and the observer comments upon the feeling of appreciation with respect to the color, rather than color serving as a means to an end. Mere recognition of color thus becomes a focal point of attention without the display leading on to an idea.

Principles Underlying Focal Point and Eye Movement.— Focal point and eye movement are themselves found functioning with respect to certain laws. Their action is encouraged or inhibited by such factors as form, balance, rhythm, proportion, unity and symmetry. Attention is largely attracted toward the form of display. If the form is not such as to conform to a pleasing sensation, attention is sustained only so long as the mental attitude is continued thru interest. Pleasing form, however, is in turn modified by an observance of proportion. Psychologically, when the parts of an advertisement are in the golden average relationship, or a ratio of three to five; when the form itself is absolutely symmetrical, as in the case of a circle, triangle and square, the display is assuming such regard for underlying physiological factors as to encourage, all other factors being equal, comprehension of the display.

QUESTIONS

1. Does display only concern itself with type emphasis?
2. Effective display depends upon what all-important factor? Discuss several ways of obtaining good display and give some corresponding dangers.
3. Name the four relations of display to the mind.
4. What is meant by unitary display? Is it dependent upon the simple, or does a long experience with complexity determine its use?
5. What prerequisites must necessarily be fulfilled before unitary display becomes possible?
6. Discuss unitary display as the Utopia to which all display should strive.
7. State the law which determines when display has reached its maximum regard for perception.
8. To be conscious of display in any form whatsoever, implies the functioning of the fundamental mind law. What is this law and how can this state be brought about?
9. Display, from the standpoint of the sense of sight alone, should employ what laws of eye movement as related to attention?
10. Summarize all of the fundamental factors of mechanical attention that should be regarded in presenting effective display.

PROBLEMS

1. Recently the Liggett & Myers Tobacco Company distributed leather Fatima cigarette cases among college students with the respective college colors and seal upon each case. No other mark of identification related these cases to the tobacco company. Analyse this situation from the standpoint of display.
2. Debate the following: The greater the need and the fewer the competitive factors, with a form of expression having once become generally recognized, the less is the need of display features.
3. Opposite you in a street car are two advertisements side by side. One advertises motor boats, the other motor cycles. Their relative display qualities are equal. Which advertisement interests you the most? Analyse why this is true.
4. In a certain jewelry window in Philadelphia all the laws of effective display have been violated. Still there is a constant stream of people visiting this window. Analyse this situation and mention several reasons why such a condition can exist.

CHAPTER XVIII

DESIRE, HABIT AND INHIBITION

Dependence of Activity Upon Need and Desire.—The two great propelling forces of all activity are expressed in the words, need and desire. We need or desire those things which seem to us at the time to be necessary, either to serve us usefully and conveniently or to increase our enjoyment in life. And in either case our response in the purchase of an article depends upon how we instinctively or impulsively feel, or, upon the conclusions drawn as a result of the processes of reasoning which have been called into play.

Influence of Heredity upon Desire.—Desire, then, as related to our instincts and impulses, is destined to be aroused if the article or proposition is such as to satisfy the pleasures which these hereditary traits elicit. The mere reading about the hunting trips of our ex-president, Theodore Roosevelt, as he plunged into the African forest, gives to him a glory immeasurable, largely because he has succeeded in calling into twentieth century consideration a tendency which the race has inherited. King Alfred and Darius are heroes in our mind-pictures of history simply because perilous bravery has been a part of our evolutionary development.

Influence of Environment.—But heredity is not the only source of our desires. The environment into which we have been born reacts upon us in a manner which helps to mould each career differently. For instance, the life of the boy reared in a time when horses were the vogue would have a love for horses not fully appreciated by the boy who has come to count the speed of an automobile with beautiful lines as of all importance. Thus, the people of one generation differ somewhat from the succeeding one, simply because the desires created by the environment give to each a different theory and emphasis in values. The country boy differs from the city boy not because his instincts are different, but because desire has been modified by different environmental factors.

Education as a Modifier of Environment.—Education is a factor of environment which also modifies our desires. For instance, many boys have a passion for " Nick Carter " stories during certain periods of their youth. But a vigilant school system will readily transform this desire into a wholesome interpretation of adventure. Our moving picture shows are continually being checked up by the critics because of a pandering to this phase of life. In so far as this instinct is recognized and yet educated into a proper recognition of its ethical relations to life, this desire should be encouraged. But the critic has not yet thoroughly outlined an. educational program which directs all tendency toward wholesome desire. The Boy Scout movement shows the force of education at work in an attempt to satisfy legitimately our desires, and at the same time to adapt these impulses to a twentieth century environment. The boys of the " Scout Movement," in regard to their desires, will greatly differ throughout their entire life from those who do not take advantage of this movement. And from the advertisers' viewpoint, there is need for a constant analysis of the classes of people to whom we are to appeal with respect to the education which has either created new desires or modified recognized instincts, impulses, or habits.

Regard Must Be Had for Individual Peculiarities.—Again, each of us has individual peculiarities which must be taken into consideration. While I might be fascinated with the idea of a country home up in the mountains for the summer time, another would desire constant travel in foreign parts. To the advertiser this means that because a single individual has already a desire or natural inclination for a certain thing, there are thousands of others who have the same desire, and in an extended advertising campaign this particular inclination should find, at some time, definite recognition in an appropriate advertisement.

Two Classes to Whom an Appeal is Made.—Thus heredity, environment, education and individual peculiarities enter into one's life experiences and create a composite picture of desire. It is the work of the advertiser to analyse the relationship existing between the goods he has to offer and the needs or desires of the people to whom he wishes to sell. Where there is no desire, advertising copy must necessarily differ from that where desire has already been created. Consequently, our appeal is to be made to two classes; namely, to those who possess desire, and secondly, to those in whom desire or need has not yet been felt.

Fig. 63 is an advertisement which illustrates these two points. There are innumerable people at the present time who do not desire a player piano. Many people think that a mechanical instrument cannot take the place of human talent. Howsoever erroneous this idea may be, nevertheless this is the opinion of innumerable people in relation to their purchase of a player piano. Consequently these people in glancing at the Apollo advertisement are merely attracted toward the artistic interpretation of the player piano. Parental instinct, as well as the beauty or even the sex instinct, is appealed to. When I begin to read the advertisement, however, I find that the writer argues regarding the cost of the instrument, while the mechanism of the instrument is also emphasized; but if I do not already have desire for an Apollo player piano, another kind of argument is necessary. On the other hand, those who are fully persuaded that a player piano would prove quite as effective as the ordinary instrument, are in the field of purchase. Thus, the form of copy in connection with the existing desire is to be modified accordingly as I wish to present my argument either to those who do not care for the piano player, or to those who are already convinced that it is a good thing. Suppose that a prospective buyer has only desire,— then the advertisement must be of such a nature as to get him to act upon this desire. At this moment I desire a new watch but for several months I have been putting off the purchase. No direct appeal has ever been presented. The avenue is paved for an immediate response if the idea of an attractive watch at a price which is not exorbitant is presented in some pleasing, argumentative form. There is the possibility that chance alone will decide just what move will be made in the purchase of this watch. It may be in response to an excellently printed advertisement, or to a display in some window. There being no absolute need for the article under consideration, it is merely the lack of a proper stimulus which keeps me from an act of pur-

FIG. 63.—The English appeal takes for granted that desire exists. The illustration tends to arouse desire.

chase. Thus, there are many groups of people in whom exists a desire for things, but the purchase of which is needlessly or carelessly postponed. It remains with the successful advertiser to bring these individuals and goods into a purchase relationship.

Advertiser's Function in the Creation of Desire.—It is the work of an advertiser to force people, first, into a recognition of goods, and then to arouse or reinforce desire by some happy phrase or eloquent command. This will possibly necessitate a campaign of advertising which will be different in nature according to the class of appeal. To give an example which is still in existence, there are women who would refuse the help of a washing machine. There is no desire for the use of such an article because real need is not felt. And this was the attitude of the mass of people when washing machines were first put on the market. The method of appeal to this class of people must be entirely different from that which is to reach the party who already owns one, likes it, and needs another. Referring to the second class, the right kind of an advertisement will appeal so as to increase desire, if improvements which further save energy and time are insisted upon. A motor machine is much more desirable than a hand machine. The advertiser's function is to make the people want it.

Necessity of Emphasizing Idea of Need.—In managing an advertising campaign it is evident that, in so far as we find new business necessary in the sense that innumerable individuals are not using our article, it is more sensible to dwell upon the idea of need. People should constantly be reminded of the fact that by non-recognition of your advertisement in the form of a purchase, they are missing somewhat of the good things, conveniences, or protections of life. The possible consumer must be reminded of a persistent need. Growth implies that constantly greater and greater numbers of people are brought to feel the need of your particular article or proposition. Those who have already tried your goods and found them satisfactory will perhaps purchase again. Those who desire and have not been compelled to buy constitute another class, and copy should occasionally be directed accordingly. The interest aroused in your campaign, however, should be other than that of mere

17

interest in the article itself; it should also appeal to the arousing of self-interest on the part of the individual.   There is a
difference between these two.   I am quite interested in the development of flying machines at the present time, and yet
have not had my self-interest so aroused as to bring a machine
into actual possession.   Conditions of life and education are
not such as to cause me to attach that particular apparatus
to the interests of my life.   Again, I am interested in the
beauty of a given home in a desirable section of a city.   On the
other hand, my self-interest is not involved, yet it is conceivable
that such an attitude of mind might stimulate me into a real
estate speculation.

Steps Leading from Non-desire to Purchase.—To summarize, then, the following steps must be considered as constitut-
ing rungs of the ladder leading from non-desire to purchase: (1)
non-desire; (2) attention; (3)interest; (4) self-interest (need or
desire); (5) action; (6) possession.

Adjustment of Desire to Monetary Conditions.—Desire
must be considered in its relation to the monetary conditions of
given groups of people.   There are many kinds of goods which
people already desire, but it is a matter of money which delays
the purchase.   There are thousands of those who would purchase
a pianola immediately if they were to follow their desires.   However, it is only when advertising arouses a self-interest in the
article by showing that it can come into their possession by easy
payments, that a purchase in many instances is likely to be made.
Thus, the copy written in connection with desire should be modified accordingly as it is possible to get people sincerely to adjust
their money relations.

Habit in Its Relation to Desire.—Habit, once acquired by
an individual or a group of individuals, is most difficult to break·
away from even occasionally, or to change.   Youth, however, is
decidedly plastic in its tendency to accept the things of its
environment.   When, then, the advertiser has succeeded in getting people into a single act of purchase, he has accomplished
much in the maintenance of persistent sales, especially if that
article is limited in competition and has real merit.   One of
the arguments which many young men have to overcome in sell·

ing goods is this: " Why should I change if my present selling relations with the firm are satisfactory and likewise the goods meet every requirement ? " This is habit operating, and habit is a factor which every advertiser must consider in connection with his competitors. To break up the habits of an individual by so-called " knocking a competitor " is one of the methods which is being condemned today. Thus, if I have an especially fine article or proposition and realize that my competitor's is not so good, it takes considerable tact and tremendous energy at times to overcome these habits, especially when they are dominated by a feeling of disregard for change, rather than reason. Thus habit, for many groups of people, seems to be the master of their actions. So habit and its relation to selling should be understood and reckoned with in attempting the sale even of standardized goods. In a competitive realm it is constantly necessary to try to win the sentiment of people away from that which is already positively satisfactory to them. When goods or articles have become worn out or ragged, there is a tendency to replace them. Unless your advertisement, in competition with earlier desires and habits, has within it that element which suggests greater satisfaction, then you are not to be placed in the class of a progressive advertiser. Habit is constantly at work modifying all purchases, and whatever has once tended to please human beings, this has found a place which insists upon constant recognition until a new desire of greater satisfaction is suggested in relation to another article.

Psychology of Habit.—Psychology says that the brain possesses plasticity which makes itself susceptible to every sense impression. There is, moreover, a tendency on the part of the brain to act in the same manner whenever a similar stimulus has been presented. A part of the advertiser's work is to step in and destroy our old habits, especially if his proposition is known to be superior. " Habit is simply a pathway of discharge formed in the brain by which certain incoming currents ever after tend to escape."

Habit differs from instinct in that it applies to those actions of the individual which have become peculiar to his life. It may be possible to appeal to an instinct to create a habit. For instance, a man wishes to sell soap and by way of illustration or argument pictures a baby in a bathtub, frolicking in glee as he lets the foamy soap slip through his fingers. The parental instinct has been aroused. The present need for soap is felt and the tendency is to buy. If, after purchase, the soap is found satisfactory, the chances are that I shall again purchase. Here an instinct has responded to an advertisement, the present need of which has resulted in the purchase of the soap, and, as a result, a habit for its repurchase has been started. If it were not for habit, our lives would daily be taken up with the conscious doing of such trivial things that it would be impossible for us to perform any of the bigger things of life. Dr. Maudsley says: " If an act becomes no easier after being done several times, no progress can be made in development." It is in connection with this theory that the retailer should act when he is engaged in selling goods. National advertising has made it possible for people to know what they wish to purchase before entering a store. When the retailer hands these goods over the counter at the request of the purchaser he is a mere order taker. True selling would imply that he try to spend the time thus saved by national advertising in the creation of new desires. Thus it is that salesmanship often becomes directly related to advertising. The most ordinary store in the poorest part of the city commands peculiar attention if its windows have a display of goods, the desire for which has already been expressed by multitudes in sales, evidenced by continuous national advertising. Because people are such inconsistent slaves of the monarch Habit is the reason why persistent advertising is often destined to success. Because many people who have once purchased goods and tend not to be persuaded or reasoned into the purchase of a competing brand is the very reason why advertising should have within it that quality which attempts to get people to act not only once and now, but also to get them to act persistently. The idea of a bargain-sale in connection with a department store is truly creative in that people buy those things which under ordinary circumstances, apart from the spirit " something for nothing," they would never be tempted to purchase. Their hoarding instinct compels them to store away what is a bargain to-day for future use. As an instance, books might be purchased at a sale for one's own benefit and afterwards be given away as presents when occasion demands; whereas, if the books had not been possessed and the present desire not exceedingly urgent, there might have been a tendency not to respond. Thus, that which tends to break up habits will be found in the passing of time not to represent a waste, but rather the creation of desire passing into new habits. It is this ability to adjust one's self to these newer methods of living and standards of comfort which make the world richer in its possession of things.

Function of the Advertiser.—The wise advertiser is he who constantly studies the habits of the mass or the particular class to which he wishes to appeal. There are habits universal and, again, habits local in nature. Christmas, Easter and the separate seasons are days which bring all people into states of mind susceptible to appeals based solely on habit. For instance, when a drug store emphasizes the Hallowe'en season and fills its windows with favors and novelties appropriate for artistic parties, they are employing the superstitious side of our nature and are insisting upon a response which is commercially desirable. However, we must remember that it is the complex feeling for the weird, unusual and artistic which urges us on into completely interpreting the feelings which have been aroused.

Consideration Should Be Given to Local Desires and Habits. —As intimated, all desires which are local should always be regarded. For instance, the Southerner does not consider Christmas worth while without fire crackers. The North can hardly sympathize with this procedure, it only looks and wonders. Again, in Philadelphia and Boston there are appeals which can be made to patriotism never possible in Chicago or Kansas City. In considering the media of a given locality, the advertiser is compelled to determine which paper, politically, the people are buying. Further, he should know whether the evening or morning paper is preferable in that particular community in which he wishes to appeal to a particular class.

The habits of the people in different localities vary, and yet each locality is susceptible to response if the right kind of a

stimulus is presented. This situation necessitates constant analysis on the part of the advertiser. People are to be gotten out
of their ruts. On the other hand, the advertiser should constantly guard himself lest he likewise be caught in the network
of habit involving only a moderate success. His nature must
ever be at war against the bend of habit which fails to recognize
a constantly changing appeal.

Inhibition.—Up to this point we have been considering the
kinds of appeal which create habit without suggesting those which
are likely to retard and to check desire. What constitutes inhibition or the checking of our desires and habits? Whenever one
idea tends to act upon another idea so as to check action about to
take place, we have what is known as inhibition. For instance,
upon reading an advertisement regarding tar roofs I am persuaded that they will meet my present needs, but suddenly I
remember being compelled to sleep under one in summer, and
the heat, which had been retained, was intolerable. As a result
of this idea, I tend to stop action in my purchase of tar roofing.
In advertising, one must be exceedingly careful not to suggest
such thoughts as will prove inhibitory. To suggest qualities of
a competitor is immediately dividing attention so that no single
idea is left for action. In the creation of desire make the advertising idea stand out with qualities that are each worthy of
immediate acceptation. If the reader's own knowledge or previous experience is such as to inhibit action, this fact can often
be overcome by means of argumentation. Do not allow your
own manner of expression to be of such a nature as to suggest
inhibitory ideas. The following outline suggests features which,
not properly regarded, introduce inhibitory ideas in advertisements:

The general appearance of the advertisements with regard
to focal point, eye movement and arrangement might be such as
to displease, and, as a result, desire is not formulated.

The thought expressed might be such as to insult our moral,
religious, political notions, or our sense for the fitness of things.
If this attitude of mind has been aroused, desire is partly inhibited.

Again, the manner of stating a thing might be clumsy or incoherent, and natural laziness is so great that whatever desire has been aroused is not strong enough to obtain action. This is often due to a lack of knowledge, clearness, definiteness, or force on the part of the advertiser in writing his copy.

Lastly, the media in which the advertisement appears might have a bad rating in the mind of the reader and, although desire has been created, suspicion will tend to check action.

To summarize, the creation of desire is thus the reason for the existence of advertisements. The advertiser must consequently remember that to create desire is his first work; to stimulate this desire into an act of purchase is his second step; and, the possible destruction, elimination or modification by fair means of his competitor's habits of purchase, is his third step. Upon the delivery of good merchandise, habit begins its operation and opens up possibilities for the continuation of happy business relations, but there is ever the possibility of a competitor stepping in to destroy old habits.

QUESTIONS

1. Name the four factors influencing desire?
2. The advertiser's appeal must be made to what two general classes? Give the three requisites every progressive advertiser must remember.
3. Starting with non-desire, give the evolutionary stages to possession.
4. Habit, to which there is an innate tendency, is instructive. Mention several.
5. What are some inhibitory factors to guard against in advertising?
6. Mention one great achievement of national advertising. Analyse from the standpoint of desire.

PROBLEMS

1. Find an advertisement in which the advertiser has created a desire, but not self-interest. Reconstruct same to bring in this element.
2. After desire has been aroused, and, purchase insures habit, formulate a brief advertising campaign to "put your goods over."
3. Locate advertisements of a firm's article, respecting locality differences and characterize each.
4. How should the following quotation influence a wise advertiser: "Habit is the enormous fly-wheel of society; its most precious conservative agent"?
5. Illustrate an instance where you believe an inhibitive factor to have entered advertising.
6. Construct an advertisement appealing to the two great propelling forces of activity.

COLLATERAL READINGS

BRIEFER COURSE IN PSYCHOLOGY, WM. JAMES, Chapter x.

CHAPTER XIX

GETTING THE WILL OF THE CROWD

Advertiser's Relation to the Crowd.—Advertising in its last analysis is successful accordingly as it gets a response from crowds. Just as the individual can be depended upon to act in connection with life's processes in a definite manner when the proper stimulus is presented, as when a drowning man clutches the life preserver which has been tossed to him, so the mass tends to respond definitely when the right kind of stimulus has been presented. In other words, there is a psychology of the mass when stimulated to an act of purchase which contains factors often not essential when dealing with the individual. The advertiser differs from the salesman in that he impersonally expresses himself thru a medium in his attempt to get people to purchase, while the salesman deals directly with the individuals, such that the personal factor tends to determine action. And just as the salesman needs to possess a certain personality as he comes in a selling touch with others, so the advertiser must, in his attempt to get the will of humanity, analyse the medium thru which he works. In other words, the medium must possess those factors which, in their unity, strike the fancy of a crowd in such a way as to suggest responsiveness. That there is a difference between the successful advertiser's point of view and the salesman's has been pointed out by St. Elmo Lewis, formerly of the Burroughs Adding Machine Company, where his advertising department permitted the salesmen of the concern to draw up a certain amount of copy for the Saturday Evening Post. He declares that the returns were quite limited as compared with the responses of those advertisements written by the typical advertiser. This carries out the general theory advanced by many, that the advertising man, in his attitude toward selling, differs considerably from the attitude assumed by the salesman. The advertiser must relate himself to the movement of the masses. The salesman relates himself to immediate individual response. Consequently, the first problem of every advertiser is to understand the psy-

264

chology of the mass. His second effort is to find out whether
or not his article has within it the possibilities of satisfying legitimate desire to the extent of producing profit for his concern.
His third effort is to study the mind of the mass and to discover
therein principles of mental reaction such that he can present his
article and at the same time hope to receive a quick response.

Crowd Psychology.—G. Stanley Lee, in his most suggestive
book entitled "Crowds," has aptly expressed this idea in the
following:

" Every idea we have is run into a constitution. We cannot
think without a chairman. Our whims have secretaries; our
fads have by-laws. Literature is a club. Philosophy is a society. Our reforms are mass meetings. Our culture is a summer
school. We cannot mourn our mighty dead without Carnegie
Hall and forty vice-presidents. We remember our poets with
trustees, and the immortality of a genius is watched by a standing
committee. Charity in an association. Theology is a set of
resolutions. Religion is an endeavor to be numerous and com-
municative. We awe the impenitent with crowds, convert the
world with boards, and save the lost with delegates; and how
Jesus of Nazareth could have done so great a work without being
on a committee is beyond our ken. What Socrates and Solomon
would have come to if they had only had the advantage of con-
ventions it would be hard to say; but in these days, when the
excursion train is applied to wisdom; when, having little enough,
we try to make it more by pulling it about; when secretaries urge
us, treasurers dun us, programs unfold out of every mail—where
is the man who, guileless-eyed, can look in his brother's face; can
declare upon his honor that he has never been a delegate, never
belonged to anything, never been nominated, elected, imposed on,
in his life? . . .

" What this means with regard to the typical modern man
is, not that he does not think, but that it takes ten thousand men
to make him think. He has a crowd soul, a crowd creed. Charged
with convictions, galvanized from one convention to another, he
contrives to live, and with a sense of multitude, applause, and
cheers he warms his thoughts. When they have been warmed

enough he exhorts, dictates, goes hither and thither on the crutch of the crowd, and places his crutch on the world, and pries on it, if perchance it may be stirred to something."

Crowds Manifest Different Qualities of Action.—*Unconscious Response.*—In studying the particular qualities possessed by the crowd with respect to the different kinds of action, the following should be considered: first, unconscious response; second, impulsive action; third, deliberate action.

To get people to act unconsciously is one of the great purposes of advertising. It is this particular quality injected into any advertising campaign which shows the faith element of the advertiser, and constitutes a factor which can never be positively determined. It is the factor in any campaign which is reckoning on the future, and it is a factor which is often left out of consideration by the narrow-minded business man. Advertising, in relation to the crowd, then, in its largest sense, is building up that kind of attitude on the part of the masses which easily paves the way for a ready response in the purchase of goods. For instance, as is often the case, your grocer does not happen to have in stock the particular kind of goods for which you have asked, and goods of another brand have been sent to you. Although you had not asked for them, they were received without a word of complaint. Why? Partly because their name had become so familiar that it was not a stranger to you, and also because your dealer, in whom you had always had a great confidence, had recommended them to you by an act of this kind. The combination of these circumstances compelled acceptance on your part without hesitation. Now, if the goods in large measure fulfilled any kind of expectancy that you had previously had, your experienced familiarity, thru general advertising, would at least start competition, not only with the article with which you had become thoroughly familiar, but with the same article of other manufacturers. Constantly advertising your particular goods, in a manner which suggests constructive judgments on the part of readers, is destined in the long run favorably to encourage sales. We must remember that people as a mass are not scanning the papers with a view of memorizing the different advertisements for possible future sales. However, when a particular kind of advertisement has been repeatedly forced upon the attention, the very nature of our mind compels its final recognition, either unconsciously or consciously. As we have intimated in our definition of advertising, it is natural for people to respond to educational interpretations of life's experiences. When the advertiser stands before the masses to teach them regarding that which, in the natural process of development, will inevitably bring to them greater convenience, happiness, or an improved environment, there is the possibility of some attention. The economic processes of life will insist that the mass be allowed to enjoy that which they greatly desire. Advertising, then, in its broadest influence in dealing with the masses relates itself to every process of business activity. The salesman, the show window, the retailer, the wholesaler, —each has a judgment in connection with the selling problem modified in some form or other by the influence of advertising.

Impulsive Action.—The storekeeper who has his goods displayed so as constantly to remind the purchaser of these articles, has aided the building up of impulsive tendencies on the part of his customer to purchase those particular goods. It is related that a certain man entered an auction sale hall and immediately began bidding upon what he thought was a Waterman fountain pen. He purchased it for 35 cents. When he received the pen, however, and saw its real name, " Waterouse," his disappointment passed into that of chagrin. The auctioneer, either thru defective speech, if we are to give him every benefit of the doubt, or by means of a slightly deficient trickiness of pronunciation, had created a wrong impression. And although that person had never used a Waterman pen, what was it that made bidding upon this particular pen irresistible? It was no other than the advertising knowledge of a Waterman pen. A pen of an unfamiliar name would not so readily have suggested an impulsive bid.

Deliberate Action.—The third type of action on the part of people is characterized by deliberation. It might be analyzed as follows: first, the individual about to purchase has two or more articles in mind; second, he possesses intelligence enough to make the choice; third, he has the freedom to act in that purchase. Now, if advertising in its largest sense has created a vogue such that his desire has become that of self-interest, deliberation implies that he immediately ask the question: Which of these several articles is most desirable? A single advertisement may arouse desire for a life insurance policy, but it is only when two or more have been considered and the choice made that this act might be characterized as deliberate. With only one object to choose from, the idea of freedom is eliminated; it is the mere necessity of circumstances, possibly based on impulse or instinct, that considers the sale. Moreover, it is this weighing and considering which make what we might term voluntary advertising necessary. Consequently, when a new article is competing with others, in the sense that a vogue for that article has already been created, it becomes necessary that your specific article be impressed upon the mind of the mass as being more desirable or, at least, just as valuable, as the other. This kind of advertising must properly interpret the article to people in terms of reason and persuasion. That advertisement which adheres most rigidly to these processes should meet with a greater response, provided reason is proven to be the basis of comparison. So far as the mass is concerned, deliberate action generally relates itself to such articles as are of high cost and the purchase of which takes place only once or twice within a lifetime; for instance, the purchase of an automobile, a life insurance policy, a home, a piano, bath room furnishings, expensive rugs, clocks, etc. In other words, when a large expenditure is likely to be involved in the transaction, our economic sense tends to check impulsive or instinctive action. While the single advertisement might have aroused desire for a specific article, when reason is working in the mind of the mass, that article will be purchased which has an intellectual appeal in it and which demonstrates the superiority of itself over another.

Thus the mind of the mass in connection with any article or proposition, from the advertiser's point of view, is often to give forth an unconscious response to a proposition or a so-called impulsive purchase. The copy should be so written as to meet the demands of that group which he is deliberately considering.

Temperament of Class Modifies Means of Approach.—But we cannot accurately calculate the response of humanity in mathematical terms. We have come to realize that humanity is not always dominated by a purely intellectual interpretation of things. On the other hand, humanity demands a semblance of logic. It is the ability to meet these uncertain issues and yet obtain results, which fascinates the successful advertiser. He begins, then, to recognize that there are different types of humanity. Moreover, each type needs an analysis with respect to its peculiar tendency of response. For instance, all of humanity does not tend to respond to the same kind of intellectual appeal. There are those minds which are captivated with a simple statement of fact, scientific in nature. Another type is lured on by a figurative interpretation involving reason. There is a class which wishes feeling alone to be emphasized. The psychologist has outlined four classes of people which are suggested as an aid in an analysis of any group of people. If a particular article is adapted to a specific group, that group must possess mind tendencies of appreciation which demand a specific form of approach. Consequently what we have to say regarding an article or proposition should be partly modified by a realization of the temperament of the class approached. Let us consider each of the four temperaments.

Kinds of Temperament.—*Sanguine Temperament.*—First there is the sanguine temperament, which is impulsive and impressionalistic in its response to a stimulus. If this class is to be won it must be made to feel the significance of the usefulness of a thing at the present moment. Full of feeling and hopefulness themselves, they respond quickly to the suggestions of the present, but they likewise proceed to forget their past experiences. Not only are they susceptible to this impressionistic copy, but they are susceptible to the command of the present moment, provided the proposition is emphasized as one which is timely in nature and which has immediate demand. For instance, if a railroad company wishes to increase its railway transportation business, it is likely to picture one of the resorts in Maine as highly desirable. The copy written for this class should tend to suggest sending immediately for a descriptive booklet. However, Fig. 64, the Big Ben advertisement, is in its entire

*If you'd rise early, just say when
And leave your call with him, Big Ben*

DOWN in our hearts we're punctual men but we can't help over-sleeping now and then any more than we can help talking in our sleep.

For man is only partly conscious when he first opens his eyes after a heavy sleep.—He needs help to get wide awake at once. He'd get up on time if he only realized the time.

Big Ben makes him realize it.—You can try for yourself. Go to sleep and sleep your best. Forget the rising hour. He'll call you on the dot at any time you say.

And if you roll over and try just one more nap, he'll remind you firmly that it is breakfast time and keep on calling until you're wide awake.

If you sleep heavily—and you very likely do, if you are a heavy worker—see Big Ben at your jeweler to-morrow. His price is $2.50 anywhere. He's sold by 16,000 watchmakers, but if you cannot find him at yours, a money order sent to *Westclox, La Salle, Illinois,* will bring him to you express charges prepaid.

$2.50
Sold by Jewelers. Three Dollars in Canada.

Fig. 64.—Appealing to the sanguine class of humanity. The object of the advertisement is to make one feel "at the present moment" that this clock is the only one worth possessing. Contrast with Fig. 69.

spirit such as to make one feel " at the present moment " that this clock is the only one worth having. We enter immediately into

Take Your Vacation at our Expense

It matters little where you wish to spend your vacation—at the seashore, in the mountains, camping, or in Europe—let us pay the bill.

Our Vacation Money Plan is quick in action and sure in results. It calls for your spare time or your whole time, just as you prefer. It can be successfully applied by any man or woman, young or old. No previous experience is necessary; no cash investment is needed. You begin to make money right at the start.

We will pay you a liberal Salary and Commission to look after our business interests in your community. The work is interesting, dignified and healthful.

Simply sign the coupon, tear it off and mail it to us. The sooner you sign and send, the more you will have to spend.

Sign the coupon *now* for a pocketful of vacation money.

Good Housekeeping Magazine

119 West 40th Street   New York City

FIG. 65.—Likewise appealing to the sanguine class of humanity. The object of the advertisement is to stimulate immediate action.

271

the spirit of Big Ben and are tempted, if we do not possess one, at least to consider its purchase. This advertisement should, from the sanguine viewpoint, have within it a sentence or two which relates itself even more directly than it does to the immediate present.

Fig. 65 is an appeal to the present in a manner which compels immediate action. This advertisement would be lost to many readers were not action to the reader suggested. It can readily enough be seen that a positive command must characterize the spirit of a so-called timely advertisement. The sanguine type should then have such appeals as suggest immediate action. It will be observed that these people are subject to all kinds of suggestions from the outside world. They are almost entirely objective in their attitude toward life. Hence they tend to be moved into feeling through an outward immediate stimulus. Sentiment is the factor which tends to create an impulsive response on the part of this group.

Melancholy Temperament.—The second type of humanity which needs consideration is that known as the melancholy class. These people are introspective in their attitude toward life, rather than objective. Opportunity for the betterment of self, and likewise an appeal to the possibility of being more valuable to the world, are characteristics of these people. " I will," " I can," " I ought " are governing factors in their decision of what they desire. Now it must be borne in mind that melancholic does not mean pessimistic, but rather a type of mind which seriously considers the individual in his ethical relations to human experience. These are likely to be governed more by ideality than intense practicability.

Fig. 66 is an advertisement gotten out by the Sheldon School, and is typical of the spirit which is appreciated by those who are conscientious with respect to their personal development. Here the average young man is pictured as in a most critical situation. A suggestion that help is to be obtained is emphasized within the text which accompanies the illustration. Those who have a tendency toward self-improvement, who wish to rise in the concern of which they are a part, or those who have a feeling of

You Must Go Up or Down!

That fact admits of no argument. If to-day you are not progressing—going toward greater things, bigger salary, greater success —you are in the same peril as a man who clings desperately to a rope suspended in mid air. You can't hold *the same grip*. You have got to assert the power within you and pull yourself upward, or slip down into the class of "Nobodies."

But you *have* the power to go up. It is within you but you must be shown how to discover it — to develop it and make it bring you more money—increases without limitation.

Ask Sheldon How

Nearly 60,000 men, in all walks of life, who have found their grip slipping have discovered the power and means of success with the aid of the Sheldon Courses in Salesmanship and Business Building. You can do the same—*NOW*.

In your spare moments you can master the fundamentals of the science that compels men to recognize your real value. You can system-atize and coordinate your mental powers, the efficiency of which determines your earning ca-pacity. If you are an employer, you can increase your profits by Sheldon's courses.

Send for Sheldon Book—FREE!

The attached coupon or a letter or postal card will bring you a copy of the *Sheldon Book* free of all expense. The contents will be a revelation to you. Don't fail to write. Start *climbing upward* today.

The Sheldon School

Gunther Bldg., Chicago, Ill.

The Sheldon School,
413 Gunther Bldg., Chicago, Ill.

Please send me free copy of the Sheldon Book and full information regarding the Sheldon course.

Name ....

Street ....

City .... State ....

Fig 66.—Appealing to the melancholy class of humanity. The object of the advertise-ment is to stimulate personal development.

constant failure, or who underestimate their value to the community,—these are the people appealed to. The International Correspondence School in its advertising appeals largely to this particular temperament.

Choleric Temperament.—The third type of mind as manifested in certain classes of people is that known as the choleric temperament. If the given group can be characterized as possessing a certain spirit, this group forcibly expresses itself in the motto " I want what I want when I want it." This is the temperament of almost impulsive action and is essentially the characteristic will of the business man. This type of man is prompt, intense, impetuous and selfish. He tends to lack sympathy with others in his present individualistic longing for conquest. In contrast with the melancholic man, he lives in the present and is moved to action by outward events. The choleric individual differs from the sanguine in that pure and often selfish reason tends to govern him in his choice of things. Sentiment is always the thing to be kept in the background and is to be employed only as he has been successful in the carrying out of some transaction. Intensity of purpose is a marked characteristic which results in a life not as broad as it might be. This man is interested in things which bring personal ease and comfort.

Anything which overcomes friction and annoyances, either in his home or in business, is welcome. He is in life for the money

Saves

Time—Ready cooked—instantly available for preparing many dishes.

Trouble—No inconvenience— no soaking—no picking—no boiling—

Money—Nothing but fish—no bones—no waste—no spoilage—

B. & M. Fish Flakes are caught in the deep cold sea waters—cleaned—cooked—slightly salted—placed in parchment lined containers—Not a speck of preservative used.

Burnham & Morrill
Fish Flakes

FIG. 67.—Appealing to the choleric class of humanity. Our business men are usually of this type.

that can be gotten out of it, and with his money he awaits a reasonable appeal for speculation and investment, all of which tend to glorify his own personal achievements. Fig. 67, the Burnham & Morrill advertisement, is an appeal to this idea, while Fig. 68 likewise offers the banishment of worry for this particular class.

Phlegmatic Temperament.—The fourth type is that known as the phlegmatic temperament. These people are so slow as to

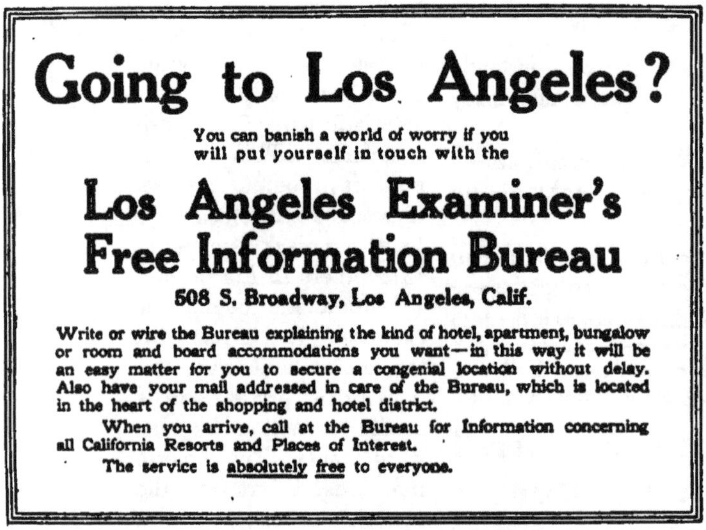

FIG. 68.—Likewise appealing to the choleric class.

lack practical effectiveness. While they employ reason, their deliberation is so long that a person of another temperament has "bounded and possibly hit the mark." Your advertisements effect them—yes. They see them all, but, you must wait their own time for deliberative action.

Fig. 69 is an excellent advertisement which illustrates the spirit of this particular temperament. While the copy is conservative, descriptive and pleasing, yet there is not within it that factor which tends to cause an immediate response to its appeal. The spirit of this advertisement is the spirit of the common sense, slow working, p h l e g - matic class. It will be noticed in comparing this advertisement with the Big Ben, what a difference there is in the personal feelings which are aroused. Nevertheless, this kind of an advertisement constantly repeated, adjusting itself to our sense of propriety, will make an impression; though it is to be d o u b t e d whether Fig. 69 will ever have the same d r a w i n g force as one which combines this particular interpretation of the phlegmatic t e m p e r a - ment with that of another.

A Precise and Kindly **Counsellor** *in* the ordering *of* your life

The Seth Thomas Bronze Doric measures the fleeting minutes with unwavering fidelity. Its simple design is representative of the attractive Doric type of architecture. Musical Westminster chimes, Westminster and Whittington chimes or a single Cathedral bell announce the hour divisions. The movement boasts the name Seth Thomas—a pledge of honest merit for a hundred years.

Your jeweler will gladly show you the Bronze Doric and other

SETH THOMAS
Clocks

SETH THOMAS CLOCK CO.
15 Maiden Lane, New York City
Established 1813

FIG. 69.—Appealing to the phlegmatic class of humanity. The copy is conservative, descriptive, and pleasing, still it lacks force which stimulates immediate action.

Advertising Appeal Should be Universal.—Now it must be borne in mind that people, generally, are not to be put into one of the above mentioned classes, as you would sort apples for barreling. It cannot be done. Humanity in mass has characteristics of all classes, but there is one temperament toward which each individual tends, and it must likewise be remembered that each article which appears in the field of commerce has within it that quality which appeals more to a certain class of people than another. It remains for the advertiser to recognize the different types and to change his advertisements from time to time, so that as many classes as possible are reached by his varied appeals.

Another factor to consider regarding our appeal to will, thru desire, is, that our desires change from one period of time to another. The natural unfolding of life from year to year, from youth to the responsibilities of a married career are such as to give us a desire for things that were formerly never considered. To meet these increasing experiences, demands that advertisers change their form of copy. Each advertisement must have a vital meaning for some one, and—who this some one is—should be thoroughly understood by the advertiser. If the goods themselves are not what they should be, not up to the advertised standard of the particular class appealed to, failure will be the inevitable outcome. The advertiser must satisfy the desires of the particular classes accordingly as he has aroused their desires.

There is a difference in the responses of men and women to the affairs of life. Temperamentally, and generally speaking, women are the first two classes named. Women are, consequently, led into the choice of things by an appeal to their sentiment or personal experience. If once desire has been aroused, price does not seem to check them in their choice of a thing, and what seems to assist them in completing their ideal is the thing to be gotten.

In advertising in connection with the masses one must be exceedingly careful not to suggest such thoughts as will prove inhibitory. To suggest qualities of a competitor is immediately dividing the attention so that no single idea is left for action. Make your idea so stand out thru specific copy that qualities are pre-eminently worthy of immediate acceptance. If the reader's own knowledge is such as to inhibit action, this fact can be remedied slightly by argumentation, but do not allow your own manner of expression to be of such a nature as immediately to suggest inhibitory influences.

QUESTIONS

1. Scientifically analyse the requisites every advertiser must respect as regards the "Mass." Discuss "Crowd" psychology.
2. What are the three responses to which the advertiser may appeal?
3. When does deliberation check impulsive or instinctive action? Choice implies freedom to differentiate. Question its validity.
4. Discuss the difference in method of appeal between the advertiser and the salesman.
5. State the advantages of the educational quality in advertisements.
6. Name the four distinct types found in society and characterize the temperament of each. To which of these classes do women usually belong?
7. Is there a difference between the melancholic and the pessimistic type of individual?

PROBLEMS

1. In a show window there are constantly advertised the same articles. What type of action-response is this building up? Mention such an incident.
2. Present twelve advertisements which distinctly appeal to each of the temperaments.
3. Construct two advertisements which illustrate the objective and phlegmatic type.
4. Illustrate by advertisements that desires change with age and experience.
5. Find an advertisement in which you feel that there is some inhibitory element.
6. In fulfilling your order the druggist has sent you Colgate's Shaving Powder rather than Mennen's, for which you asked. Discuss the advertising significance.
7, Construct your advertisements selling the same article to each of the four temperaments.
8. Name articles or propositions which seem particularly adaptable to each of the four temperaments.

COLLATERAL READINGS

Æsthetic Education, Chas. DeGarmo, Chapter vii, "Formal Orders of Beauty."

Crowds, G. Stanley Lee, (A most suggestive work for every advertiser).

CHAPTER XX

THE ENGLISH OF ADVERTISERS—ESSENTIAL ELEMENTS

Function of English in Advertising.—The ultimate end of advertising is to obtain the public's buying judgment for an article or proposition. While an illustration without reading matter often carries conviction in creating desire, nevertheless, a large part of the power of advertisements consists in the ideas forced by means of the varied uses of English. The mere fact that a statement appears in print becomes to many an eloquent appeal for truth. This class, however, is comparatively limited, yet it serves to show the force of the printed word. Again, recognizing that advertising is a force which demands results, it is found that advertisers may be twofold in classification: one class whose writers have eloquent power of expression, definition and description, but who fail to get returns; while the other group is composed of those who compel attention and incite action on the part of the reader. It is the man of action, one who can get the maximum of returns with minimum amount of effort, who is being sought after by the business world. The ideal advertiser, then, must have the ability, through his written word, to make things happen as certainly as though specific orders had been sent into the firm by its salesmen.

The Fundamental Qualities of a Progressive Advertiser.— The fundamental qualities of a progressive, successful advertiser, including the written English essentials, then, are personal sincerity and adaptability, belief in one's house and proposition, and a written style characterized by clearness, force, and precision. If these characteristics are based, in each instance, on the kind of truth which emphasizes the merit of an article or proposition, and which leads the reader to think of this newer thing favorably, it is only a more competent competitor who is to be feared.

The important question for each young advertiser is: How may I become possessor of those qualities which unite to create productive copy? It is an answer to this question which should rivet his attention at the very beginning of an advertising career.

Advertising, analyzed from the consumer's viewpoint, is an art. The advertiser has studied principles in order that they may be put into actual use. Now an artist is largely successful accordingly as he lives in the spirit of his work. " The letter killeth but the spirit maketh alive " is as applicable to the art of advertising as to any other phase of human experience. The advertiser must live in the spirit of the article which he is to present to the public. The details and associated ideas of it should become a part of his mind-fabric. His attitude should be creative in nature, and it should be the thought of giving an original interpretation teeming with the spirit of life that is to be considered primarily, rather than mere technique. Nevertheless, every advertiser should understand the principles involved in the writing of clear, forceful and precise English. The more these principles are instinctively correlated in attempting to interpret an advertising idea, the easier, more natural and effective the advertising copy is likely to be.

Every successful written advertisement is reducible to certain clearly defined principles, and for these to become a factor in creative writing implies an effective appeal.

Each Business has Its Own Peculiar Vocabulary.—An examination of a large number of advertisements relative to the sale of different automobiles shows that the choice of words used by each tends to be similar. This is true when considering the vocabulary of a given article as a whole. Each particular business, however, has it peculiar vocabulary. In connection with a given article there are also certain expressions peculiar to that trade. It is the duty of the advertiser to study each possible expression in the description or explanation of the goods to be sold. When one has gotten his spirit in harmony with the article to be sold, then the discriminated expression must come. When he finds it, he is conscious of its appropriateness and he tends to like it; and when he tells others, they, too, will fancy it. When an advertiser is really original, his choice of words in the description of a thing is strong and different in contrast to one who lacks creativeness. Moreover, it is not only choice of words which is important, but the particular viewpoint selected for the public's approval. Thus to know what constitutes the best talking point;

how to change that viewpoint at the psychological moment,—this calls into play the critical faculty; and it is this checking up of the advertiser's own efforts which is destined to keep his copy sane and unique in appeal.

Value of "Catchy" Words and Phrases.—A word which catches the imagination of people at a glance is the one sought after for popular advertising. "Uneeda," "B. V. D.," "Educator," "Goody!" "Presto!" are typical examples of words which catch the fancy only to lure the reader into a further perusal of the text. Of course the kind of type as well as the punctuation has considerable to do in re-emphasizing the significant word.

Words, however, which within themselves are powerful in their grasp upon the imagination are comparatively rare. On the other hand, the same effect upon the mind can be obtained by using phrases or clauses. To find one which can be read with effectiveness at the psychological moment is undoubtedly the *sesame* which opens many doors for the advertiser. The human mind enjoys thought succinctly expressed. "A case of good judgment" in connection with Edelweis beer; "Hasn't scratched yet" associated with Bon Ami; "Spotless Town" as symbolic of the absolute cleanliness of Sapolio; "He won't be happy till he gets it," related to the famous Pears' Soap advertisement; "Listening to his Master's Voice," in conjunction with a Victor Talking Machine; or "The Machine you will eventually buy," as well as "Eventually"—these and a score of others have become a part of the public mind. So individualistic are they, that any new advertisement which does not compare in happy moods or suggestiveness is at a great disadvantage with these older competitors.

"Corn Puffs," a new food, is now thrusting itself upon the market (Fig. 70). How apropos the statement "Now the Curtain Rises"; the word "Now" is exceedingly expressive; it takes us into the theatre and introduces us to the moment just before the curtain goes up; the very atmosphere is hushed with expectancy. Yes, we have been properly introduced.

Emphasis Secured Thru Punctuation.—As stated before, single words, phrases or clauses teeming with suggestive thought usually occupy prominent places in any given advertisement. Punctuation is often one of the methods by which their importance is emphasized. The right thought in connection with a question mark, quotation marks, underscoring, exclamation point, with variation of type,—these are the specific methods of assisting in " getting the thought over." It will be noted that the absence of punctuation marks also tends, at times, to reëmphasize the text. At the present stage of development the advertiser does not adhere to the conventional ideas of punctuation. Nor does the public expect it. If the advertisement has that which is clever within it, such that the thought predominates in attention, the crowd is loath to go back into a criticism of the form of the message. Consequently if we wish to formulate a conservative judgment relating to the unauthorized punctuation of advertising, as condemned by good literary form, it might be said : *Those advertisements which contain such form variations as become merely secondary in emphasizing thought are to be justified; when, however, such criticisms arise as tend to lead one away from the thought intended, the unusual form is likely to be an inhibiting factor.*

Simplified Spelling.—While discussing the subject of words, it is well to consider the question of spelling. Our language is in a process of spelling change. A few years ago Theodore Roosevelt gave to the printer an authorized revised list for spelling. While many of the older school hesitate to accept the revision, there is a tendency on the part of the business world to adopt it. It is the conviction of many that fifty years from now will have brought the method into operation by a slow absorption process. The advertiser will have his part to perform in this change. Since many scholars and authoritative people have recognized the newer method, there need be no fear on the part of the advertiser that he is transgressing the laws of good English. In every movement there must be the pioneer. Being the leader of a new trail involves the criticism of its followers by the old school. But in the case of reformed spelling, the trail already has enough increasing followers to insure absolute recognition.

Now the Curtain Rises on a New Corn Food

Corn Puffs — with a New Corn Flavor. Flaky, Bubble-like Globules of Corn

The queen of foods is ready for you at most grocery stores today. Drops of corn—airy, floating, fragile pellets, toasted as corn was never toasted before. Made from corn hearts—the sweet hominy part. Made by grinding, cooking, forming into pellets, then exploding those pellets by steam.

It took eight years to perfect this food. And the man who did it is Prof. A. P. Anderson, the man who invented Puffed Wheat and Puffed Rice.

Now, in another grain, he explodes every food granule. He makes digestion easy and complete. And in crisp, flimsy, toasted morsels he gives you the most delightful corn product the world ever knew.

It is not like any toasted corn you know. Most toasting is done by a modest heat. But these pellets of corn, sealed up in huge guns, are toasted before their explosion in an over heat of 550 degrees. And that multiplies the flavor. You'll find it entirely new.

No other such dainty has ever been offered for your morning table. Serve it with sugar and cream—mix it with fruit—float it in bowls of milk. Scatter the pellets over a dish of ice cream. Season them with melted butter for hungry children in the afternoon.

One taste will tell you why the first who enjoyed them called them "The Witching Food."

"The Witching Food"

15c per Package

Don't wait to enjoy it. Most grocers now have it. Telephone for yours, and he'll send it or get it for you.

Expect it to be a revelation in a food delight, and you'll not be disappointed. In all our years of cereal making we have found nothing so good as Corn Puffs. Nor have you.

The Quaker Oats Company

Sole Makers

(961)

FIG. 70.—A unique method of presenting a new article. Note the effective employment of punctuation, words, phrases, and clauses.

Primary Purpose of Punctuation.—Primarily, punctuation is to make easy the reading of any text. In advertising we find tho ordinary usage of punctuation entirely disregarded. The advertiser attempts such combinations as will produce striking effects. Therefore, we may say that the advertiser is permitted to employ marks in any way whatsoever, if by doing so his advertisement gains in attention qualities, clearness or emphasis.

Forceful Language Requires Simple Words.—Too much emphasis cannot be given to the fact that the public's vocabulary is comparatively limited. The simpler and yet more suggestive the use of words, the more likely its hold upon public attention. An advertiser wished to use the word " optimist " in a certain advertisement. A clerk of the establishment said not to do it, that the mass to whom the appeal was to be made would not understand it. A test was made and several customers questioned regarding the meaning of optimist. The majority did not know its meaning. This word prominently printed meant absolutely nothing to them. The incident has its lesson. The class of people to whom an appeal is to be made should be studied most carefully with regard to its vocabulary and general ideas of things. The introduction of a strange word or peculiar figure should be educational enough in influence to explain itself somewhere in the text. People do not like the use of long words. Anglo-Saxon usage seems to carry the most forceful effect. Words should be regarded as to meaning and only those chosen which convey a definite concept.

Words and the Creation of Mind Impressions.—Our use of words, phrases and clauses, either literally or figuratively employed, is to create a definite impression upon the mind. In advertising any article or proposition, scientifically, it is necessary from time to time to change the viewpoint of appeal. The following classification becomes possible. An article may be made to appeal to: (*a*) emotion; (*b*) environment; (*c*) utility. These are realized by means of : feelings or personal sentiment, reason, imagination, or suggestion.

For instance, if I am about to advertise Supreme Auto Oil for the Gulf Refining Company, I may appeal to the emotional phases of its existence by introducing a reference to poor oil, which has often disconcerted the crowd dependent upon " quality " for a happy motor trip.   Or I may call attention to the *speed* which carries the car easily over the mountains.   In this second instance the environment becomes an influencing factor in emphasizing the excellence of Supreme Auto Oil.   Again, I may scientifically and with a well-descriminated vocabulary show the processes of refinement through which the oil passes in order to serve the autoist satisfactorily.   This classification suggests, having once determined upon a talking point, that an appeal may be made either to the sentiment, the reason or the imagination of the public mind.   Sentiment here refers to the personal feelings which control each individual's life, such as love, beauty, sorrow, humor, etc.   Reason regards an accurate scientific statement of the facts properly emphasized.   Imagination carries the reader into a larger realm where he pictures the article in relations often more fanciful than real.   Thus it is given to the advertiser to determine what should be his phase of appeal as well as the particular quality of mind which he wishes to respond to his advertisement.

Classification of Separate Mind Phases.—The following analysis is a classification of the separate mind phases:—

Sentiment	*Reason and Suggestion*	*Imagination*
" Cut-Glass, The Gift that Never Fails a Welcome."	" Simplicity — Accessibility—Economy "	" My Policies "
	" Built for Severe Service."	" Ready—Aim—Fire."
" Don't Overlook the Health, Happiness, Comfort and Convenience to be Secured by the use of the Ajax."	" It is So Easy to Claim Too Much."	" Aunt Phœbe."
		" Special Extra! "
		" Spotless Town."
	" Ask the Man Who Owns One."	" Lest You Forget."
" We therefore take this means of bringing this Special Sale to Your Personal Attention."	" A Rapidly Moving Stock."	" Nature's Royal Road to Health."
	" The Facts Speak for Themselves."	" The National Joy Smoke."
	" Don't Let the Opportunity Go Away."	
" Found faithful after ten years' exposure."	" A .Legal Guarantee with Each Garment."	
" And he hasn't changed a bit. Same Old Penrod, only more so."	" It's the Process."	
	" Peerless—All that the name implies."	

These excellent expressions are typical of those found in every phase of advertising.   There is a decided improvement in any advertisement when the reader is assisted into a large thought-appreciation by the introduction of an appropriate figure of speech. Just as a touch of color in many an advertisement adds effectiveness for the eye; so a figure of speech, consistent in its interpretation of the text, will add to the power of the imagination.

Thought Should Be Easy of Comprehension.—The length of sentences should be seriously considered in all advertisements. Those which are too long cause one to hasten on. Thought should adopt that kind of form which adjusts itself readily, easily, or curiously to the eye or mind of the reader. Thus, form and brevity of the thought expressed become interrelated in their effect on the mind. Notice the following forms combined with brevity:—

Have	A Difference and no Difference
You	A Difference in the Price but no
The	Difference in the Diamond
Elgin	From the Atlantic
	to the
With	Pacific Ocean
The	
49	You Can Buy
Dial?	The Oliver Typewriter
	for 17 cents a Day!

The adroit use of form really suggestive of brevity, and which leads one on, is typical in the following paragraph taken from a Van Camp advertisement. " Now he is chef to the millions— to the millions who have formed a new ideal in baked beans. Countless housewives—when they want a quick, hearty, delicious meal—simply call on this chef to serve it. That is, they heat a can of Van Camp's and it comes to the table with all the fresh oven flavor."

Paragraph Form.—Analysis of the form of advertisements shows each paragraph possessing power either to attract or to detract in attention value. Paragraphs too long in form and which contain complicated sentence structure tend, at first glance, to discourage attention. In such paragraphs it is only an overpowerful thought which can command attention. Many advertisements lose in effectiveness because of too lengthy paragraph structure. If the thought is involved or uninterestingly

combined in a long paragraph form, attention is discouraged
from the very start. Short paragraphs which conform to pleasing and forceful eye adjustment are likely to prove most effective.

Summary.—To summarize, then, the correct and emphatic
choice of words, phrases or clauses; the figurative presentation
of thought; the proper appeal of an article with regard to emotion, environment or utility; the adaptation of thought to impressive arrangement and punctuated emphasis,—these are certain fundamentals in increasing the English efficiency of advertisements.

QUESTIONS

1. What is the general twofold classification of advertisements from the business English standpoint?
2. From this same standpoint designate seven qualifications that aid in increasing English advertising efficiency.
3. Name some current succinct words.
4. What advertisement can you recall suggesting brevity in form and thought?
5. Analyse the following quotations and classify them according to sentiment, reason and suggestion, or imagination:—
   " First thing in the morning since 1830."
   " Why covet your Boss's Job? "
   " Count the cost."
   " Health and Happiness—you owe it to yourself."
   " Let the Gold Dust Twins do your Work."
6. By what means may we appeal to emotion, environment, utility?

PROBLEMS

Here is a graphic representation of the fundamental elements in increasing English advertising efficiency:—

Fundamentals in
increasing
English
Advertising
Efficiency

1. Correct and emphatic choice of $\begin{cases} \text{words.} \\ \text{phrases.} \\ \text{clauses.} \end{cases}$
2. Figurative presentation of thought.
3. Proper appeal of an article with regard to .... $\begin{cases} \text{emotion} \\ \text{environment} \\ \text{utility} \end{cases}$
4. Adaptation of thought to $\begin{cases} \text{impressive arrangement.} \\ \text{punctuation emphasis.} \end{cases}$

1. Create an advertisement which illustrates the three points of view
   utility, environment, emotion.
2. In connection with your advertising campaign create:
   Three possible slogans.
   Five figures of speech.
   Four emphatic sentences irregularly punctuated.
   One succinct word.
3. Find two advertisements, poor in punctuation and with the too intricate
   use of sentences. Suggest improvements.

CHAPTER XXI

THE ENGLISH OF ADVERTISING—STYLE AND DISCOURSE

Quality of Style is Essential.—To quote Spencer: " A reader or listener has, at each moment, but a limited amount of mental power available." And in turn this power must be utilized in three ways. First, in recognizing and interpreting the symbols presented; second, in combining and arranging these symbols in the mind; and finally, only that part left can be utilized in understanding the thought conveyed. Thus, going upon this analysis of our thought processes, we see at once how essential quality of style is in writing advertisements.

Clearness.—Clearness aids the interpreter fully to comprehend the meaning of what is expressed. Precision limits that which is said or written, finitely, or it tells the truth, the whole truth and nothing but the truth. On the other hand, force causes the buyer to *feel* and incites him into action.

It is herein impossible to discuss all the violations of clearness, precision, and force, but there are a few typical errors in connection with these qualities of style which need to be called to our attention.

1. Avoid the ambiguous use of the demonstrative pronoun. Construct your sentences so that there can be no possible doubt as to the antecedent of these pronouns; nor the relative.

Suggested Violations of Clearness (Extracts from actual business letters and advertisements) :—

Original: " In reply would say, the prices you quote on wheat are satisfactory and this causes me to award you the contract."

Improved: In reply would say the prices you quote on wheat are satisfactory, *a fact* which causes me to award you the contract.

Original: " The Insurance Company should have done more to obtain an estimate which was very incomplete."

Improved: The Insurance Company should have done more to obtain an estimate *for the latter* was very incomplete.

2. Clearness often becomes indistinct through the omission of necessary words; over-condensation is to be avoided.

Original: " Your specifications call for a ceiling 32 ft. at its widest point."

Improved: Your specifications call for a ceiling 32 ft. *broad* at its widest point.

3. Place the participle so that there can be no doubt as to what word it modifies.

Original: " Dear Sir: I saw our former business sign when in Boston this morning walking down Huntington Street."

Improved: While in Boston this morning walking down Huntington Street, I saw our former business sign.

4. Keep words and clauses that are grammatically connected reasonably close together.

Original: " We would bring to your attention, in Mr. Conklin's life insurance policy the advisability of incorporating the ' Right of Revocation ' clause."

Improved: In Mr. Conklin's life insurance policy, we would bring to your attention the advisability of incorporating the " Right of Revocation " clause.

Force.—1. Use no more words than are necessary fully to express the idea. Avoid closing sentences with unimportant words, which tend to decrease attention. Likewise, to gain force, where possible, keep up the element of suspense. Remember, however, that suspense should be relieved at the psychological moment.

Suggested violations of force :—

Original: " They are made to fit the shoulders, without binding, and to give perfect comfort and one year's service to all. Your dealer may not have them so send directly to us."

Improved: They are made to fit the shoulders, without binding, and to give perfect comfort. One years' service guaranteed. If your dealer hasn't them, send to us direct.

2. Emphatic words or phrases should come in emphatic places. But, while stress is essential, guard against letting your interest involve you in exaggerations, affectation, the use of large words, and too general terms.

Original: "Accept no other. All imitations are falsely representing us. Avail yourself immediately of this preponderous opportunity."

Improved: Now is your opportunity to get a great bargain. Many imitations misrepresent us. Beware! Accept no other.

3. Although force is often gained by repeating a prominent word, generally avoid repetitions, except in the more difficult forms of exposition. Even here, it is possible so to expand and repeat that, as Phelps says, "the thought is suffocated by the multitude of words employed to give it life."

Original: "In reply to your question concerning the abolition of the Local Utility Committee; it is a question that must be looked at on all sides; it is a question that cannot be thoroughly discussed by mail; it is a question that demands long and serious consideration."

Improved: In reply to your *query* concerning the abolition of the Local Utility Committee; this is a question that must be looked at on all sides; it cannot be thoroughly discussed by mail; moreover, it is one that demands long and serious consideration.

Precision.—1. Words should be used in their proper sense.

Original: "The advertiser should not mete the agencies' initiative."

Improved: The advertiser should not *limit* the agencies' initiative.

2. Distinguish between the auxiliaries " shall " and " will " and " may " and " can." The following table clearly illustrates, in most cases, the usages of " shall " and " will."

Future of Expectation	Future of Determination
I shall go	I will go
Thou wilt go	Thou shalt go
He will go	He shall go
We shall go	We will go
You will go	You shall go
They will go	They shall go

Original: " If we look to see what business houses are striving toward coöperation we will find that those firms of a monopolistic type are not among those interested."

Improved: If we look to see what business houses are striving towards coöperation we *shall* find that those firms of a monopolistic type are not among those interested.

3. " May " suggests permission or possibility; " can," the ability.

Original: " Can we publish an advertisement detrimental to our competitor ? "

Improved: *May* we publish an advertisement detrimental to our competitor ?

4. Often we fail to differentiate between concrete and abstract words and forms of the same word.

Original: " What we need are increased advertisements in specific fields.

Improved: What we need is increased *advertising* in specific fields.

5. Avoid the use of the preposition as a connective.

Original: " We regret to inform you that your credentials are not valid without they are signed by the proper official."

Improved: We regret to inform you that your credentials are not valid *unless* they are signed by the proper official.

Four Types of Discourse.—*Description.*—The aim of description is so " to represent a scene in words that the reader becomes, for the time, an actual observer." In a word then, vividness is the first essential to good description. The general shape of the object described should be made perfectly clear in the mind of the reader or observer. Thus vividness in the creation of the mental picture assists in our immediate understanding of the proposition.   However, it should be remembered that because of their very nature, it is difficult to impress upon us the real form of many objects; as, for instance, the spindle or the gyroscope.   The best way to appeal in this latter instance would be thru the imagination by means of an illustration.   Again, vividness of description may be ascertained by recalling human feelings naturally associated with certain objects.   Finally, we should not confuse description with narration, for although the

A

Continental Motors

Continental speed and power are attained by superior theory, put into better practice.   Continental crankshaft bearings are ground to 95% of bearing surface, smoother than a mirror; pistons are balanced to a pennyweight; connecting rods are lightened to a mathematical niceness; valves are seated-in with a faultless exactness; cylinders are polished to a flawless luster.

"He lives down on the river road, in the shabby, weather-beaten house on the left.   You can't miss it."

Shabby and weather-beaten!   A striking landmark, no doubt.   The porter at the railroad station didn't mean to give the place a black eye, but that is what he did.   Too bad the owner hadn't used

Dutch Boy White Lead

B

Fig. 71.—Description.

one is often dependent upon the other, there is a marked distinction.

Figs. 71 A and B are examples showing the value of description.

Narration.—(Fig. 72).—It should be remembered that narration is to *time* what description is to *space*.   The aim of narration is so to print the picture upon the mind that the reader will feel himself actually present at the scene.   Narration thus has a two-fold advantage over description: first, it employs human personality and sympathy with a constantly changing scene of action; second, narration uses the power of suspense in leading the reader to any appropriate climax.

As a suggestion to the advertiser, get a clear mental picture of the story to be related and conform to its intensive action as nearly as possible. Then be sure that your ideas are climatically arranged. This interpretation of action should result in an advertisement which unifies our appreciation of the thought contained. See example 72.

Persuasion.—(Figs. 73, 74 and 75).—Bain's definition of persuasion as applied to advertising would read as follows: Advertising endeavors to obtain the coöperation of man's free or aroused impulses for some proposed lines of conduct, in connection with the purchase of an article or proposition, by so presenting it in language as to force the reader into desired action.

Persuasion necessarily

Found faithful - after ten years' exposure

A remarkable story of Elgin durability comes from Oklahoma, and is vouched for by a lawyer of that state.

"In 1904 I was United States Attorney for the Central District of Indian Territory and prosecuted one . . . . for a murder alleged to have been committed in the Kiamitia Mountains in the old Choctaw Nation, Indian Territory, some ten years prior to the date of the prosecution.

"The body of the deceased was found in the mountains ten years after he was killed, and was certainly identified by the remains of a gun marked for identification, some marked coins, and a certain Elgin watch carried by the deceased. Although the watch had lain by the skeleton in the mountain, exposed to the sunshine, rain, sleet and snow, for ten years, when it was discovered and picked up it began running and clicking off the time as perfectly as though it had been wound the day before."

Ten years of exposure to the elements, yet unharmed! What a gruelling test for such a delicate piece of mechanism! What a convincing proof that lifelong service may be expected of Elgin Watches — either men's or women's models!

ELGIN Watches

Fig. 72.—Narration.

---

consists of two steps: exhortation and argumentation. The former implies that the *end* in view must be desirable by arousing personal feelings, as like, dislike, gain, comfort, ease, etc.; the

⌐More Money This Year⌐

CAN YOU EARN IT?

Or is it to be the same old grind of hard work, uncongenial employment and only small pay?

Is it to be another twelve months of standing still while you watch other men get the advancement *you* hoped to get?

Or will you make it a year of real *achievement?* Will you realize *now* that the better job goes only to the man who has the *training,* and will you take steps *now* to get the training that better jobs require?

If you really want the coming year to count for something, let the International Correspondence Schools help you to make your progress *sure* and *tangible.*

It is the business of the I. C. S. to raise salaries. For 23 years the I. C. S. have been training men for success in the kind of work they like best.

Let the I. C. S. help **you,** too. Join the army of well-paid men.

FIG. 73.—Persuasion. Emphasis related to feeling.

Why POSTUM
Instead of Coffee

Better Nerves	**Better Digestion**
Less Biliousness	**Less Headache**
Sound Sleep	**Clear Brain**

Steady Heart Action

FIG. 74.—Persuasion. Emphasis related to pure logic. This advertisement suggests the line of argument which each should apply to himself.

No Excuse *for* Cold Rooms

THERE is no longer any excuse for cold rooms. With a PERFECTION SMOKELESS OIL HEATER rooms without regular heat can be made comfortable in short order.

Business and professional men, merchants and builders, all find the PERFECTION HEATER a most useful and necessary device.

In the home a PERFECTION HEATER is indispensable. It banishes chill from cold rooms and cold corners— portable warmth and cheer, that's what it is.

The PERFECTION HEATER costs little to buy and little to use. It burns kerosene, a fuel that is ideal because it is low-priced, efficient, easy to handle, and everywhere available. One gallon gives ten hours' glowing warmth. Think of it! An hour a day for ten days. It is made so that it will not smoke or smell. It is handsomely finished.

FIG. 75.—Persuasion. A combination of feeling and logic.

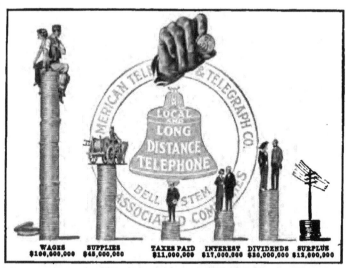

| WAGES | SUPPLIES | | TAXES PAID | INTEREST | DIVIDENDS | SURPLUS |
| $100,000,000 | $45,000,000 | | $11,000,000 | $17,000,000 | $30,000,000 | $12,000,000 |

How the Bell System Spends its Money

Every subscriber's telephone represents an actual investment averaging $153, and the gross average revenue is $41.75. The total revenue is distributed as follows:

Employes—$100,000,000

Nearly half the total—$100,000,000—paid in wages to more than one hundred thousand employes engaged in giving to the public the best and the cheapest telephone service in the world.

For Supplies—$45,000,000

Paid to merchants, supply dealers and others for materials and apparatus, and for rent, light, heat, traveling, etc.

Tax Collector—$11,000,000

Taxes of more than $11,000,000 are paid to the Federal, state and local authorities. The people derive the benefit in better highways, schools and the like.

Bondholders—$17,000,000

Paid in interest to thousands of men and women, savings banks, insurance companies and other institutions owning bonds and notes.

Stockholders—$30,000,000

70,000 stockholders, about half of whom are women, receive $30,000,000.

(These payments to stockholders and bondholders who have put their savings into the telephone business represents 6.05% on the investment.)

Surplus—$12,000,000

This is invested in telephone plant and equipment, to furnish and keep telephone service always up to the Bell standard.

AMERICAN TELEPHONE AND TELEGRAPH COMPANY
AND ASSOCIATED COMPANIES

One Policy   *One System*   *Universal Service*

FIG. 76.—Exposition aided by an illustration; likewise Exposition in form.

latter implies that the *means* must be conducive to that end, or pure reason-why copy. It should be borne in mind that each persuasive advertisement emphasizes either the feeling, the logical quality, or a combination of both.

The advertiser in preparing persuasive advertising copy should consider the following factors in assisting him to form sane, true, and yet forceful judgments.

Persuasive discourse should clearly consider at the outset the affirmative of the proposition advanced; it should give due consideration to the other side of the question; it should anticipate all possible objections; it should avoid overargumentation; and finally, every good persuasive a d v e r - tisement s h o u l d summarize its data.

Figs. 73, 74 and 75 are advertisements showing the power of persuasion with respect to (a)

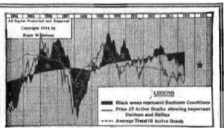

How Babson Service Helps the Investor

You can invest with safety only when you *know* trade, labor and market conditions. Babson Service keeps you reliably informed and enables you to anticipate the future.

Eliminate worry. Cease depending on rumors or luck. Work in accordance with a definite policy based on fundamental statistics.

For particulars—which will be sent gratis—address Dept O-4-40 of the

Babson Statistical Organization
Advisory Building. Wellesley Hills, Mass.
Largest Statistical Organization of its Character in U. S.

FIG. 77.—Exposition.

feeling, (b) pure logic, (c) a combination of both.

Exposition.—(Figs. 76 and 77). Hill defines exposition as "consisting in such an analysis of a general term as will make clear to the mind the general notion of what it is the sign."

Undoubtedly a purely expository advertisement is the most

difficult to represent by written words. For this reason it is generally advisable to accompany the written copy with an illustration. However, altho the most difficult form of discourse to master, we find it used most frequently. Therefore it is well to remember that as " exposition is the discussion of the essential attributes of some abstract or general theme," certain definite limitations should confine exposition's magnitude.

Our first requisite in setting up the limits of exposition should be to compile exact information. Second, condensation is fundamental. Third, as nearly as possible, avoid using the other types of discourse. Finally, constantly check your copy up by asking yourself whether you are clearly explaining the "how" of your article or proposition. When we explain the " how " of a proposition or article, we state the forces which give it unity ; we make clear the relationship of the various parts which go to make up the whole. In other words, we attempt to create the picture of an article or proposition with a suggestion of the underlying laws of its existence. We attempt to justify it as a " thing " worthy of a place in consciousness.

Figs. 76 and 77 are expository advertisements greatly aided by effective illustrations.

QUESTIONS

Improve the following business sentences and determine what suggested violations of Clearness, Force, or Precision, influenced your decision.

1. " I interested our party when I was in Boston this morning upon a business proposition."
2. " Gentlemen: By indomitable perseverance, in spite of every obstacle, and contrary to the desires of many, you must admit the Bell system has triumphed."
3. Gentlemen: We suggest that the stockholders assemble to draw up a code of laws and vote upon each by ballot."
4. " In the lower part of the City you will find the Pomeroy Company's business."
5. " Our bookkeeper shall render you a statement to-morrow as per your request."
6. " For rent or sale, by C. T. Heppe & Sons, a piano with excellent tone qualities, in mahogany."
7. " Mr. Henry—' What is to be done' to repeat your own words, can better be determined by you."
8. " For many years you have conducted an inconspicuous tobacco store. We respectfully offer you an opportunity of consolidating with us."
9. " Dear Sir: You must develop plasticity and encourage reciprocity if you continue as our representative."

10. " Our inability to comprehend the situation renders articulation tedious."
11. " The advertiser must create a desire for an article which did not exist before."
12. " It will not be necessary or required of you to pass any efficiency examination."
13. " We do not clearly understand what the contents of your letter mean to say."
14. " For Sale. A Scotch terrier, by a lady, with curly hair."
15. " A firm should be cautious about retarding a salesman's progressiveness."
16. " Whether the recent advancement of railroad rates is a violation of the Interstate Commerce laws is what we want to know."
17. " Sink your shaft 60 ft. deep back from the banks of the ocean and you will find a nice vein."
18. " After having noted the contents of your letter of recent date we beg to advise you—"
19. " You are requested to appear before the Committee and render your financial report to them."
20. " Dear Sir: The flaw in your diamond is inconspicuous."

PROBLEMS

Apply the following table-summary to the letter below and determine which of these violations of Clearness, Force, and Precision it contains.

Clearness	Demonstrative and relative pronouns. Antecedents of demonstrative and relative pronouns. Omissions. Over-condensations. Participles. Sequence of words and clauses.
Force	Useless words. Weak sentence endings. Suspense and relief. Emphatic words and phrases. Exaggerations. Affectations. Large words. Too general terms. Repetitions.
Precision	Use words in proper sense. Shall and will. May and can. Concrete and abstract words. Prepositions.

1.

Mr. A. J. Hill,
    Port Deposit,
        Maryland,

The proposition we made you in our message of a few days ago, was so beautifully attractive we are a little surprised we have not heard from you before this.

No technical training nor past experience is necessary to fulfilling this position. All we want is a man that can do things—a man who is not contented with a mere living—a man with personality and aggressiveness—the type of man who is willing to work and put forth his best efforts, sometimes to the point of sacrificing present remuneration for increased future compensation.

The House Cleaning Business is not a fairy tale. It is simply a new and modern method of doing work which has been done for ages and will be done for ages to come. This method of cleaning has come to stay and people are becoming fast educated to the efficiency of the house cleaner. It is only a question of time when every house will use them, simply because it's easier and cheaper to let a gas engine clean the house than to do the work with pure raw muscle and hard work.   ,

We feel that we can be of considerable assistance to you as you are in close touch with the latest cleaning ideas and the most reputable health inspectors in your territory advocate our installation.

So many people have written recently asking if we could not make the payments $5.00 a month, this small amount bringing the cleaner within their reach and making purchase possible, we have decided to permit such payments when, in our salesmen's opinions, financial leniency is feasible.

We want to warn you against being discouraged should you meet with no results at first. Our salesmen average 7 calls to get one order; in other words they talk the House Cleaning Business proposition over to 6 persons who do not purchase in order to get one who does subscribe.

In closing we again wish to re-emphasize, that the House Cleaning Business is still in its infancy, thus holding out the possibilities of great future development. We want to let you in on the ground floor. Act, Now!

This is our third letter, and without we receive an answer to this, we shall think, as indeed we would be justified, that there was no sincerity back of your inquiry.

Respectfully yours,
ONEIDA VACUUM CLEANING CO.

ETV/H.

2. Analyse the following advertisements and classify them from the standpoint of the four types of discourse: Figs. 78, 79, 80, 81, 82, 83 and 84.

REFERENCES

BRIEFER PRACTICAL RHETORIC, CLARK.
PHILOSOPHY OF STYLE, HERBERT SPENCER.
RHETORIC, BAIN.
SCIENCE OF RHETORIC, HILL.

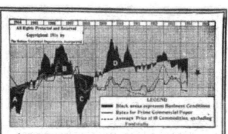

Fig. 78.—State the kind of discourse.

Fig. 79.—State the kind of discourse.

Try this easy way to clear your skin with

Resinol Soap

Bathe your face for several minutes with Resinol Soap and hot water, working the creamy lather into the skin gently with the finger-tips. Then apply a little Resinol Ointment. Let this stay on ten minutes, and wash off with Resinol Soap and more hot water. Finish with a dash of cold water to close the pores.

Do this once or twice a day, and you will be astonished to find how quickly the healing, antiseptic Resinol medication soothes and cleanses the pores, removes pimples and blackheads, and leaves the complexion clear, fresh and velvety. After the first few treatments, the Resinol Ointment can probably be omitted.

Resinol Soap costs but twenty-five cents at all druggists and dealers in toilet goods. For a guestroom size trial cake, with a miniature box of Resinol Ointment, write to Dept. 31-G. Resinol, Baltimore, Md.

FIG. 80.—State the kind of discourse

What the Little Beaver Saw

EIGHT years ago very few people knew that they could build better walls and ceilings with BEAVER BOARD than with lathe and plaster. But even then the little Beaver foresaw the growing, insistent demand for this pure-wood-fiber material that would not crack or crumble like plaster; that was quickly put up, at any season, without dirt or litter; that made rooms warmer in winter, cooler in summer, brighter and more attractive.

Today he sees a vast international organization distributing BEAVER BOARD all over the United States and Canada and in many foreign lands. He sees buildings of every type, new and remodeled, with beautiful paneled and painted BEAVER BOARD walls and ceilings that need no repairs or wall-paper.

He sees BEAVER BOARD a standard building material which has been made better and better from year to year, and is suited to the needs of all who build or remodel.

Visitors to Buffalo and Niagara Falls are cordially invited to visit our Buffalo offices and get a first-hand acquaintance with BEAVER BOARD quality, beauty and co-operative service.

Write for free booklet, "BEAVER BOARD and Its Uses," and painted sample.

The Beaver Board Companies

United States : 317 Beaver Road, Buffalo, N. Y.
Canada :   517 Wall Street, Beaverdale, Ottawa.
Great Britain :   4 Southampton Row, London, W. C.

FIG. 81.—State the kind of discourse

With a Victrola every home can enjoy the world's best music

The Victrola is the "open sesame" which admits you to the enjoyment of all the music of all the world.

It reveals to you in their grandeur the musical gems of the ages. It brings to you the art and personality of the most famous singers and instrumentalists. It presents an endless variety of melody and mirth to suit your every mood.

FIG. 82.—State the kind of discourse

Let Us Pay Your Expenses to the Exposition in 1915

You will never have another opportunity to see so many interesting things in California as you will in 1915.

Think of traveling on solid vestibule trains all the way from Chicago to Denver, where a short stop will be made, then to Colorado Springs, with a drive through the Garden of the Gods to Manitou, at the foot of Pike's Peak; thence a trip over the mountains to Cripple Creek and the Gold Mines.

Then through the Royal Gorge and over the Rocky Mountains to Salt Lake City, to Los Angeles, Santa Barbara and the Coast Line to San Francisco.

Then a week or more in the delightful climate of California—days spent in studying the wonders of the Exposition or in strolling in idle enjoyment through the endless mazes of its attractive amusement section.

What a liberal education!—what pleasurable memories to carry through a lifetime!

And the return home—via the Mount Shasta Route to Portland, then to Tacoma, Seattle, and thence into Canada and through the mountains to Calgary, Regina, Winnipeg, then back to the States to St. Paul, Minneapolis, Chicago and home! What prospect!

We will pay all your expenses from the time you step on the train at your home station until you return—24 days in all. There is no competition. It is a straight out and out offer that depends entirely upon your own efforts.

Sign the coupon and let us tell you how you can earn a free trip to the Panama-Pacific Exposition in 1915. Send it to us today.

Cosmopolitan Magazine

119 West 40th Street   New York City

FIG. 83.—State the kind of discourse.

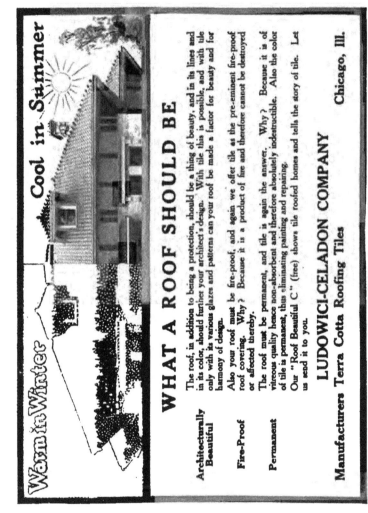

Fig. 84.— State the kind of discourse.

CHAPTER XXII

FACTORS IN SUCCESSFUL LETTER WRITING

Advertising Power of the Letter.—From an almost insignificant beginning in the business world, direct advertising or letter writing has grown until to-day more than $107,000,000 is spent annually in the United States on this form of publicity. Letter writing has become the second most important kind of advertising in business; and because of its vast importance and great expense, it is essential that we direct our efforts toward producing the best possible letter. The average business man has often doubted the power of the well-written letter; for heretofore his business has grown by personal contact with his trade. Some, however, have been manifestly successful thru letter writing alone. Thus two large Chicago mail-order houses do an annual gross business of $140,000,000 thru correspondence. The Addressograph Company of Chicago sells systems, machines, and materials for the sole purpose of collecting mailing lists. The business man is learning that there is a tremendous power in well-planned letters, and each year he is spending more time and money on this form of selling.

The Function of Successful Letter Writing.—The function of successful letter writing is the ability to create the same picture, desire or activity in the mind of the reader for a particular article or proposition as is intended by the writer. The commercial correspondent should have three fundamental ideas in mind when he dictates a letter. He should be careful regarding the arrangement and form; he should consider the best use of English; third, he should introduce those elements which stamp his letter with individuality.

The Form.—The least courtesy that can be paid to any customer by a salesman is the neatness and correctness of his dress. Due emphasis should always be given to the form of expression. The well-written and neat letter is likely to indicate the character of a company as much as does the dress of a salesman. A letter head $8\frac{1}{2} \times 11$ inches makes possible a neat appearing page for business correspondence.

The first essential of a correctly written letter is that it will be well balanced. The contents of many letters are scattered over the entire page instead of the factors of balance and space being duly considered. In other words, we like to feel instinctively that the letter has been well centered. The following example adheres to these principles of nicety of form without seeming stiff or overly dressed.

Drake Smith & Co.,
Newport,   (Heading)
R. I.

August 3, 1915. (Date)

A. L. HERRING,
Frisco, Va.   (Introductory Address)

Dear Sir: (Salutation)

....
....
....
....
....
....
....
....
....
....
....
....
....
....

(Complimentary Close)   Sincerely yours,

        (Signature)   DAVID SMITH,
                                        President.

Standard usage warrants the elimination of indentations in the introductory address since it saves time for the stenographer and does not mar the beauty of the letter. The indentation of the paragraph beginnings is yet maintained to give facility in reading.

When the business heading appears on the paper, the date heading contains just the date. If, however, the case arises where the heading is written in conjunction with the date, this should occupy at least two lines and at most three. Each part is separated with a comma and the entire heading closed with a period.

The following are correct:

1214 Thomas St., Louisville, Ky.,
June 20, 1915.

or

1214 Thomas St.,
Louisville, Ky., June 20, 1915.

or

1214 Thomas St.,
Louisville, Ky.,
June 20,1915.

With respect to the date, many correspondents use June 20th and in the body of the letter refer to it as June the twentieth, or " our letter of the twentieth inst." All of these forms, however, are unnecessarily long. There is nothing wrong with June 20, both in the date and in the body of the letter; and it is decidedly more simple. The introductory address and the salutation mark the left margin for the body of the letter, while the right end of the date forms the margin for the corresponding edge of the letter. This gives an equal margin on both sides. It is better form that the first sentence of the paragraph be indented, since this breaks up the mass of the letter and suggests easy reading. The complimentary close and the signature are written so as to give a finished balance to the letter. It is customary to use double spacing between the different divisions of the letter, while single spacing is used between the parts of each division.

The one central idea which should dominate the correspondent is that the letter be perfectly balanced in all of its several parts. This can be done with form letters as easily as with typewritten or script letters; for the address on the former can be added without spoiling the effect gained by an otherwise perfect balance.

The same idea of balance and space should be followed on the envelope. The conventional size envelope is $3\frac{1}{2} \times 6\frac{1}{2}$ inches, which permits a well balanced arrangement. The outside address should be written without indentations; and excepting the fact that postal clerks read indented addresses more easily, largely thru habit, the non-indentation saves time for the stenographer, and is in harmony with the form of the enclosed letter.

Thus the form of the letter concerns itself principally with a perfect mechanical arrangement upon which it depends for its first favorable impression.   For example, a young man's application for a position in the sales promotion department of a large mail-order house was selected from among many letters because it was distinctive in appearance, in that it was well planned and mechanically correct.

The English.—The mechanical make-up of a letter may be correct, but if its message lacks convincing English its purpose has failed.   The important point of all letters is the thought motive that has caused their creation.   The letter that wins must have a particular idea to cover, a specific point to attack, a certain truth to expound; and the manner in which these conditions are fulfilled determines the strength of the letter.

Let us again quote Spencer in his essay, " Philosophy of Style," and apply his thought directly to letter writing.   " A reader or listener has, at each moment, but a limited amount of mental power available.   To recognize and interpret the symbols presented to him requires part of this power; to arrange and combine the image presented requires a further part; and only that part which remains can be used for realizing the thought conveyed.   Hence, the more time and attention it takes to receive and understand each sentence, the less time and attention can be given to the contained idea, and the less vividly will that idea be conveyed."

Thus, the quality of clearness becomes of paramount importance in attempting to influence the mind of another individual thru the written word.   On the other hand, clearness depends upon the right choice of words.   If your own definition of a given term is contrary to the prevailing notion and you fail to regard the fact that you have a more highly discriminated vocabulary, this discrepancy within itself will often cause a misunderstanding.   This results in unnecessary, extended correspondence.   Those who are vitally associated with the inside workings of a given concern are likely to have a vocabulary which is more discriminating than the average individual would have.   Hence, in all letter writing we should be careful to consider from the other man's point of view what we are trying to say. Words are the links which form the chain of thought throughout the letter. Their individual and collective strength determines their final selling efficiency. Therefore, words in their technical meaning and use should be studied in connection with the class to be reached. Avoid long words where short ones will answer. The phrase, " You are not permitted in this shop," may be sufficient warning to most men, but the sharp command, " Keep Out," will bring better results. When in doubt, use the simpler Anglo-Saxon word in contrast to a lengthy Latin form. Complicated sentence structure, too lengthy paragraphs, and non-punctuated sentences, each, if disregarded in connection with the larger thought which you are attempting to express, will often tend to inhibit responsiveness on the part of the reader. The same principles of style as suggested in the chapter on the English of Advertising will hold in connection with letter writing.

Individuality.—It may be possible to express one's thought in English that is quite clear and yet the message not " get over." In other words, letter writing to be successful in nature should relate itself to the mind of the reader in such manner as to suggest individuality on the part of the writer. To make one feel the importance of your letter from the very moment of its arrival should be the thought of the writer. It is only by a careful consideration of individuality that this can be obtained. Thus every correspondent faces the problem—how to get and hold the attention from the very start. Many good letters with excellent selling points fail because the opening sentences are weak. The writer should strike at the vital fact immediately, or at least his opening sentence should be so engaging that the reader is unconsciously lead into an appreciation of the message intended. There is entirely too much, " I have your valued favor of the 15th instant and wish to say in reply——" in the average business letter. If I were in the market for building material it would not concern me that you heard indirectly that I was " contemplating the erection of a large 4-story building." What really would be of interest to me, and to every builder, is the price and quality of the materials which you are selling.

The following letter is to be characterized as individualistic in nature in that the paragraphing is unique; the thought is expressed in a manner not found in ordinary good writing, while there has been a strict adherence to the principles which constitute good narration.

Dear Sir:
A three-line letter did it.
—brought back the $48.25 owed him for ten months by a personal friend of R. E. Brown, a Chicago business man.
Mr. Brown had tried every means he dared to collect what was due him. All had failed. He did not wish to sue—even threaten—a friend. Finally he examined a copy of our New Book, " How to Collect Money by Mail."

The particular associations which you bring into your letter, apart from the one idea which you wish to convey, often make your letter vitally individualistic in nature. One of the most common expressions of individuality in connection with the sale of any kind of goods is the sane and suggestive regard for passing events. Every economic condition in the business in which you are engaged should be utilized whenever the correspondence can be enriched by apt illustrations. Thus, current events often give the right thought motive in order to get in touch with the prospect. The following letter from a skilful correspondent illustrates very successfully the use of current events in the selling of fire clay bricks.

The European War makes it impossible for any more German Clay to be shipped to this country for a long time.
But manufacturers of Glass House Pots and Flux Blocks who have been using German Clay in their batches should not be alarmed. Even if you never find it possible to secure another pound of German Clay, that fact need not cause you worry or inconvenience.

WE'RE READY WITH THE REMEDY!

For several years we have been developing, testing and *using* a clay known as 69-B Clay, which is far superior to German Clay for making Pots and Tank Blocks.
This Clay is mined right here in America. We have an unlimited supply and can take care of your requirements promptly and satisfactorily.
Repeated analyses show that our 69-B Clay is higher in Silica, lower in Alumina, Iron and Alkalies, and has greater tensile strength, both raw and burnt, than the German. *It is uniform throughout.*
Investigate now! Don't wait until you are in actual need, but write to-day for prices and full particulars of this good clay.
Yours truly,

Thought Analysis of Correspondent's Letter Should Be Thorough.—The chief function of all business letter writing is to get certain kinds of responses from people. It necessarily follows that the writer of these letters must be able to select the right kind of thought attitude necessary to get the results desired. For example, given a list of persons whose interest in a particular article has been manifested in answer to an advertisement, the right pulling power letter can be depended upon to sell to a certain percentage of the number. On the other hand, a letter whose thought has not been thoroughly analysed with respect to the particular group of individuals who have written, will greatly reduce the possible return.

Classification of Thought Attitude.—Many writers fail to succeed in that they attempt to impress too many ideas upon the mind of the prospect. The reader thus becomes confused with respect to the original purpose of your letter. The thought of any letter of a business concern becomes modified accordingly as it applies to the four following situations: first, the fact that it is a letter addressed to a previously unknown individual and regarding whom there is entire ignorance apart from the name; second, the fact that the group to which you are writing is highly specialized, as physicians, teachers, lawyers, etc.; third, the fact that individuals had answered a specific advertisement would indicate such a state of mind on the part of the writer as would bring home a message entirely different from that kind of a letter where the reader was being appealed to for the first time; fourth, the fact that the individual who has written inquiringly has a general knowledge of the reputation of your house. Again, it must be recognized that letters to specific individuals, where many personal qualities are known, would differ considerably from those letters which are written to groups of people. Likewise, an appeal to any group might differ considerably from an appeal made to a specific individual. Thus, the first questions every good writer should ask are, " What is the main idea which I wish to get over ? " " Is this idea of such a nature as to appeal to those individuals, immediately, because of the recognition on their part that I am in sympathy with them either as individuals or as members of a given group ? " Thus it becomes necessary that a good correspondent study his prospects with respect to the personal knowledge, the previous business transactions or the chance relations which have made letter writing at all possible.

Kinds of Letters.—In the business world to-day there are three clearly defined types of letters that are being written daily. These three kinds of letters are involved in the progress of any successful concern. They are addressed to one of three groups: either to the members of the concern itself; to people who are likely to become prospective customers; or, in the adjustment of complaints on the part of these customers. Thus we can justify a three-fold classification: First, intradepartment educational letters relating to: (a) knowledge of house policies, (b) changes in house policies, (c) encouragement to greater efficiency, (d) complaints and (e) general inspirational letters.

Second, the "offensive" letter which tries primarily to sell goods and which may be classified as follows: (a) initial letters to prospectives on mailing list, (b) letters in answer to general inquiries, and (c) letters in answer to advertisements.

Third, defensive letters relating to the house policy in the case of needed adjustments, which include: (a) collections, (b) complaints regarding shipments, (c) complaints regarding style of goods, (d) complaints regarding quality of goods, (e) complaints relating to damages in transit, and (f) complaints with respect to prices.

From a selling standpoint the three letters which are most important are first, those which relate to initial prospectives found on mailing list; second, those which relate to answers to advertisements; third, letters to the various members of the house itself, the motif of which emphasizes that which encourages selling efficiency.

The Mailing List.—Every well-organized large city house working thru salesmen, men who canvass the trade, keeps a complete card file of customers, present and prospective. In making up the mailing list every possible bit of information is obtained regarding the person to whom the letter is to be sent. It is quite easy to find the kind of business, profession or trade in which a man is employed. This, in itself, is indicative of certain mind tendencies and permits of an introductory sentence at least interesting. Mail order houses have much detail information regarding their trade and it is partly because of this that they have been able so well to compete with others. A knowledge of the kind of work in which a man is engaged or his hobbies which have come to be known, these permit a variety of letters. A good mailing list is the most important factor in the distribution of all literature. It is not pleasant to feel that a large percentage of the names have not been honestly or intelligently selected and that a heavy loss must be counted upon.

Letters Indicate the Power of Advertising Copy.—Letters of inquiry in answer to advertisements reveal how good an impression has been made, as well as the weakness of the advertising copy. The fact that a question is asked regarding a certain unexplained point might indicate that the advertisement was not good. But this need not necessarily be true, for the size of the advertisement might not permit an insertion of details into the text. At any rate the advertiser should, by a careful analysis of the letters which are received, be able to tell quite accurately, what effect his particular advertisement is producing. This permits of an intelligent change of copy to further increase the power of the advertisement. If the people are learning something really important about the article, the letter will not be filled with questions but will oftener immediately ask for the goods. The coöperation of the letter writer and the advertiser thus produces a combination which can intelligently help to estimate the pulling power of each advertisement from the standpoint of interest.

The Intradepartment Letter.—The so-called intradepartment letter is sent to different people within a concern, giving them information, encouragement and instructions regarding those policies which make for greater efficiency of the working force. For the members of any movement to receive this kind

of information from authoritative sources means the creation of
new ideals. Men soon grow to know what is expected of them
and, furthermore, to be kept alive in the development of their
own business field. This kind of letter writing necessitates accurate knowledge and great sympathy on the part of the writer.
Again, there must be the element of personal appeal where each
feels himself, upon the reading, to be a part of a truly progressive
establishment. Then, as one man begins to succeed above another, the poor salesman or clerk may come to realize that it is
inefficiency, not favoritism, which permits this greater success.

Reproducing Letters: Propriety of a Duplicated Letter.—
When it becomes necessary to reproduce letters in large numbers,
the important thing for the correspondent or business man is
to use a method which is efficient and at the same time economical. It is a rather curious fact, in connection with letters sent
out by the business world, that the one which by its mechanical
make-up suggests duplication, is often looked upon suspiciously.
In fact when a letter is recognized as a copy, there is a tendency
on the part of many to throw it into the waste basket. This
attitude of mind, however, is entirely unjustifiable when we come
to realize that any large and prosperous concern must in our
day, talk not to a single individual in connection with a proposition, but to thousands. The notion that a letter has been put
thru a duplicating process should not within itself suggest
the idea of a lack of interest on the part of the sender. However,
if the reproductive process has been such as to turn out a letter
which is mechanically imperfect and which suggests carelessness
on the part of the sender, the reader has reason justly to condemn the evident discourteousness. So long then as a condition exists in the business world where the reproduced letter is
looked upon suspiciously, it becomes necessary for the correspondent to reproduce a duplicate which should, as closely as
possible, resemble the original. Apart from the idea that the
duplicated form should resemble the original, the fact is that if
the original is excellent within itself and duplicated properly,
it is in spirit the original. It is only when a letter has been sent
to an individual, the contents of which are not applicable, that

one has a right to criticise the contents. As business men we must come to appreciate the fact that in our dealings with thousands of people scattered over the entire country, there are hundreds to whom the message is as applicable as it is to ourselves and that, from a business economic standpoint, a duplicated message is as efficient and necessary in giving a message as if each letter were written individually upon the typewriter.

Process for Duplicating Form Letters.—There are several processes for duplicating form letters on the market today, and all of the machines used in these various processes are more or less efficient. Some machines, of course, are more widely known than others. There are three main divisions into which the different processes of duplicating letters naturally group themselves. These different divisions are as follows:

```
Type Machines:
    Rotary  .... Multigraph
                ( Writer Press
    Flat Bed . { Printograph
                ( Mulstedt Press or Multicolor
Stencil Machines:
    Underwood Revolving Duplicator
    Rotary Mimeograph (Dick)—Dermatype
    Rotary Neostyle
    Rotospeed
    Flat Mimeograph
    Flat Neostyle
Gelatine Machines:
    Schapirograph (gelatine roll)
    Commercial (gelatine roll)
    Beck Duplicator (gelatine roll)
    Lawton Duplicator (gelatine pan)
    Hecktograph (gelatin pan)
```

Analysing the outline above, all of the duplicating processes have been grouped accordingly as they fit under the respective heads, as for example, type machines, stencil machines and gelatine machines. By selecting from each of these different groups a typical machine, one can easily understand the process of duplicating which is involved.

The Multigraph.—The Multigraph represents that type of machine which prints from individual type characters. This machine prints from sliding type set up on a revolving drum thru a ribbon, so that the result is practically as good as any typewritten page. The type rack is on the left hand of the drum and the place for setting up the type is on the right hand, so that an operator simply moves the type from the left hand to the right hand side of the drum, being able to set up practically one line of type in two minutes. When the type is once set up, there is no limit to the number of letters that can be duplicated. When the required number of letters has been printed, the type can easily be returned to its proper racks on the left side of the revolving drum almost as rapidly as when the type is originally set up for the printing of the letter. Another type machine on the market to-day is the Mulstedt Press machine, or the Multicolor. In this case instead of type being on the rotary drum, the type is on a flat or moving bed and the paper is on the drum or cylinder.

The Rotary Mimeograph.—In the rotary Mimeograph machine, made by the A. B. Dick Company, and machines of a similar character, for example, the Underwood Revolving Duplicator and the old Neostyle machine, the printing is done through a specially prepared paper. This paper, which is evenly covered with wax, is placed in a typewriter, where, without the use of ribbon, the type forms are cut in this wax preparation, which forms what is known as a stencil. The prepared stencil is then fastened on the cylinder drum, and moistened with ink from the inside. When the drum is pressed against a sheet of paper, the result is a facsimile page of the stencil. When more than eight or nine hundred copies are to be made from a stencil, instead of a wax stencil a dermatype sheet is used. This sheet is practically indestructible and can be run an almost indefinite number of times. As there are two types of type machines, so there are two types of stencil machines; the rotary Mimeograph, which is now using the dermatype sheet and the flat Mimeograph, where the stencil is placed on a flat pad instead of being put on the hollow drum.

The Gelatine Machine.—The third and last style machine, into which all duplicating processes have grouped themselves, is the gelatine machine. This, as in the other two types of machines, divides itself into two parts—the gelatine roll and the gelatine pan. The gelatine pan machine is nothing more than the composition gelatine, upon which the specially prepared ink—which is of a purple color—can be transferred. This transferred page of writing can then be retransferred to possibly 50 or 60 clean pages. The only difference between the gelatine roll and the gelatine pan is that the composition gelatine in one case is a roll, upon which the freshly prepared sheet is transferred, and the other is a gelatine pan.

There are a great many more duplicating machines on the market at the present time than have been listed above, but these particular machines which have been mentioned are merely named as representative of the different styles of machines for reproducing letters.

The Addressograph.—In handing large mailing lists some successful scheme of addressing envelopes becomes highly important. To meet this need the Addressograph Company of Chicago has developed a machine known as the Addressograph for this kind of work. When any names are to be placed on your mailing list, they are referred to the Addressograph operator. She or he then takes a blank addressograph name-plate for each name, and places it in a graphotype. A graphotype is a machine operated somewhat like a typewriter, the function of which process embosses typewriter-style type on metal plates. After this operation, which can be performed by a young boy or girl almost as quickly as addressing an envelope, an impression is made on a special card and both the card and the name-plate are inserted in the metal holder measuring 5 inches by 3 inches— regular card index size. Cards are supplied with various rulings to meet every advertising need. After classifying the name-plate, it is placed in a filing drawer for further use. When it is desired to use the plates for addressing, the drawer is placed in the Addressograph and the machine automatically selects the plates and addresses the envelopes, cards, etc. The plates after being used are automatically replaced in the drawer so that no time is lost in returning plates to their original places. An individual with a typewriter can address 750 addresses a day at an average cost of $2.50. The Adressograph can produce 25,000 addresses a day at an average cost of 7 cents a thousand.

QUESTIONS

1. What are the functions of successful letter writing?
2. What is direct advertising? Wherein does it derive its importance in business?
3. What are the essential qualifications of an efficient correspondent?
4. State the difference between the thought and the function of a letter.
5. What is meant by "Individuality" in correspondence?
6. What is the value of a mechanically perfect letter?
7. Mention the different methods of reproducing letters.
8. What is meant by an "offensive" letter? A "defensive" letter?

PROBLEMS

Criticise the following answers to the "original" letter.

ORIGINAL LETTER

PHILA., PA., January 1, 1915.

F. W. SWARTZ & Co.,
   318 Michigan St.,
   Buffalo, N.Y.
Dear Sirs:

Last September I began business as a retail hardware dealer. Upon starting, I asked you to send one of your salesmen to me to aid in stocking up my store as I knew little about the business.

Your salesman, Mr. Johnson, stocked up my store, but in doing so he sold me a large amount of unnecessary and high priced goods, such goods which are not demanded by my trade.

Now, I have a lot of dead stock upon my hands and would like to know if you can take the unnecessary goods off my hands and in return give me the real necessities, such necessities I will outline with the amounts wanted upon receiving a favorable reply from you. This proposition seems fair to me and I hope you will grant it.

Yours truly,   C. H. RHEINER.

ANSWER

Dear Sir:

Your letter of the 1st instant to hand and the contents of same noted with a great deal of interest. We regret very much that the conditions as outlined in your letter have occurred, and beg to advise that it will give us pleasure to rectify error or a misjudgment which our salesman might have made.

We believe that it was with no intention that our salesman, Mr. Johnson, overstocked you with a high-priced line of goods and feel confident that in having persuaded you to install the stock was prompted through his having apprized the situation before having approached you upon this matter.

Kindly return goods which you have in stock which you feel that you cannot dispose of and we will gladly replace same with material which will be more to your liking.

Yours very truly,

Dear Sir:

In reply to your letter of January 1st we regret very much the difficulties you have had with our goods. This may have been caused by our salesman, Mr. Johnson, misjudging the territory in which you were to handle this material. We trust by this time, however, that you are able to judge for yourself the kind of goods and the trade you are to deal with and

will send our representative to you in the very near future in order to go into detail in this matter. We will be glad to make any adjustments that we feel are reasonable and trust you will be willing to do the same.
Very truly yours,

Dear Sir:

Yours of January 1st at hand and would state in answer to your letter that at the time of our salesman calling at your office you were requesting the goods that you ordered. Had you advertised, as you stated to our representative, no doubt the goods would not be on hand in stock as you have at present. If you have any trouble in disposing of the articles on hand, we would be glad to take up a proposition with you and giving you a rebate and restocking in a lower priced article. We hope, however, to have you advertise as we have stated, and hear more favorable replies.
Very truly yours,

Dear Sir:

Replying to your letter of January 1st, I note that you believe our goods which Mr. Johnson sold you to be too high in price. We really don't think you mean high in price comparing the quality of the material but believe that if you will consider the advertising we are doing in connection with this material you will find that there will be a sale later which will warrant your giving it a trial. However, if you believe it not to be what you desire for your particular trade, we will grant you permission to return same and upon receipt of your list of necessities will make you a proposition on that grade of material.
Very truly yours,

Write a letter refusing to do as requested by Mr. Rheiner.

Write a letter accepting Mr. Rheiner's viewpoint.

Admitting the salesman to be at fault, have the Sales Manager write a letter to Mr. Johnson, the salesman. Remember that his failure has meant " loss to the house."

Write three different letters in answer to the following. Justify your motive in each :—

ORIGINAL LETTER
PHILA., PA., January 1, 1915.

THE ROCKFORD SALES CO.,
    Boston, Mass.

Dear Sirs:

We have been advised by the express company of the return of your Fall order. The same has been returned too late for our acceptance. for our Fall trade is entirely past and we have no possible way to dispose of these goods.

As a dealer in this line you ought to be familiar with the fact that at this time of the year, the manufacturers have started on their Winter work, and that it would be impossible to accept this returned order.

This matter lies between you and the express company and we advise you get in touch with them and secure the return of that stock.
Very truly yours,
FORD MFG. CO.

CHAPTER XXIII

ECONOMIC AND SOCIAL IMPLICATIONS OF ADVERTISING

Twofold Effect of Advertising.—Selling, encouraged and enhanced thru advertising and salesmanship, has had a two-fold effect on human affairs. One is economic, in that increased selling has wrought considerable change in business systems; the second effect is social, in that the desires of people have created new relations and standards of living. It is the object of this chapter to analyse, from the advertising seller's viewpoint, the significance of these phases of change.

The Present Necessity for Creative Advertising.—Under the old competitive system business men were seen cutting prices, with advertising as an aid in self-preservation. The extreme of this particular method of out-doing a competitor is now characterized by the expression "cut-throat competition." But intensive competition, as such, tended to carry in its wake considerable destruction, with only the strongest surviving. A new method of conducting business affairs has developed, known as that of monopoly control, and the results have been a gradual tendency toward the standardizing of goods. Coöperation has resulted in gigantic business enterprises, with its promoter made the cynosure of all eyes. Credit has been given him for his successful manipulation of funds and his successful control of human ability in the creation of trusts and monopolies. The result of this organization has had a two-fold effect upon selling: first, a tendency to stifle competition; second, a tendency toward price maintenance. As competition has been stifled so as to insure a steadily increasing output and at the same time an increase in profits, the producer has come more to consider the necessity of standardizing his product. The ability of a single concern to turn out great quantities of goods for people scattered over the entire country necessitates a recognition of the value of creative advertising to which the business world has readily responded.

320

A Standard Appeal for a Standard Product.—But the idea of profits is not the main thought of the advertiser in his attempt constantly to increase his sales. He ever holds before him the idea of standardization and is only interested in the question of production and price maintenance as they prevent or encourage him in creating and continuing standardization.

Price Maintenance.—Now the advertiser and salesman being directly involved in the process of selling are vitally interested in the various phases of price maintenance as related to the standardization of goods. The insistence of profits, on the part of investors in a given business concern, depends primarily upon the idea of selling at a profit.

Desire in Its Relation to a Universal Demand for an Article. —As one class of people after the other is supplied with a given article of consumption, there is insistent need, if progress is to be insured, that new desires be created for a still larger output on the part of the producers of that article. Thus it would seem that advertising based primarily upon the idea of intensive competition, where the attention of the public is being constantly directed toward the price of a thing, is vastly inferior to the coöperative system encouraging the idea of standardization, where publicity attempts to create desire for the quality of a proposition or thing, with the price idea of secondary consideration. The production of a given article of sale in our own country does not, as yet, seem to have those elements within it which retard output. In other words, a coöperative method of manufacturing seems to have the possibilities of supplying an article universally, if only enough desire is created, and enough money is possessed for purchases by the prospective consumer. Thus, selling under our trust or monopoly system, based on the idea of coöperation, makes progress accordingly as the right advertiser, in conjunction with the executive, is allowed expression, the executive on the one hand estimating profits, while the advertising man is struggling for the standardization of his article.

Let us analyse for a moment the automobile situation. Glance at the main highway in any one of our large cities, and you will see, standing there, scores of automobiles. Many of

21

them represent the salary of a chauffeur; all of them represent
hours of possible usage wasted. Thousands and thousands of
people are constantly passing by them, with the idea, either
consciously or unconsciously expressed, " This is waste. Why,
in my need to eliminate time and space in the carrying out of
ideas, am I thus handicapped when others are thus over-liberally
supplied ? " My theory, in connection with the development
of the automobile business apart from competition, depends
upon the creation of that kind of a machine under such working
conditions as can be used by the greatest number of people,
either in necessity or pleasure. Under the present system in
the United States, it is given to a few classes to enjoy the use
of the automobile. This is not true universally, however, for
London, Paris, and Berlin do otherwise. Foreigners, as far
as the masses are concerned, seem to have solved the automobile
questions much more satisfactorily than ourselves. In our own
cities, the automobile thus far is for special classes. That
automobile manufacturer who first realizes that given classes of
people are supplied, thru desire, with automobiles, and who has
the possibility of increasing his output, will begin so to adjust
the manufacture and price of his automobile as to reach still
larger classes. It is at this point that the advertiser must standardize his article in the minds of a still larger group. In our
own country, we find, however, different automobile manufacturers who have thus far been contented with supplying only
certain classes with automobiles; but, when Ford came into the
market, he analysed the situation,—" the best automobile for
the greatest number under present conditions." And the Ford
automobile, in its extensive sale, is the envy, as a business venture,
of all progressive business men. Carrying out the idea logically,
then, the introduction of a taxicab at a price which will meet
with favor on the part of the vast mass of humanity, incapable,
under present conditions either of owning or even using an
automobile, will be the next great automobile business step in
advancement. The present jitney situation is perhaps the opposite extreme. The progressive advertiser sees this condition in
advance. He realizes that advertising implies, not stability of

business, but progress thru standardization for a constantly
increasing number of people. More goods, greater factories,
greater profits, are the combination of ideas which impel him
on in the creation of greater desire.

Interdependence of the Executive and the Advertiser.—
Under the monopolistic method, then, we find a tendency for
the man who has created a trust or a monopoly to function more
and more as an executive in the management of his large business, while a new type of man is needed to disseminate knowledge
and create desire, in order that the output of a particular industry might be increased. The fact of the necessity of advertising is no longer disputed. Just what type of man should
be chosen for this work; what his relationship should be to the
vast organization of which he is a part; what should be the
nature of the form thru which he is to function, are among the
questions not yet entirely settled. Perhaps they will never be
settled definitely so long as progress is noted, for the future
might reflect an addition of such features as entirely to change
the present form of procedure. He may ever be the follower
of that which is expedient and thus is often uncertain in his
career. But, with respect to the present, there are undoubtedly
many concerns which are handicapped in progress by their wrong
interpretation of advertising, as well as their wrong consideration of the advertiser. For instance, the question often arises,
whether an advertising agency should write the copy and prepare the campaign for a larger manufacturing plant or whether
a specific business attend to its own advertising.

**The Advertising Agency Compared with the Advertising
Department.**—Now advertising in its last analysis, represents
a certain state of mind on the part of the advertiser in his
attempt to unite an article or proposition, a business concern,
and the consumer or purchaser. A real solution, then, of the
question suggested would relate itself as to whether an advertising agency, with every conceivable device for the gathering
of news, experienced in the analysis of innumerable enterprises,
with men at the head who have acquired their proficiency and
so-called scientific data in the school of rugged experience, is

stronger than a department which might be organized within a specific business, whose man at the head thought and studied conditions for his business alone, and whose assistants think only in terms of this specific business. And so advertising has created these two departments: one, an agency which attempts to make a complete investigation of conditions and which outlines a campaign accordingly; the other, a department within an organization which specializes in an intensive analysis of the conditions of that business and upon this bases its advertising campaign. The present tendency seems to be a greater appreciation for the agency. It is their claim that their wider experience in many fields can serve more efficiently than a department which exists in a single field. In addition, they claim that with their larger working force constantly alert to many changes, that greater efficiency both of analysis and expression can be maintained.

The Business Bourse Idea.—But a third kind of organization is beginning to assert itself in business life. This is typified in an organization of New York City, known as the Business Bourse. It is their particular function to investigate business problems, a knowledge of which will allow a particular concern to modify its selling plans so as to produce increased efficiency. This concern likewise is interested in á scientific analysis of problems related to selling. A journal is issued monthly which gives statistics regarding these questions of universal interest. While an agency considers many of the same questions, yet the Business Bourse idea is larger, in that it attempts to specialize in an investigation of general as well as specific problems. And so we find the development of institutions, regarding the field of advertising, to be somewhat different in theory of organization. Yet there is a tendency for each to appreciate the value of the other. They themselves find that there is an interdependence of relationship, and each is found to be learning from the other. There is also a tendency on the part of universities to investigate business and to assist in suggesting greater selling efficiency.

The Need for a Business Psychologist.—The most profitable method of realizing advertising is to consider the largeness of a

concern. It seems that the larger the concern, the greater the
need for a special department in advertising, rather than absolute
surrender to the advertising agency. Again, salesmanship and
advertising are becoming peculiarly interrelated. At one time the
advertiser attempted to advertise goods; the salesman to sell; each
disregarded the other. At the present time, however, there is a tendency for the executive to insist that the advertiser know what the
salesman is doing; and, likewise, that the salesmen appreciate
what the advertising department is attempting to realize. As the
significance of the relationship between advertising and salesmanship increases, there must necessarily arise, as a result of the functioning of these two departments of work, a man who can
sympathize with both phases of the question. He it is, then,
who becomes, in the truest sense of the word, the head of the
selling forces of an establishment. Again, it seems that the
larger the concern, the greater the demand for a man who can
properly interpret every phase of that particular business relating to selling. He should be called a business psychologist. He it is who measures the degree of desire in connection
with his proposition and who regulates his actions accordingly.
If the concern is large enough to demand many people in the
carrying out of ideas, it seems to me better that an advertising department be allowed to function in conjunction with an
organization which investigates special problems related to advertising. On the other hand, if the concern is not large enough
to employ a great number of efficient working people, this business psychologist should be made to coöperate both with the
advertising agency and the existing, more highly specialized
organization.

It again becomes necessary to emphasize the difference between the executive of an organization and this so-called business psychologist. The work of the executive is decidedly different in nature from that of the advertiser. The executive is
one who keeps the various parts of an organization functioning
normally and interrelatedly. He should be in sympathy with
each particular part and be ever ready to encourage such movements as will assist in the progress of the whole organization. The

business psychologist is really the efficiency man in the *selling* organization, his plans being modified accordingly as he tends to function out of relation with other parts. It is, moreover, the business of this psychologist, not only to analyse situations in connection with selling operations, but also creatively to overcome whatever difficulties present themselves. He must not only be in touch with the prospective consumer in his purchase of an article or proposition, but he likewise must be ever alert to the efficiency in kind and degree, manifested on the part of the various people connected with the selling department of an organization. The demand in the business world at the present time is for efficient men with so-called personality,—a man who impresses others as an individual in his acts, one who has commanding force enough constantly to keep up a spirit of progress in selling.

Influences Inhibiting Business Progress.—But in the problem of progress, in connection with a given concern, there are always set going certain forces to inhibit an advancement of the ideal. The element of jealousy, a fixity of wages, and a non-sympathetic executive are three factors working in many large concerns which often create a real problem. For instance, a manager of a large corporation puts it in this way:

"Mr. X, we do not want you to come to our concern as an instructor in efficiency, and so develop Brown's working capacity that he becomes dissatisfied with his $1200 job, having aroused him into a realization that he is now worth $2000. We do not want you to develop a $1200 man into a $2000 man. What we want you to do is to get an exceedingly efficient $1200 man who will be content to remain at a $1200 proposition."

Again, a concern seeks the employment of a young man who can efficiently function in a certain phase of work. They wish a man with a so-called all-around personality, whose working efficiency is likewise visibly resulting in profits to the concern. Yet, oftentimes, when such a man is put into the position, the one who is at the head of the department looks a little bit suspiciously upon the progressiveness of his new man. Real problems arise and Brown is seen to vie with the head of the department in an interpretation of the difficulty. Brown seems to succeed in the solution of the problem better than the head of the department. Jealousy and fear for one's position set going a series of circumstances, which often result in the ousting of our most efficient friend Brown.

The Element of Salary.—The element of salary is a serious consideration in connection with the progress of an individual career. In advertising, perhaps more than in some other departments, the true selling type is the man who is constantly on the alert with respect to what is happening in life. He is the observer type who brings judgment into execution because he has observed. He is ever ready to meet present conditions. Insofar as he has been thoughtful and analytical, with respect to his past, he is likely to act more correctly in the present. He it is who measures his ability by what he is capable of making. To give a concrete example: A student whom I have in mind was working for a large concern, where his creative selling ability had been recognized because he had been able to sell three times as much goods in a given day as the young man in competition with him. When he entered the employment of this concern, he engaged his services on a commission basis; but, his salary began to be out of proportion with the work of the regular man, whereupon the firm immediately attempted to reduce his salary. The result was that he left that particular concern and engaged his services to another where the real worth of his creative ability was more justly recognized.

Real Value of Creativeness.—Thus, there is a tendency on the part of many concerns to fail in their recognition of the fact that great creativeness on the part of an individual demands compensation. The very functioning of his life is primarily based on the idea that he wishes to sell more goods in order that he, himself, might have more money. A nature of this kind is unhappy and non-efficient accordingly as it is compelled to function automatically, or in accordance with precedent. The demands of this kind of life in the possession of things are greater. Essentially an active individual, one who is thinking in terms of time and in space or in the elimination of both, he finds money as the only means of creating a condition whereby he can realize his desires. Hence, the concern which fails to consider the idea of salary in proportion to the creative ability of an individual, is not solving its problem of progress wisely, and when a young man can leave the employment of one concern, who is declared viciously incompetent in that concern because he has not adhered to the idea of precedent, and yet can fill a position with a competing firm so as to produce greater results because he is given a fair wage opportunity,—this betokens the lack of a psychological analysis on the part of the business executive in that concern. There must be the oversoul whose appreciation of each individual's condition is all comprehensive and fair in its grasp. It is this condition which creates a province for the business psychologist.

The Non-Sympathetic Executive.—The third condition relates to a non-sympathetic executive. There is a tendency on the part of many executives to become fixed in their ideas of the functioning of their business, particularly if that business has become large and seems to be working automatically. The executive may tend toward one of three attitudes of mind in his methods of administration. First, he is ready to consider the saving side of his business as emphasized in the facts presented by the accountant. The executive who over emphasizes the necessity of saving is likely to be pessimistic in his consideration of promotive problems. A second tendency on the part of the executive is that of too much consideration for the promotive element of the business. This is likely to result in an expenditure of money and effort which inflicts serious problems upon the business. The third tendency is to keep sanely these two forces of economy and promotiveness functioning harmoniously, —a man is needed who is capable of adjusting the financial difficulty to the idea of progress, and who can manipulate, in his allowance, both factors, enough to feel optimistically the growth of his particular enterprise.

Thus, with respect to the economic development of business, as related to the question of selling, which includes advertising in its various phases, departments or business enterprises have arisen, whose aim is scientifically to analyse conditions of selling, in an attempt to function more efficiently and progressively; second, the force of selling has developed different types of mind, in connection with the business data, a regard for which has not yet been largely recognized. A new type of man, the business psychologist, is demanded, in order to sympathize sanely with the human factor seen functioning in an initiative individual. In other words, we need a type of man who can place people in the kind of work for which they are most fitted, in connection with selling, and whose financial compensation in this form of creativeness ought to be recognized as necessarily larger than for the type of man who is merely a clerk. As an advertiser, in his aim he is so to correlate the various interests as to realize the standardization of his article among constantly increasing numbers of people.

Sociological Effects of Selling Forces.—Primarily, the social consideration of any movement implies a regard for the welfare of the greatest number of individuals. We might, then, ask in what different ways selling, as manifested either in advertising or salesmanship, is affected by, or is affecting, the life of the community. Now advertising in its cumulative effect upon people tends to socialize their manners. And so effective has become the power of advertising in creating habits of action in the purchase of goods that the effects of these habits are being brought under severe scrutiny. Thus experience under analysis reveals a feeling on the part of great numbers of individuals that there is great waste in advertising; many even doubt the efficiency of advertising as a selling force. Many deplore, from a selling standpoint, the great amount of human force that is necessary in the distribution of goods. They maintain that this has an effect on the price of goods. They also maintain that a high price for goods is a bad thing. This class argues that, because the price of articles is high and because it has taken so much money to advertise this price in order to create a demand, the advertiser is partly to blame for the high price.

Social Need of Advertising.—Now the explanation of these viewpoints forces one into a study as to why we have advertising as a process at all. Psychology in connection with economic process, as related to desire, offers the best argument for the maintenance of advertising as a necessary force in progress. It would maintain that life is a process. The action of this process involves our various senses,—heat, cold, smell, touch, taste, sound and sight. The inference regarding our senses seems to be that they have been developed in order to save us as creatures having life. But not only are we conscious of the saving quality which they possess, but also that the senses in their expression afford pleasure to the individual possessing them. Thus we find ourselves inclined to develop them; and we conclude, that accordingly as each one is trained to live in a harmonious sense life, he lives rightly and sanely. To live without an expression of any one of the senses is commonly regarded as a calamity. Accordingly we are considered sane when we invent a stove to burn the coal that has been dug by an also inventive miner. Our temperature spots are thus given a regulating medium, while during the process of getting comfortably warm, a miner's family has been fed, a manufacturer has been able to pay off his help, and at the same time a bank president gets his automobile, while all sit about a comfortable fire. Thus a feeling for the necessity of things in order to meet the demands of our senses has so far seized upon the actions of men, that under fair economic conditions, to be without a stove or what it represents in evolution, is a sign of unintelligence or of primitiveness.

To cite another example: the English people use very little ice, and it is difficult for them to appreciate the apparent excessive demands of the American for this product. But let a protracted hot summer extend over the Kingdom and they immediately begin to realize why Americans desire cold drinks, ice preparations, and refrigerators. Or, again, an Englishman has either accidentally or by means of an advertisement seated himself at one of Selfridge's ice cream tables to be waited upon. The result is that he tastes that which has been accepted as palatable to a kindred nation, and experience proves that he is inclined to declare the Americans a discriminating and sensible people, while he himself is induced to adopt a newer custom.

To continue, either by chance, necessity or ingenious fore-thought a new article is invented which saves much labor, let us say a safety razor or a carpet cleaner. Many people have found in either of these devices those factors which have re-sulted in a saving of energy, time and money. The result is that these articles brought before their attention, either by means of advertising or the recommendation of friends, find a sale, and these newer products, which make happier or easier life of man, are thrust into the world's markets.

These examples analysed reveal three factors: first, that ac-cordingly as we enter into consciousness of a thing realm, we develop as human beings; second, that growth implies an accep-tation of those things which create a more harmonious sense relationship; third, that acceptation of these various things implies power of adaptability. When we search for the physical power of adaptability, we find it in the plasticity of the brain; the psychic manifestations of plasticity are then realized thru such tendencies as curiosity, desire, necessity or initiative.

Granted a "thing" world necessary for a person's visible existence; granted that he grows accordingly as he continues to accept these things and to harmonize their relationship; granted that adaptability to this thing realm is made possible by means of certain universal human qualities,—we have a fourth factor created as a result of our threefold classification; namely, the necessity of a factor which would make realizable the process of continuing to live in a thing realm—a factor which en-courages human growth—a factor which assists human adap-tability and which is powerful enough to arouse curiosity, to realize necessity, to stimulate desire or to compel initiative. This factor is practically known as advertising. It is philo-sophically termed education. Thus, again, we see that in a reaction between a thing world and a human mind there is a factor which brings these two together, and which acts apart from mere chance.

Economic Effects of Advertising: Big Business.—If we are justified, then, in saying that advertising has a psychological basis and is, consequently, a necessary factor in the develop-

ment of our appreciation of a thing world, it becomes necessary
to analyse certain effects of advertising. First, it might be
said that advertising has been a factor in the tremendous growth
of many concerns. This growth has resulted in a feeling on
the part of the community that big business is a dangerous
thing, for big business means the crowding out of the less successful competitor. It means that the masses of the people are
buying goods of the larger concerns at the expense of the smaller,
and this transition from small business to large business has
brought its economic problem as manifested in an attempt at
government regulation.

Insofar as advertising is discovered in helping to create
these problems it has received condemnation from those who
regard monopolistic rule as detrimentally affecting prices. But
as stated before, it is the work of the advertiser to create a
vogue, standardize his goods and increase profits thru constantly
larger sales. If the means by which these things are done are
revealed as non-ethical and injurious for the social welfare in
the sense that undesirable habits are created, advertising as
a *process* is not to be condemned. It is the pernicious *manipulation* of principles of advertising in the creation of manners,
or in falsehoods inhibiting social progress, which need rebuke
from the critic, and remedial measures from the advertising
world itself.

Cost of Living.—Inasmuch as either creative or competitive
advertising has entered nearly every phase of economic advancement, its cumulative effect has tended to associate itself in the
public mind with the general statement, " The high cost of
living." What is actually meant by the statement " The high
cost of living? " This is a question that is under discussion in
every social group. Rich and poor, in one way or other, feel
its significance. But all classes of society are not regarding
the statement—" high cost of living "—in exactly the same way.
For instance, a man who is earning $20 a week and is support-
ing a wife and three children, and who has the ideals of a
workingman, justly complains about the high cost of living
on the basis that eggs are forty cents a dozen, butter fifty cents a

pound, and beef is running as high as twenty-four cents. He has a family budget. He finds that at the end of the week he cannot give to his family the necessary things for a decent existence. He raises a cry of indignation, and he protests.

On the other hand, the man who is earning $2000 a year, or even $10,000, also complains about the high cost of living. Does he object on the basis that potatoes are costing forty cents a peck, that gasoline is twenty-one cents a gallon, or that books are selling at two dollars which are in reality worth only one dollar and twenty-five cents? His judgment regarding the high cost of living has an entirely different mental background. He is one whose sensitiveness with respect to *living* is highly developed. Things which to the workingman are a luxury, have become to him an absolute necessity, and so rapid has been the increase of things necessary for the complete enjoyment of a human life that this high salaried man finds it impossible to enjoy these better things without entirely depleting his yearly budget.

Thus an analysis of the high cost of living reveals these two aspects. One where the very necessities of life cost more than the individual is able by means of his weekly earnings to pay for; the other, a notion of a high standard of living, or, in other words, a desire on the part of the individual to possess so many of the good things of life that his pocketbook is likewise depleted in the purchase. This analysis forces us to a serious consideration of the significance of things in our life. Is it wrong to desire to live fully? Has advertising sinned when it encourages me to open up a credit account and by means of it live six or eight months ahead of my time? Is advertising wrong when it attempts to force every one into a greater appreciation of this " thing realm "? The old question arises, are things made for profit or are things made to be used? If things are made only for profit regardless of humanity, then our advertising is to be justified on the basis that a single class benefits. If, however, things are made to be used and the world has a right to demand those things which can be made, then advertising as an educational force is to be justified in favor of the mass. In either case, we see that, for progress in our ideal, advertising is a necessary factor.

The question now arises, in what way does this advertising affect the cost of the high standard of living? Does the consumer pay for this advertising? Many interested in the direct force of advertising, as such, believe advertising not to increase the cost of an article. They believe that advertising scientifically applied is the faith element in the business world, which, somehow or other, changes the conditions of the business world so that every one has more than he had before. Advertising is a creative element whose factors result in greater happiness or in the possession of more things. We might put it in this way: A father spends $3000 or $4000, in the education of his son at a university. Does he feel that by this procedure he has deliberately thrown away $4000? On the other hand, is it not true that he feels his son to be a more valuable member of society, capable of greater earning capacity, and worthy of a higher place in life because of this peculiar training? In the same way if goods are to be used, if goods mean increased happiness to mankind, if life would be less progressive because of the elimination of a single thing, the force which brings these things into possession of mankind certainly should not be counted as an element which is to be figured as a cost loss, but really as an element which makes possible the possession of that which brings increased happiness. Advertising thus becomes a socializing factor whose emphasis is related to the intrinsic value of a thing in its service to mankind, rather than to the other problem of monopolistic business.

Advertising as an Educational Factor.—Again, to criticise certain phases of advertising, a competitive advertising system has had a psychological effect in the creation of desire and habit with respect to the purchase of many articles which prove useless. Advertising as a force renders itself to the play of the imagination to the bizarre, and to originality. And people are often involved in an exchange of values which are needless or wasteful. In spite of advertising we need to realize that new things are not needed with every change of season; fads are not necessary in order to be considered an up-to-date member of the community. Advertising sins when it attempts thus to mislead people. And yet the advertiser is in part subject to these very whims and fancies of people in order to sell his goods. When people become scientific in their buying, the advertiser will become sane in his production and sane in his sale of an article. It is a better solution of these problems which is to place advertising on a higher plane of expression. This higher plane must insist upon a regard for such manners of expression on the public mind in the creation of habits as will not disclose advertising to have been the means of injury. For instance, the public should be taught to appreciate the installment plan not as an advertising argument to lure multitudes into the purchase of luxuries, the expenditures of which drain the family budget; they should be made to understand that paying on time has an element within it which should consider the present moment in relation to the future.

Dignity of Advertising.—Again the advertiser is often overly eloquent and deceptive in the use of his argument. He gets people into wrong habits of action in their purchase of goods. False judgments are formed in the minds of people by the extravagant use of English in such phrases as "Just as Good," "Bargain Day," "Remnants," "Near Silk," "Half the Price" and "Worth More." These false judgments, however, are giving greater significance to the word "Guarantee," the effect of which tends to produce closer relations between producer and consumer. Because of a change in sentiment, due to a larger appreciation of advertising, as well as a change in our distribution system in the form of the Parcels Post, the middleman is already beginning to see a part of his profits going to the consumer.

Progress in advertising has become more dignified as it has recognized the social elements in its nature. The present discussions among all interested in advertising relates to an insistence upon honesty. The Baltimore Convention of Associated Clubs of America, which met in the year of 1913, was characterized by its spirit of insisting upon honesty. The newspaper, with respect to its circulation; the agency, with its price in connection with purchaser of copy; the retailer, in connection with his publicity campaign; the manufacturer, in his price maintenance clause in connection with the retailer—all are found insisting upon a program of action where honesty is found functioning. A part of the discussion of any business at the present time, when meeting in a convention to discuss methods for greater efficiency, always culminates in each group, at some period or other, in a discussion of honesty. The consumer is beginning to demand that exaggeration be eliminated and that the truth be spoken in connection with the article or proposition in which he is about to invest money. The business man, in his relations with business men, is beginning to insist that honesty be at the basis of every transaction.

Honesty Minimizes the Idea of Prices.—The socializing effect of honesty will directly result in greater sales to the upright firm with truthful advertising copy, but will react to the detriment of a concern turning out poor goods whose advertising is exaggerated. Honesty helps the man who has a good proposition, but is detrimental to the one who has inferior goods. As far as the public is concerned, honesty has culminated in the guarantee idea so that those concerns which advertise " guarantee," have attained a stage of development enviable in the eyes of poorer competitors. Thus changes in the form of expression are the result of sentiment interpreted in terms of social progress.

With a change in sentiment from false advertising to honesty, the idea of price in many advertising campaigns is beginning to be considered a secondary factor in the distribution of goods. Quality and service are being emphasized. We are buying goods because they will serve us honestly. The honesty of a concern is forced upon the public mind by its appeal to the guarantee argument. But the guarantee argument, carried logically to its end, suggests most peculiar difficulties. If several articles are competing for sale from an honesty standpoint, and one is superior to the others, and if the idea of quality governs purchase rather than price, these two factors, quality and guarantee or honesty, must result in the greatest number of sales. Thus, on a basis of honesty, business would find itself insisting that only the best articles be sold that would serve the greatest number of people. Only the guaranteed article would be found to survive, while inferior articles would be condemned. Now this social attitude of mind, which declares for the superior article, and condemnation for the inferior one, is not true to the facts of life. Thus, the idea of substitution should have a· prominent part in the mind processes involved in the purchase of goods. Habit with respect to the purchase of a specific article should not be so insistent in expression that it fails to recognize the merits of other propositions under conditions where a real saving is involved. For instance, if it could be shown conclusively that a certain number of those now owning an automobile at an expenditure of $100 a month for maintenance, including an occasional purchase of a new machine, could more cheaply employ the use of a taxicab to accomplish the same results, this kind of substitution should be looked upon favorably. Cheapness, and even lack of durability, might be just as serviceable and elegant for certain conditions as a larger expenditure of money. The man who declares, " I want only the best," has often lost the useful interpretation of life, unless usefulness implies a long period of time where quality is demanded. There is the temporary phase of life which needs to be emphasized; and an idea, in the mind of the community, that at all times and under all circumstances it should buy the best, is not treating fairly concerns which turn out an inferior quality yet whose goods prove serviceable under certain conditions.

Upon this theory of substitution the public mind needs to be educated with respect to the service that an article or proposition is to give. A summer cottage need not, for the happiness of the crowd, be equipped with the latest electric system. A candle stick is quite as serviceable under certain conditions.

" **Reason Why** " Copy.—Again, in the writing of copy, or in statements made by individuals in an attempt to sell goods, there is a tendency on the part of the Americans to insist upon so-called " reason why " copy, or statements of mere facts, apart from the adornment of those facts. The American type of

22

mind is afraid of exaggeration. Whenever an exaggeration pictures the impossible, a feeling of dishonesty or a lack of sanity associates itself with the concern. But those who sell must ever remember that a community does not usually purchase with the mere presentation of a thing; it must be forced into a recognition. Consequently, a certain amount of exaggeration or over-emphasis is often necessary to gain the attention. The wise advertiser is he who escapes the condemnation of his critics, by accurately discriminating between that state of consciousness which differentiates the force that carries conviction, from the force that embodies dishonesty or the sheer fanciful.

Growth of the Guarantee.—The conditions of the American business world at the present time in its concept of honesty merely emphasizes the general theory advanced, that honesty is an acquired characteristic, the functioning of which has not yet been determined in all departments of business expression. The present criticism of the solution of honesty in selling is that business men, even in their attempt to be honest, are still selfish in their attempt to develop this characteristic. It may be that selfishness will always modify the influence of honesty in the business world, to keep back a condition where a scientific knowledge in goods distribution could prevail. But at the present time, those who emphasize the guarantee idea, with honesty at the basis suggesting quality, are the rising group. The man who cannot compete on this basis is experiencing difficulty. If he is to survive, it is necessary, as suggested above, that he show to the public the real serviceableness of his goods, in relation to time, and that they are just as serviceable, proportionately, as the article of superior quality. In fact he has not yet awakened to realization of a possibility of a guarantee of his own in connection with the output of his goods under certain conditions. The consciousness of this theory will undoubtedly bring many changes in the form of the advertisements that are to appear in the future.

Blending Utilities.—Again, advertising as a force, if it is to accomplish greatest results, should recognize the possibility of blending utilities. This is aptly typified in the automobile situation as suggested above. If the community is to purchase

automobiles, but finds as at the present time, the expense of
a car too great because of inferior roads, poor city streets, bad
hotel facilities, poor ways of reaching congested parts of a city,
it is necessary for the advertiser to have such laws passed as will
compel the necessity for improvements to meet the selling demands of his proposition. Thus, a seller is found insistent in his
study of the means by which his goods can be distributed to
the larger number. And, gradually, as the public mind wants
those goods, it in turn enables these laws to be passed, by which
service is extended. This is concretely shown at the present
time in the use of the communion service in the average church.
They are not using individual cups. The wise advertising man,
for a concern turning out individual communion service, is he
who sees that from a sanitary standpoint an individual cup
should be used. With this scientific fact as a foundation, he
has a perfect right to insist that the state legislature pass a law
condemning the use of the old method of service. The community is often deceived as to the real motive of the passing
of a law, especially if the arguments for its passing are put
on a scientific basis. Nevertheless, this method of selling goods
is one by which the entire community is served. If only the
public could be made to feel its relation to all the factors involved in a complete enjoyment or use of a thing, advertising
could more easily include a complete scientific attitude toward
the factors which involve social progress. But under present
conditions where whim, fancy, imitation and necessity are often
the only sources of action, the advertiser is frequently compelled
to do many seemingly needless things. It is only as people come to
think in terms of change that these difficulties will be largely
overcome. One of the means by which the public in general
is encouraged to purchase by means of advertising is that of the
part-payment plan. The public is encouraged to realize its
ideal thru the many installment plans established. The installment plan, entering an average family, has the effect of systema-
tizing the family budget. More care is taken in the distribution of funds. When a family has possessed a pianola for several
months, and they have grown to value the instrument, desire
for possession alone encourages constant payment. This frame

of mind is careful so to regulate the financial account as to realize final payment. The installment plan is a sane way of allowing people to live happily in the present, of regulating the future in the encouragement of faith on the part of the community in the working out satisfactorily of life's issues. The installment plan, again, has undoubtedly influenced large groups of young people in their outlook upon life. Were it not possible to purchase the furnishings of a four- or five-room flat on a time payment plan, many a young man would become discouraged, but where his monthly salary can support another life and at the same time live comfortably, a realization of this, indicated in an advertising street car card, often suggests immediate action.

Right Buying.—The real problem which includes a recognition of the individualizing of taste on the part of the consumer relates itself to the question of right buying. The force of selling, which attempts to put into the possession of an individual, an unsatisfactory article, is a force set operating which does not result in public good. So the wrong article to the wrong man creates a condition of mind not favorable to progressive advertising; but the right article to the right man, or the right article to the greatest number of people, under conditions whereby all are benefited, should be the true analysis of the present.

Individual Factor in Selling.—Large production with a tendency toward the standardization of an article should not fail to recognize the individual factor in salesmaking whenever it is possible. For instance, clothing is now turned out by the thousands of suits and by the same pattern. Now individuals naturally resent accepting that which is exactly like others; they wish some change adapted to their individual tastes or needs. Hence the selling of goods under such conditions as will allow advertising to recognize the factor of individualized taste, is necessary wherever choice is involved. And the more each individual feels that his particular wants and tastes are to be most carefully considered, the more pleased is that person.

At the present time innumerable individuals resent the idea of being dictated to with respect to the way their weekly allowance should be spent.   We find many programs for living published in the daily papers, yet there are thousands of people who never once consider the advisability of being taught how to purchase correctly.   The future advertising man will find, more seriously than at present, among his many problems this one:—How to teach people, as families or as organizations, to spend most profitably their money in order to get the greatest good, and at the same time recognize the necessity of encouraging individual tastes.   Waste, in the use of unnecessary things, would in this manner become eliminated; and when the idea of waste has disappeared, necessity holds sway, and whatever is necessary becomes right.   Thus his work will be to teach people how rightly and yet individually to buy, considering the income which is to be expended.

Publicity is Magnified Advertising.—The social implications of advertising have thus far been considered in the standardizing of goods, the socializing of manners, the individualizing of taste, the idea of substitution and the blending of utilities.   *Advertising* has related itself more specifically to the direction of individual human habits.   In contrast with advertising, the idea of *publicity* presents itself, which involves all of the processes of advertising, the principles of which, however, operate on a higher plane and in a larger way.   Thus, *advertising per se* makes itself felt in the creation of a vogue for a particular article or proposition, while publicity enters as a factor in developing the environment in which man can live.

Functions of Publicity and Its Possibilities.—Publicity, as a force, shows itself functioning in the political realm.   Men whose characters are beyond reproach, whose ambition to serve humanity is great, who feel that they can be truly creative in their service to the state, are beginning to realize that frankness, honesty, sincerity, and ability, properly presented to the community, will assist in the possibility of election or appointment. The public mind is susceptible, under the idea of an honesty campaign, to this kind of a plea.   Thus advertising in the larger sense of publicity is a factor in our political life, and he who would sway public opinion must needs know somewhat of its principles.

Religion has not yet universally accepted this larger interpretation of advertising. The conservative in religious movements, or in churches, abhor the idea of advertising *per se,* and properly so, but there is no reason why they should be averse to temperate publicity. Nevertheless, we find various church organizations in large cities contemplating so-called religious advertising campaigns; these campaigns would lose the stigma of the name advertising if they were looked at from the publicity standpoint. Insofar as these movements reveal to the community the possibility of bettering itself by association with these organizations, just so far will they be successful. A few of the present campaigns are not based on the idea of publicity or that of education. They still teem with the spirit of selfishness, creed, or individual opinion. Religion and politics will find advertising their greatest power in approaching the mass, accordingly as they become true educators with respect to their proposition. Moreover, their propositions must have at basis that which people should and would, once educated, like to have.

Another, the field of education, has found itself successful in the selling of itself to the community, accordingly as it has wisely considered the subject of advertising. Education, in some of its forms, attempts to be exclusive in nature. Either the money idea makes it so, or the society idea. When, for instance, a young man purchases a course in salesmanship and is compelled to sign a contract, which prohibits him either from showing those books to another or reselling them, it is in greater part purely a commercial transaction from the standpoint of the seller. Again, whenever a school is so exclusive that it will not advertise at all but depends upon its good name, we have a school based on the idea of mere exclusiveness, the inference of which is that money is a secondary consideration. To what extent publicity will assist this kind of business in the future, is rather uncertain; but the spirit which insists upon a democratic interpretation of things, is likely to modify the action of both these kinds of institutions.

Again, the motion picture has within it wonderful publicity possibilities. People are brought into a knowledge of the manufacturing processes of goods made in other lands. Indirectly, these factors are changing public opinion in their purchases of goods. The whole world is becoming a store in which people can buy. No longer are we satisfied with the inefficient thing of our neighborhood, for efficiency can be recognized in an output from a foreign land. There is a certain cosmopolitan type of mind being created accordingly as it realizes often, thru motion pictures, a newer or different interpretation of what are the products of all the earth. It has just been announced that Paris is to have advertising motion pictures displayed in stations. This is, at least, a recognition of a possible force apart from mere entertainment. At the present time there seems to be a tendency to attribute the decline of magazine advertising as partly due to motion pictures. If statistics can prove this, the next move on the part of advertisers should be better to utilize these entertainments. Life insurance companies are already suggesting in story form the values of their different policies.

Summary.—Thus, by way of summary, honesty is in the process of making, largely by means of advertising and publicity. The larger social movements of life, as religion and politics, are beginning to appreciate the possibilities of conquest thru publicity. Education, which directly appeals to the idea of personal advancement, has still a greater field for operation. The advertiser is to change the surface of the earth and the minds of people, if necessary, in order to get the greatest number of goods into the hands of the greatest number of people, at a profit. The high standard of living is to be encouraged, insofar as humanity is actually served under present conditions. An advertising man, who recognizes the fact that the time element is a necessary factor in a wise distribution of his goods, is most faithfully serving the present generation. The social concept, as related to advertising, still insists on the idea that the vast mass of humanity are to be benefited. The wise advertiser, then, is he who studies his proposition in connection with the social and economic progress of humanity.

INDEX

CPSIA information can be obtained
at www.ICGtesting.com
Printed in the USA
BVHW051001021019
559808BV00035B/1762/P

9 781376 531138